FACING THE
BUREAUCRACY

FACING THE BUREAUCRACY

Living and Dying in a Public Agency

Gerald Garvey

Jossey-Bass Publishers · San Francisco

Substantial discounts on bulk quantities of Jossey-Bass books are available to corporations, professional associations, and other organizations. For details and discount information, contact the special sales department at Jossey-Bass Inc., Publishers. (415) 433-1740; Fax (415) 433-0499.

For international orders, please contact your local Paramount Publishing International office.

Manufactured in the United States of America. Nearly all Jossey-Bass books and jackets are printed on recycled paper that contains at least 50 percent recycled waste, including 10 percent postconsumer waste. Many of our materials are also printed with vegetable-based ink; during the printing process these inks emit fewer volatile organic compounds (VOCs) than petroleum-based inks. VOCs contribute to the formation of smog.

Library of Congress Cataloging-in-Publication Data

Garvey, Gerald, date.
    Facing the bureaucracy : living and dying in a public agency / Gerald Garvey. — 1st ed.
      p.   cm.—(The Jossey-Bass public administration series)
    Includes bibliographical references (p.   ) and index.
    ISBN 1-55542-502-X
    ISBN 1-55542-712-X (paperback)
    1. United States. Federal Energy Regulatory Commission.
    2. Energy policy—United States.   3. Bureaucracy—United States—Case studies.   I. Title.   II. Series.
HD9502.U52G374   1992
353.0087'22—dc20   92-30630
                                               CIP

FIRST EDITION
HB Printing   10 9 8 7 6 5 4 3 2 1   *Code 9306*
PB Printing   10 9 8 7 6 5 4 3 2 1   *Code 9479*

**The
Jossey-Bass
Public Administration
Series**

**Consulting Editor
Public Management and Administration**

**James L. Perry
Indiana University**

Contents

ix

Part Two: A Case Study in Organizational Innovation

Part Three: Whither Bureaucracy?

Preface

Our sprawling government contains dozens upon dozens of agricultural marketing services, bureaus of land management, offices of producer and pipeline regulation, and similarly titled units. The work of officials in these agencies touches all of us. From food inspection to policing the nation's pension programs to energy price setting to . . . well, you get the idea: the bureaucrats in executive departments such as Agriculture and Labor, and in independent commissions such as the Federal Energy Regulatory Commission and the National Labor Relations Board, affect our day-to-day lives in thousands of ways.

Facing the Bureaucracy tells the story of the birth, brief flourishing, and ultimate death of a major project in an important agency of the U.S. government. During the period in which the recounted events unfolded at the Federal Energy Regulatory Commission, I moonlighted from my regular position as a professor of politics at Princeton University, serving as a consultant to various

FERC officials. My personal experiences provide the basis for the case study around which the book is organized. Ostensibly, the story is about the computerization of the regulatory process. In reality, the story has a *human* focus; it describes the bureaucratic maneuvering, the Washington politics, the personal agendas that affected the FERC automation project.

The sense that one has a tale to tell is rarely justification enough for an author to write a book—let alone for a reader to invest his or her time with it. Let me therefore enlarge a bit on my own motives.

I have never found it very easy, in the American government courses that I teach at Princeton, to turn students on to the subjects of bureaucratic practice and organizational behavior. Most students sign up for classes in government because they want to learn about the great issues of state—the politics of global change, progress on civil rights, and the like. What goes on at places like the Federal Energy Regulatory Commission inspires little interest.

The lack of curiosity about such so-called old-line agencies, although understandable, is regrettable. Given the impact that officials in these agencies have on all of our lives, we might be expected to show more interest than we sometimes do in the problems that our bureaucrats face, the atmosphere in which they work, and the motivations that spur them. I therefore present the case study and analysis that follow out of a combination of my personal involvement as an "expert adviser" to public officials, my pedagogical concerns as a teacher of the U.S. political process, and my sense of the informational needs of all citizens.

Purposes of the Book

Above all, I hope to give readers a feel for the texture of life in a public bureaucracy and thereby to both stimulate and satisfy curiosity about behavior in government agencies. Moreover, I hope to convey this "feel" in a way that contributes to contemporary social science theory and, specifically, to an important body of unfolding theory in the field of organizational and management studies.

The Texture of Life in a Bureaucracy

Activity in the Federal Energy Regulatory Commission is for many purposes typical of life in most public bureaucracies. The work of FERC's bureaucrats is specialized and very technical, and it occurs in environs that many would find more than a bit offputting. The office-cubicles in the agency's leased buildings at 825 North Capitol Street—a skid row section of Washington within view of the Capitol dome—are crowded, grungy, and poorly maintained. An aura of dullness hangs about the place. This aura ensures against regular scrutiny by journalists or scholars.

Herein lies an irony worthy of notice. FERC officials regulate three major U.S. industries: interstate natural gas transportation and portions of gas production, hydroelectric generation and interstate sales of all commercially produced electricity, and interstate oil transmission by pipeline. Much of this regulatory activity occurs in adversarial proceedings. Within FERC's second-floor hearing rooms, elaborately ritualized procedures—identical in all essential respects to the procedures of every other federal regulatory body—theoretically guarantee the openness and fairness of the agency's decision-making processes. But the nature of administrative proceedings makes much of the work seem boring to conduct and stultifying to observe. Therefore, procedures that were intended to ensure fairness drive audiences away. By insulating the agency from day-to-day public oversight, these procedures bring about results exactly opposite to the ones intended. Since, apparently, few observers want to know what goes on in agencies such as FERC, little public pressure exists on the bureaucrats who staff these agencies to work with the diligence and regularity that might be expected if an attentive citizenry monitored their activities.

I hope in the following pages to show that administrative proceedings in a government bureaucracy are not so dull after all. The stakes are high. The cast includes some colorful individuals of rare ability. Even the ritualized procedures display a certain fascinating logic to the viewer who can decode them. Those who appreciate the texture of life in our public agencies are not only more likely to understand how government works (and whom it works for!) but also why better pay and working conditions promise to improve the service that citizens get from their career public officials.

Illuminating Practice with Theory

The second purpose of the book is to sharpen our understanding of bureaucratic practice, using a case study developed against the backdrop of two contrasting theoretical approaches. I identify these approaches as the Old Theory and the New Theory.

Both the Old Theory and the New are my own constructs. The terms are presented for expositional purposes and do not purport to summarize the intellectual history of public administration as a field of study. Scholars of bureaucracy may be familiar with Martin Albrow's (1970) catalogue of seven ways in which analysts have viewed bureaucracy: bureaucracy as rational organization, bureaucracy as organizational inefficiency, and so forth. Each characterization is suggestive, but none fully captures the bureaucratic phenomenon. The point is to use such characterizations as literary foils and not to pretend that any one of them is analytically rigorous or complete.

The Old Theory, as I use the term, was the theory that guided America's progressive reformers in their agency-creating effort of a century or so ago. These reformers sought to promote efficiency in government, prevent special interests from infecting bureaucratic practice, and limit the discretion that bureaucrats could exercise. In the following pages, I accent certain progressive premises that today seem benighted. But I do not mean literally to suggest that the theorists of a complex movement in our history were innocents in the ways of the real world or that every progressive thinker agreed with every other one. Certainly, the reformers whom I group together as Old Theorists were realistic enough to know that their highest hopes would probably never be attained in full.

Set against the Old Theory is a new one, drawn from microeconomic theory and the rational choice model in political science. The New Theory can be used to explain why, some critics think, the progressives' institutions have evolved into structures displaying characteristics exactly opposite to the ones that their founders expected.

I identify in some ways with the New Theorists, but I also disagree with certain of their conclusions. Following the example of the political scientist Terry Moe (1984), whose summary is a classic of lucidity and compression, I have assigned my New Theorists somewhat artificially to a single "school" containing pioneers of organizational theory (Ronald Coase, Herbert Simon), classical scholars of management science or public administration (Chester Barnard, E. Pendleton Herring), contemporary formal model builders (Mathew McCubbins, Oliver Williamson—though the latter probably deserves a category to himself), and empirical political scientists (Hugh Heclo, Herbert Kaufman).

Audiences

First, *Facing the Bureaucracy* is addressed to professionals in public administration and organizational studies, including: (1) practitioners of public management; (2) executives in private sector organizational settings; (3) consultants, practitioners, and teachers in the automation and data processing fields; and (4) teachers and researchers in public administration, management studies, and organizational theory. Though not a how-to book, the work should help these professionals deal with, for example, problems of organizational renewal in aging institutions, particularly through the use of special task forces as vehicles of constructive change; issues raised by the issue-network environment of bureaucratic activity; and the design of procedures to reduce transaction costs within an organization.

My hope, however, has been to reach well beyond the circle of professionals and to produce a book of interest to general readers and accessible to students. This hope motivated my overall presentational strategy—especially my adoption of the (admittedly overstated) Old Theory-New Theory framework and my use of an informal story-telling style in Part Two.

I envision use of the book in both graduate and undergraduate courses in public administration, administrative law, bureaucracy, political economy, and government regulation. Teachers are always searching for ways to demonstrate that theory really does illuminate empirical material; my explicit intent has been to help

satisfy this criterion of textbook adoption. Mimeographed versions
of the book have been used (and, thus, have been "teaching tested")
in two graduate courses at Princeton's Woodrow Wilson School.
The manuscript was revised based on student feedback, with an eye
to ensuring its value in the classroom as well as in the professor's
study or the practitioner's office.

Overview of the Contents

A brief introduction sets forth the essentials of the Old and New
Theories and the bearing of each on the problem of organizational
change.

Part One gives an overview of the federal agency structure in
general and the Federal Energy Regulatory Commission's organization in particular. Chapter One describes the evolution of the
federal bureaucracy. It then elaborates on the Old and New Theories
as they help us to understand the federal administrative structure.
Chapter Two locates the formal agencies of government within the
vast private-contracting industry and the complex of trade associations that have grown up in Washington, D.C.

Part Two presents the case study of organizational change in
a public bureaucracy in the form of a memoir drawn from my own
experiences at FERC. Chapter Three develops the place of the Federal Energy Regulatory Commission in the Washington scene, emphasizing the external pressures (from the president, Congress, and
private industries) and internal pressures (from career civil servants)
that bear on the commission's activities. Chapter Four describes the
decision to computerize the procedures that FERC officials use
when they set the prices that the nation's big pipeline companies
charge for moving natural gas from the oil-patch states where it is
produced to the cities of the North and West where it is consumed.
Chapter Five describes the launching of the FERC automation project, setting events in the more general context of conditions—such
as change-resistance within the ranks of permanent employees—
that an "entrepreneurial leader" in a large bureaucracy is likely to
encounter.

Chapter Six presents an analysis of the task force as a vehicle
of change. Few career civil servants pass many years on the job

without an assignment to an interagency task force or a special project team. The *ad hoc* group has become the technique of choice for modifying routines and structures in many complex organizations. This chapter focuses on the reasons for, and the psychology of, task-force thinking in agencies such as FERC. Chapter Seven points up the central roles of negotiation and compromise in contemporary public management, emphasizing the negotiating process within the litigative framework that has evolved under the federal Administrative Procedures Act. Chapter Eight recounts the allegations of criminal wrongdoing in the midst of which the FERC automation project eventually self-destructed. This chapter focuses on the psychology of the investigative process.

Part Three draws lessons from the case study, interpreted in terms of the two theories introduced in Part One. Chapter Nine considers four related phenomena—institutional aging, bureaucratic discretion, the rise of issue networks, and susceptibility to corrupt practices—as natural tendencies in public bureaucracies and then critiques the administrative controls that have been developed in the attempt to limit discretion and prevent corruption. Chapter Ten draws out certain lessons of the FERC case study for public sector leaders and managers, and notes in particular the bearing of the phenomena discussed in Chapter Nine, the limiting effects of administrative controls, the role of "good people" at both the senior managerial and working levels of our public bureacracies, and the contemporary relevance of the progressives' call for an ethic of public service.

Some Disclaimers

The secret of change within organizations is often to be found in the mechanics of bureaucratic politics and the chemistry of personalities. Hidden agendas, personal feelings, private interests, and even subconscious motivations may dominate the rational or "public-interested" aspects of bureaucratic behavior. I have therefore tried in the case study recounted in Part Two to give glimpses of partisan political forces, business interests, organizational procedures, and above all the emotions of individuals who affected the FERC automation effort.

The players in the story are real people, and I have used their real names. But because I am not, as the expression goes, "afflicted with total recall," I have attributed quotations only when I have felt sure of their accuracy. Although I have not knowingly compressed chronologies, I have omitted accounts of events or persons to the extent that they seemed not to illustrate more general problems or principles of bureaucratic practice.

The FERC automation project challenged those staff members within the agency who opposed computerization. The nature of the activity was such as to bruise some feelings, engender some resentments, and inspire some divergent interpretations of what computerization did or did not achieve. Nevertheless, I do not consider the case study to be an exercise in kiss and tell. My purpose is instruction, not titillation or ledger squaring. If, in telling the story of those who opposed the project as well as those who supported it, I have at any point permitted emotions to affect my characterizations of bureaucratic adversaries, I regret it—not only because personal unfairness is never justified but also because meanly motivated passages must undermine the credibility of a story that deserves to be truly told.

Congressional inquiries, journalistic exposés, and prosecutorial probes are common, if nerve-wracking, occurrences in Washington these days. At FERC, an investigation prompted by allegations of corrupt actions by top officials, some of whom were figures in the automation effort, created fear and paralysis throughout the agency. In this environment, support for continuance of the computerization project proved to be unsustainable. The reader should know right off, though, that the allegations, which were not really very lurid to begin with, for the most part turned out not even to be true. Notwithstanding which, the charges and ensuing investigation profoundly affected individuals' careers. I have tried to convey the impact of such charges on personal lives and to explain how investigative episodes affect the conduct of government business.

The technicalities of government procurement procedures, the constant requirements for apology (whether in testimony before Congress or in seemingly routine sole-source justifications for government contracts), the conundrum of political motivations in precincts that are supposed to be dominated by technical expertise—

these realities invite game playing, even cynicism. In evoking the ambiguities of bureaucratic practice, I may have revealed more about my own role than I should have preferred. As a paid consultant and a friend of key agency officials, I had a personal, a professional, and a financial stake in the indefinite perpetuation of the computerization project. I have tried to judge whether my role fatally undermines my ability to tell the story in an impartial way, and I certainly respect my readers' right to make the same judgment. If, despite good-faith efforts to do so, I have failed to rid the text of self-serving rationalizations or score-settling references to others, well, maybe my own ultimate inability to rise above self-interest will help make the larger point of the book.

Acknowledgments

Finally, I want to extend my most sincere thanks to those who have read the manuscript in whole or in part and offered so many helpful suggestions: John Burke; John DiIulio; Jameson Doig; George Downs; Edward Garvey; George Garvey; Thorson Gregory Garvey; Robert George; John Glascock; Jeffrey Goldstein; Richard Shuman; David H. Rosenbloom, whose observations based on readings of early extracts from the manuscript were helpful—and humbling in their depth of knowledge in the field of public administration; James L. Perry and Alan Shrader, consulting editor and acquisitions editor, respectively, for the Jossey-Bass Public Administration Series; the Jossey-Bass referees, Donald Kettl and Eugene MacGregor, both of whose suggestions were enormously valuable, and who kindly consented to have their names revealed after all revisions were completed; and my wife, LouAnn Garvey.

Princeton, New Jersey   Gerald Garvey
December 1992

For my son,
Thorson Gregory Garvey

The Author

Gerald Garvey is a professor of politics at Princeton University. He received his B.S. degree (1959) in aeronautical engineering from the U.S. Air Force Academy and his Ph.D. degree (1962) in politics from Princeton University.

Garvey is the author or coauthor of *Economic Law and Economic Growth: Anti-Trust, Rate Regulation, and the American Growth System* (1990, with G. E. Garvey); *Strategy and the Defense Dilemma* (1984); *Nuclear Power and Social Planning* (1977); and numerous other books, scholarly articles, and government-sponsored reports. He is a former editor of *World Politics* and a member of the editorial boards of *Review of Politics* and *Socioeconomic Planning Sciences*.

Garvey teaches public management in the Princeton University Woodrow Wilson School core graduate curriculum. His research interests are currently focused on contemporary formal theories of organizational and bargaining behavior.

Cast of Characters

C. M. "Mike" Butler
Chairman of the Federal Energy Regulatory Commission during the early years of the Reagan presidency; a Texan by birth, a conservative Republican, and a strong proponent of free-market economics and accelerated deregulation of the natural gas industry.

Charles Curtis
Butler's predecessor as FERC chairman. (Between Curtis's departure and Butler's accession to the post, Commissioner Georgiana Shelton served briefly as acting chair.) Curtis had been a senior aide of Congressman John Dingell, whose sponsorship was a key element in Curtis's elevation to the top job at FERC by President Carter.

John Dingell
Congressman from Michigan, chairman of the House of Representatives Committee on Energy and Commerce, and the most impor-

tant legislator in Washington in terms of power over FERC; an opponent of accelerated deregulation.

Gerald Garvey
Professor of politics at Princeton University who, while serving as a part-time consultant to FERC, designed and helped install the Pipeline Rates Division's computerized rate-making program; see "The Author" p. xxi.

Lawrence "Lonnie" Lebow
Assistant general counsel for gas and oil litigation at FERC in the mid 1980s; brought to FERC from the Interior Department by Robert Satterfield.

James Lighthauser
A senior employee of Computer Data Services, Inc. of Rockville, Maryland; chief programmer for the FERC automation project.

Albert Linden
Deputy administrator of the Energy Information Administration at the U.S. Department of Energy during the period of the FERC automation project.

William G. McDonald
Executive director of FERC, 1977–1986, and the initiator of the FERC automation project.

Raymond Madden
Special agent of the U.S. Department of Energy inspector general's staff; responsible for investigating certain charges of official misconduct made by Lebow against McDonald.

Eileen Mason
Executive assistant to Executive Director McDonald.

Robert Means
Director of regulatory analysis and chief economist at FERC under Chairman Butler; a former University of Texas law professor and

a proponent of the free-market approach in the natural gas
industry.

Charles Moore
A Texas lawyer appointed by Chairman Butler as general counsel
at FERC (a predecessor of Satterfield in the job).

John Moriarty
A midlevel official at FERC; in charge of an effort to computerize
rate-making that had been initiated at the agency before McDonald
launched the automation project described in this book.

Joe Neubeiser
One of Executive Director McDonald's senior recruits on the FERC
administrative staff; had major responsibilities in procurement and
personnel, which became objects of investigation.

Raymond O'Connor
Butler's successor as FERC chairman; came to FERC from a background in energy law (Consolidated Edison of New York) and fi-
nance (Citibank, Bache-Halsey) and returned to New York
(Citicorp) after resigning the chairmanship in 1985.

Kenneth Pusateri
One of McDonald's senior recruits on the FERC administrative
staff; promoted to acting executive director of the agency after
McDonald's departure from the office.

Robert Satterfield
General counsel at FERC under Chairman O'Connor.

Anthony Sousa
O'Connor's successor as (acting) FERC chairman.

Victor Stello
Executive director (formal title, general manager) of the U.S. Nuclear Regulatory Commission (NRC); had been McDonald's supe-

rior at the NRC just before McDonald received his promotion to the executive directorship at FERC.

Kenneth Williams

Director, Office of Pipeline and Producer Regulation—the FERC bureau with primary regulatory authority in the federal government over the U.S. natural gas industry; resigned from FERC in 1985 to join the energy-consulting firm of Brown, Williams, Quinn & Chinn.

Williams's main deputies and assistants included:

Raymond Beirne. Williams's deputy throughout the period of the FERC automation project; eventually resigned from FERC and joined his former boss at Brown, Williams, Quinn & Chinn.

Donald Champagny. Bierne's subordinate throughout the period of the FERC automation project; in charge of the branch responsible for cost-of-service estimation; eventually resigned from FERC to join his former bosses at Brown, Williams, Quinn & Chinn.

Robert Scarbrough. Bierne's subordinate throughout the period of the FERC automation project; in charge of the branch responsible for rate design; eventually resigned from FERC to join his bosses at Brown, Williams, Quinn & Chinn.

FACING THE BUREAUCRACY

From Bureaucracy Building to Bureaucracy Bashing

Large organizations, for the most part bureaucratically structured, are dominating institutions in modern life. Big corporations are the representative economic entities of industrial America, and the public sector bureaucracies that have emerged during the past century—many of them to regulate economic and industrial behavior—affect activities that range from the labeling of baby food to the disbursement of retirees' pension savings.

Managers in these private and public sector organizations constantly confront the challenge of change. New problems emerge. New technologies must be absorbed, new ideas accommodated. Every day, organizational planners have to choose among competing strategies of growth, adaptation, and contraction.

The Coming—and Possible Going—of Progressivism

A century ago, the choices must have seemed simpler. What Stephen Skowronek (1982) called the New American State had nowhere to

1

go but up. The United States adapted to industrial change and
continuing corporate growth by expanding—and bureaucratiz-
ing—the federal government (Hays, 1957). An expansion of government in the states paralleled the institution-building process at the
federal level. Lawmakers first expressed a new regulatory activism
in direct legislation and then began to delegate authorities to state-
level public utility commissions. The progressive impulse was
equally pronounced at the municipal level, most notably in the
widespread appearance of reformist administrations and the adoption of the city manager approach to urban governance.

To the progressive architects of a rapidly expanding public
sector, bureaucracy was not a dirty word. Nor was the growth of
government to be feared. Between 1890 and the mid 1920s, the Agriculture and Interior departments, arguably the most influential federal agencies of the time, grew rapidly (Hays, [1955] 1975). The same
years saw the creation of the Commerce and Labor departments and
the establishment of the first independent regulatory agencies. The
New Deal, often considered the final phase of progressivism (Goldman, 1952), added its own set of "alphabet agencies" to the nation's
stock of public bureaucracies.

Woodrow Wilson, Louis Brandeis, Herbert Croly, and Frederick Winslow Taylor equated bureaucracy with the rational distribution of specialized functions. In this view, they anticipated Max
Weber's classic explication of the bureaucratic model. And although the progressives concentrated on the potential of public
administration, they were also sanguine about the applicability of
the new rationality to private industry, as the advocacies of Brandeis
and Taylor particularly demonstrated (Wilson, 1887; Croly, 1909;
Weber, [1910] 1946a; Taylor, [1911] 1947; Mason, 1946; Haber,
1964).

The progressives expected appointive civil servants to bring
a "science of administration" and techniques of "scientific management" to the government offices they were creating at the federal,
state, and municipal levels. Applicants were to qualify for these
positions by merit alone. Candidates for government work would
also come imbued with an ethic suited to their high calling. Because
they would bring the true professionals' standards of performance
to their offices, they could be trusted not to "play politics"—that is,

not to substitute goals of their own for those of their legal superiors. To do otherwise would violate their specialized training, their professional commitments, and their ethic of service (see Weber, [1918] 1946b).

Two Competing Theories

The progressives' theory of administration—we may call it the Old Theory—has undergone a marked declension over the years. Faith in rational decision making based on expertise has given way to a view of decision making as unarguably political and based on bargaining (Herring, 1936; McConnell, 1966; Allison, 1971) or to a theory of incremental decision making based on "satisficing," "muddling through," or "groping along" (Simon, 1947; Lindblom, 1959; Behn, 1988). The decades have seen a dramatic reversal of approach, from the confident bureaucracy building of Wilson to the bureaucracy bashing of the 1980s; from the progressives' clear-cut distinction between public administration and private management to the "iron triangles," "adhocracies," and "issue networks" that today connect public agencies with private industries by lines of reciprocal influence (Heclo, 1977, 1978; Mintzberg, 1983).

Advocates of privatization and of deregulating the government argue that public agencies as we know them may no longer be up to the job (Henke, 1987; Wilson, 1989). The growing tendency to rely on private contractors for work that the progressives would have assigned to public servants underlines a trend toward the displacement of government bureaucracies by decentralized, market-based decision-making structures (Kettl, 1988; Osborne and Gaebler, 1992).

Paralleling the changes that have occurred at the level of attitudes, as well as those in our public agencies' actual patterns of performance, have been changes in analytical concepts. A new theory has emerged to help explain why institutions created under the inspiration of the progressive doctrines seem, to many, to have produced structures displaying characteristics opposite to the ones originally expected. The New Theory, as the term is used in this book, elaborates the "realistic" approach to organizations and management pioneered by Chester Barnard (1938). To Barnard's teachings, four Nobel laureate economists—Kenneth Arrow, James Buchanan,

Ronald Coase, and Herbert Simon—have added a curiously hetero-
dox set of doctrines selectively drawn both from conventional
microeconomic theory and from certain criticisms of traditional
microeconomic assumptions.

From the canon of economic teachings the New Theorists
derive their two key premises: humans are strongly rational and
they are dominantly driven by self-interest. Yet the New Theorists
have been willing to criticize other widely accepted microeconomic
principles. These theorists' major contribution, an analysis of institutions that emphasizes attempts by decision makers to minimize
transaction costs, rests on their rejection of the traditional assumption that markets are "frictionless" (Williamson, 1985).

Members of Simon's Carnegie school of management, named
after Pittsburgh's Carnegie Institute where these scholars taught or
studied, and a handful of academic political economists, mostly
headquartered at West Coast universities, picked up where the early
New Theorists left off and worked out the main patterns of the
approach (Simon and March, 1958; Cyert and March, 1963; Williamson, 1975, 1985, 1990; Moe, 1984; McCubbins, Noll, and Weingast, 1987).

The New Theory by no means covers all of the ground that
students of organization and management have explored since the
days of Wilson and Weber. For this reason, the Old Theory–New
Theory dichotomy neither summarizes the history nor suggests the
doctrinal richness of American public administration theory.

An intellectual history of the postprogressive contributions
to administrative theory would have to recognize, at a minimum,
the "generic management theory" school of Gulick and Urwick
(1937); the "human relations" school, including the theorists of
organizational culture (Mayo, 1933; Roethlisberger and Dickson,
1939; Selznick, 1957; Maslow, 1962; Argyris, 1964; McGregor, 1966;
Ouchi, 1981a, 1981b; Peters and Waterman, 1982); the school of
Appleby (1945, 1949) and Waldo (1948, 1955), together with the
many contributions—particularly those emphasizing democratic re-
sponsiveness—that these two scholars have inspired in a generation
of influential colleagues and students; and a diverse set of philo-
sophically oriented critics of organization and bureaucracy, includ-

ing Habermas (1987), Handler (1990), Scott and Hart (1979, 1989), and Weick (1979).

The New Theory, then, presents only a partial view of organization and management theory. Nor is this partial view an unchallenged one, even within its own limited purview. So why feature it so prominently as the foil of progressive thought? Because, in a way that none of the other theories do, the New Theory gives a peculiar conceptual structure to the belief currently held by so many Americans that somewhere, somehow the progressives' vision has failed. In brief, the New Theory can be taken as a kind of intellectual manifesto of the bureaucracy bashers.

A "Rationalist Rationale" for Bureaucracy Bashing

Unlike the human relations theorists and the proponents of organizational culture (though like the progressives), the New Theorists advance a strongly rationalistic interpretation of the world. As if to underscore the point, Kenneth Arrow (1974) once wrote that among academicians, economists think of themselves as the peculiar guardians of rationality. But although they accept certain of their progressive predecessors' key assumptions, the New Theorists come to conclusions that subvert rather than support the early reformers' optimistic assessment of the potential of bureaucracy.

The New Theorists, for example, share the progressives' expectation that bureaucrats will be experts in fields ranging from food chemistry to railroad rate setting. But the New Theorists reason that because experts work mostly on specialized problems, they develop specialized skills and vocabularies. Their expertise also lets them develop convenient shortcuts through approved procedures whenever the driving force of self-interest suggests that they will feel better off if they do so. Bureaucrats can easily use the specialized information that they possess to erect defenses against intrusion by outsiders. The same kinds of defenses can also often be used to shield bureaucrats from close surveillance within the organization. Any large, technically oriented agency or business firm, the New Theorists argue, is filled with informational black holes. Under these conditions, bureaucrats can bend rules unobserved. They can also find niches in which they are safe from the scrutiny of superiors who might try to observe their detailed work.

Abuses of discretionary power become relatively easy within these protected niches. It is also easy for civil servants who are inclined toward sluggishness to shirk their duties, because their expertise permits them to withdraw almost at will into the surveillance-proof recesses of the organization.

Shirking responsibilities need not always be egregious or obstructive; it is not even always conscious. It may involve simple carelessness, or it may stem from a worker's habituated incapacity to adapt when changed circumstances call for changed patterns of work. The "faceless bureaucrat" then falls into the kind of change-resistant "mindless routine" that many citizens think is endemic in bureaucracy. The point at which chronic resistance to change becomes terminal marks the onset of institutional old age.

Resistance to change in aging agencies should be of particular concern to Americans, if only because most of the public bureaucracies in the United States have now had ample time to grow old. The New American State is no longer new. All of the Progressive Era public agencies have existed for at least sixty years, and the oldest of them go back to the nineteenth century—easily long enough for symptoms of institutional senility to appear. Pertinent here is the metaphor of an organizational life cycle that culminates in a state of debility and bureaucratic stagnation (Bernstein, 1955; Kimberly, Miles and Associates, 1981). Given the senior status of so many of our government agencies, constructive change in the public sector may be especially difficult to initiate because it typically must occur in an environment constrained by both an aged organizational structure and habits of inertia and routine within the workforce.

The New Theory, then, helps us explain how those supreme values of Weberian bureaucracy—functional specialization and technical expertise—can lead to outcomes that the progressives would have found abhorrent: institutionalized inefficiency, abuses of discretionary authority, an inability to adapt. This line of analysis obviously undermines confidence in the efficiency of large organizations. And it directly challenges the progressives' assumption that an internalized ethic of public service would motivate government experts to work the will of their political superiors.

Transaction Costs, Issue Networks,
and Administrative Controls

The New Theory also helps us understand the origin of that fundamental structure of modern governance, the issue network (Heclo, 1978). Whenever decision makers become aware of a buildup of avoidable transaction costs in their relationships with one another, they are likely to respond by organizing an informal issue network. Public officials and private decision makers, noting the need for constant coordination and exchanges of information, develop informal but continuing and cooperative relationships. Networking can be viewed as a perfectly natural response to problems, especially the problem of coordination across the public-private interface, that are inherent in modern governance.

Once in existence, an issue network may facilitate change, resist it, or, more likely, present positive and negative opportunities at the same time. Because a network is a ready-made (if informal) communication system, a network member who has a new idea to sell may be able to use the preexisting patterns of cooperative relationships to get the word out. On the other hand, the participants in an issue network do not communicate with one another for communication's sake but rather to advance certain interests. The advancement of one's own interests may call for the formation of coalitions within the network to block others' agendas. So to the extent that an organizational entrepreneur's agenda conflicts with other network members' perceptions of their respective interests, change will encounter more, not less, organized resistance.

Although networks can be used to communicate interests, some people fear that they may also regularly be used to exert undue influence. Public officials may come to identify their personal interests with those of the private actors with whom they deal on a regular basis. Within the issue network's circle of public officials, legislators may interfere with executive appointees' impartial administration of the law, or senior civil servants may bend to appeals by lawmakers who seek special treatment for their constituents. The most commonly noted danger of all—that industry representatives will take advantage of their continuing relationships with public actors and bring pressure to bear on these officials—must be assessed with reference to another persistent problem of governance, the vesting of discretionary power in government decision makers.

In the United States, we do much of what we do at the porous boundary between the public and the private because we still value the progressive reformers' vision of governance by experts untainted by private influence. To that end, we multiply administrative controls of all kinds. Because discretionary power is abusable power, the greater the latitude that an expert official—a bureaucrat—enjoys, the greater is the danger that the official may come under the sway of private interests. Hence (the logic goes), the greater the perception of available discretion, the greater must be the effort to monitor and discipline officials' actions. If a hermetic separation of public from private were possible, so that private actors would find it more difficult than they do to reach their public sector counterparts, or if civil servants' abilities to act with discretion did not make their openness to private importunities as dangerous as it is, there would be much less need to control the interactions of government officials and private businesspeople with one another.

The American "culture of legalism" (Mashaw and Harfst, 1990) favors judicially reviewable procedures to discipline both the formal conduct of officials and their informal contacts across the public-private interface. It is unfortunate, though, that new controls almost always increase transaction costs for those who must follow them. The ever-growing web of regulations accounts for much of the sluggishness and stodginess in our public bureaucracy. As a consequence, the networking process, which was initially undertaken to improve efficiency in the administrative process by providing a means to cut down on transaction costs, tends to end up interfering with efficiency.

Regulations and restrictions certainly slow the gears of government. But do they work in the sense of improving fairness and probity in public administration? Do administrative controls actually limit the discretion of public officials in the ways that are expected? The case study presented in Part Two suggests that individuals who are set on pursuing goals of their own ("self-dealing," in the language of the New Theorists) often find ways to circumvent or even pervert any set of rules. What is more, the ingenuity needed for covert rule bending, like the human trait of self-interest itself, seems to be well represented among public servants and private businesspeople alike. Hence the effort to straiten conduct at the permeable membrane between government and the private economy may cost us much in lost efficiency while gaining us relatively little in the way of improved rectitude.

The background materials, the case study, and the analysis to follow should suggest some answers to the questions raised by these problems—questions about the role of self-regarding interests in American governance, about the avoidability of inefficiency in our public bureaucracies, and about the abusability of official discretion by our civil servants, particularly under pressure from private sector members of issue networks.

Public Administration Between the Old Theory and the New

The reformers' ordination of a separate cadre of public officials, imbued with an ethic of service and insulated by civil service protections, probably represented a sensible enough solution to problems of governmental corruption and inefficiency, given the times and the stock of concepts with which the reformers approached their task. The notion of a superior ethical standard also resonated with the late-nineteenth-century liberals' equation of formal education with "enlightenment," and enlightenment with a presumption of moral rectitude (Hayes, [1941] 1983). Alas, we are unlikely to see again the kind of bureaucracy-building binge that the progressives initiated—or for that matter the kind of willing suspension of disbelief that they displayed regarding both the possibilities of bureaucratic efficiency and the prospects for a new standard of public virtue, to be set by professional civil servants.

But neither is indiscriminate bureaucracy bashing what we need today.

Though they may not have delivered exactly what they expected from their New American State, the progressives have much to teach us about the demands of citizenship, even today. And despite the shortcomings of their organizational theories, the reformers' high-minded assumptions—not only about governance but also about human nature—add a dimension to our understand-

ing of the organizational experience that is missing from the New
Theorists' doctrine of rational self-interest as well as from the
familiar legalistic arguments for administrative controls.

But let us see now if the story itself does not make the essential point without much need for additional editorial commentary.

□ **part I**

Our Public Bureaucracies— In Theory and in Practice

chapter 1

Old
Versus New
Theories of Bureaucracy

Washington hands use "old line" to summarize a common attitude toward many of the long-established agencies of the federal government. The term refers mainly to a style of bureaucratic behavior, one characterized by dullness and routinized, highly specialized work (such as meat inspection within the Agriculture Department or rate setting for the gas pipeline industry at the Federal Energy Regulatory Commission). It is not mere age that makes an agency old line. Age, however, is almost always a factor, since the symptoms of bureaucratic stodginess usually become evident only at an advanced stage in the agency life cycle.

The metaphor of an agency life cycle derives from the work of Marver Bernstein (1955). Bernstein argued that a new bureau typically comes into being in the midst of excitement and optimism. Political leaders want to fix some grievous wrong or exert control over a rising new industry. Whatever the motivation, the creation of a new agency is accompanied by much political hoopla. But the sense of crisis that may initially have been brought on by abuses or rampant growth cannot be sustained indefinitely. Public concern wanes. The pressing problem that led Congress to create a new agency ceases to press, though the nation remains stuck with the bureaucracy that was set up to deal with it.

According to Bernstein, the élan of the founding period then gives way to a phase of debility and decline. This phase is at once terminal and interminable. The excitement of the founding period becomes no more than a distant memory. The years of debilitation stretch into decades, and the familiar functions of the now tired old agency continue to be performed with the appearance of monotonous, metronomic routine.

The Formal Bureaucracy

Agencies with old-line reputations are represented within all categories of the formal federal bureaucracy. To gain some appreciation of the old-line style in any one of them is, therefore, to gain some insight into the inner workings of big government itself.

At the center of the formal Washington bureaucracy are three kinds of agencies: the cabinet-level executive departments, the so-called independent regulatory commissions, and the subcabinet presidential agencies. The four most senior cabinet departments—State, Treasury, Defense (incorporating the army, the navy, and, a post–World War II creation, the air force), and Justice—trace their origins to acts passed by Congress in 1789, during its first legislative session. Jobs in these departments carry disproportionate shares of the prestige, power, and glamour that is to be found in nonelective government service.

Because the first four departments have existed since the beginning of the nation, they are sometimes referred to as "old line," but not with the usual connotations of the term. To get to the agencies that convey the stodginess associated with the common usage of "old line," one must move down the list to the departments that follow Justice in the official order of precedence. These are the departments of Interior (established in 1849), Agriculture (set up as a federal commission in 1861 and elevated to cabinet status in 1889), Commerce (established in 1903), and Labor (split off from Commerce in 1913). Following Labor in the federal pecking order are the executive departments created since World War II: Health and Human Services, Housing and Urban Development, Transportation, Energy, Education, and Veterans Affairs. This order is a ceremonial ranking as well as an index of departmental seniority. The State, Treasury, Defense, . . . Veterans Affairs ranking corresponds, for example, to the order in which cabinet officers march into the House of Representatives for the president's state of the union speech every January.

Some of the newer departments—Energy, for example—retain a bit of the verve of bureaucratic youth. But they have the feel of old-line agencies in the making. The specialized and often rather routine work of their employees leads to the same kind of lassitude that one finds in much older departments, such as Interior and Agriculture.

The Great Era of Bureaucracy Building

Given the bad repute that the term bureaucracy has taken on over the years, it is easy to forget the optimism of the "scientific managers" and "good government" partisans of the Progressive Era. The call of public service beckoned some of the nation's best and brightest—the Gifford Pinchots, Frederick Newells, and Harvey Wileys of the day—to the burgeoning bureaucracy.

As was suggested in the Introduction, the growth of the Interior and Agriculture departments through the addition of new bureaus and the upgrading of existing ones was perhaps more pronounced between the mid 1880s and the late 1920s than during any other period. It was during these years that Pinchot, with much public adulation, led in the professionalization of the Forest Service (created in 1879 as the Division of Forestry in the Agriculture Department). Newell took the Interior Department's Geological Survey through the great national resource inventories that Congress mandated in 1888. Meanwhile, over years of service beginning in the 1890s, Wiley was decisively shaping the Bureau of Chemistry, a sister bureau of the Forest Service within the Agriculture Department, into what became the Food and Drug Administration (so named and given expanded duties in 1906).

Similar upgradings occurred in other executive departments
and in the vast apparatus that would eventually be titled the Executive Office of the President. The Commerce and Labor departments came into being, and so did most of the great independent
regulatory agencies, beginning with the Interstate Commerce Commission (ICC). In virtually all cases, the pattern of agency creation
was the same—a pattern of industrial counterpart organization.

Industrial Counterpart Organizations and Iron Triangles

The heyday of federal agency creation spanned years of enormous
economic volatility and, for the most part, of dramatic industrial
growth. As the economy changed, the focus of attention shifted, too,
from one new problem industry to another. Not surprisingly, each
new agency was typically established as a direct counterpart to a
particular industry in which progressive lawmakers saw actual or
imminent potential danger. The pattern was not conducive to
agency-building on the basis of a coherent plan.

If X industry seemed a candidate for regulation or promotion
(or both), Congress typically set up a counterpart agency—a "federal X commission." And for good measure, Congress often simultaneously created a new X subcommittee in the Senate or House of
Representatives. The subcommittee would oversee the work of the
new X commission and periodically consider whether additional
legislation might be needed to keep X industry on track. In this way,
congressional subcommittees proliferated along with the agency-
by-agency growth of the regulatory bureaucracy itself.

Thus too did the so-called iron triangles of American government first appear: a new bureau (vertex one of the triangle) linked
to a new legislative subcommittee (vertex two) as well as to the firms
in the counterpart industry (vertex three). The iron triangle imagery
of tightly linked bureaus, subcommittees, and counterpart industries has become familiar in political scientists' accounts of the
workings of public bureaucracy. It appears prominently, for example, in popular introductory texts (Lineberry, 1989; see also Ripley
and Franklin, 1989).

The more sanguine of the progressive reformers, believing as
they did in the possibilities of human rationality, might have pre-

ferred a less piecemeal approach to national industrial planning
(Croly, 1909; Hays, [1955] 1975). Nevertheless, the counterpart pattern proved eminently consistent with Americans' pragmatic, solve-
problems-as-they-come approach to policy making (Graham, 1976).
And in some ways, the progressives' faith in the possibility of an
ethic of public service actually supported the ad hoc pattern, for it
underwrote the reformers' confidence that public sector decision
making could be insulated from the potential corruption of private
sector influences. This naiveté contributed to the emergence of certain patterns of public-private interpenetration that the counterpart
pattern facilitated but that the original progressives had intended to
prevent.

The Independent Regulatory Commissions

The bureau-subcommittee-industry pattern reproduced itself many
times over, not only with the addition of specialized bureaus to the
executive departments but also in the creation of the independent
regulatory agencies—"independent" because they lie outside of the
president's direct chain of command. As the railroads, oceanic shipping, hydroelectric power, radio broadcasting, and other problem
industries successively became candidates for regulation, Congress
set up separate counterpart agencies: the Interstate Commerce Commission; the Shipping Board, which became the Federal Maritime
Commission (FMC); the Federal Power Commission (FPC); the Radio Board, which became the Federal Communications Commission (FCC); and so forth. Or else Congress simply expanded the
jurisdiction of an existing agency by adding a new bureau to regulate an industry that it found to be in need of federal control or
assistance.

Two other major independent agencies, the Federal Reserve
System (the Fed) and the Securities and Exchange Commission
(SEC), were also products of the Progressive Era. Technically, the
Fed and the SEC are independent commissions on the pattern of the
ICC, the FCC, and the others. However, the Fed and the SEC may
be too glamorous and too much involved in newsworthy actions
(such as deciding whether to expand or contract the nation's money
supply; bringing well-publicized lawsuits against stock market ma-

nipulators) to qualify as old-line agencies in the normal usage of
the term.

The legal separateness of agencies such as the ICC and the
FCC from the executive branch not only makes them independent
but also distinguishes them from the major subcabinet presidential
agencies. Included in the latter category are the Central Intelligence
Agency (CIA), the Environmental Protection Agency (EPA), the
General Services Administration (GSA), and the National Aeronautics and Space Administration (NASA). These organizations all resemble the executive departments in that they are large, important,
and belong to the president's immediate chain of command. But
they have administrators or directors instead of full cabinet officers
at their helms. The CIA, EPA, GSA, and NASA also lack something
of the stature of, and generally have smaller budgets and staffs than,
the cabinet-level departments do.

Principles of the Old Theory

So vast, sustained, and pronounced a development as the emergence
of the bureaucratic state could hardly have occurred in the absence
of a coherent set of principles to guide it—principles that inspired
faith in the organizational solution and gave the reformers a conceptual template to use as they structured and staffed the new agencies. The term for the theory that fired the progressives' excitement,
the *Old Theory*, suggests not only that enthusiasm for bureaucracy
has faded among most students of government but also that certain
premises of the progressive theory have now been pretty generally
repudiated.

The progressive reformers accepted most of the major tenets
of nineteenth-century liberalism. They believed in the ameliorative
potential of education and science, in expertise, and—as the name
of their movement suggests—in the possibility of almost limitless
human progress. The progressives emphasized that organizations
can be made efficient by the rational distribution of specialized
functions combined with a scientific plan for the flow of work. To
keep public administration—that is, the work of what became our
old-line agencies—not only efficient but also apolitical and uncor-
rupted by special interests, the Old Theorists focused on the distinc-

tions between the public sector and the private, and between politics and administration. The fact that few students of public management accept either distinction as very defensible today gives some measure to the intellectual course that we have traversed since the days of progressivism.

Bearing in mind that the expression is only a reference term and not a precise analytical category, we may apply the catchall term *New Theory* to the critical ideas that emerged through the 1970s and 1980s to explain how the progressives' bureaucratic edifice gradually slipped into decline.

Expertise and the Problem of Discretion

The Progressive Era legislators foresaw the need for volumes of detailed new legislation to cover the technical issues of industrial promotion and regulation. Under democratic theory, elected representatives had to remain in charge of the nation's overall industrial policy. But because members of Congress possessed neither the specialized knowledge nor the time to oversee the day-to-day workings of U.S. industries, they appointed expert administrators and commissioners to exercise authority in their place. The senior appointees to the new agencies and commissions were, in turn, backed up by bureaus of expert staffers (Hays, [1955] 1975; McConnell, 1966; Ackerman and Hassler, 1981).

The progressives' theory of delegated authority gave rise to a structure with a built-in problem, the problem of discretion: how to keep the top-level administrators and commissioners accountable to their superiors in Congress while not denying them room to exercise expert judgment, and, further, how to keep the actions of those lower-level civil servants—the expert staffers of the new agencies and bureaus—in line with the instructions of their bosses, the agency heads and bureau chiefs.

Owing largely to the influence of Lord Alfred Dicey, the leading British constitutional commentator of his day, a strict interpretation of the "rule of law" principle governed legal thinking throughout the period that is called Victorian in British history and Progressive in U.S. history (Shapiro, 1988). In line with the Diceyan view, most late–nineteenth-century liberals abhorred discretion as

"the law of tyrants" (Pound, 1922). If the reformers feared any outcome more than they did the law of tyrants, it was probably rule by
petty tyrants, that is, by midrange bureaucrats who arbitrarily modify the laws and regulations that they administer.

The best way to solve a problem is not to let it appear in the
first place, and to a degree, the intellectual climate of Progressive
Era America convinced many prophets of bureaucracy that the
problem of discretion could be forestalled through education, professionalization, and conversion of civil servants to the gospel of
good government. The Old Theory was an ethical theory in that it
relied on the internal values of well-educated public servants to
discipline the conduct of government business. Under this ethical
theory of the civil service, bureaucrats were expected to behave with
probity and rectitude primarily because they would want to—not
out of fear of punishment and not merely because they were chasing
the carrots of promotions and pay raises.

Frederick C. Mosher (1968) characterized the period 1883–
1906 as an era dominated by the idea of "government by the
good"—*the good* referring to the politically incorrupt. Only later
did the scientific managers inspire the broad-scale shift to an imagery of "government by the efficient," a dispensation that Mosher
found dominant in the federal service from 1906 through the New
Deal years of the 1930s.

The Organization of Work by Classification

The premier date in Mosher's categorization, 1883, refers to the year
of the Pendleton Act. This act framed the personnel system of the
new bureaus and laid a basis for the detailed classification system
under which the work of the federal bureaucracy was to be organized (Pendleton Act). A complex pattern of goals and political
pressures underlay the civil service reform movement (Van Riper,
1958; Skowronek, 1982). At the center of this pattern was a provision
for the appointment of selected federal career officials on the basis
of merit alone. A candidate's qualifications would have to be demonstrated by the passing of a civil service test or the possession of
formal academic credentials, and often by both.

Because demonstrated mastery of a technical skill or specialized intellectual discipline was supposed to be the criterion of appointment, recruits to the federal service would have self-selected, by their own prior educational choices, into professions other than that of "mere politics." Top graduates of the nation's colleges and professional schools would come to government imbued with true professionals' standards of performance. The progressives simply did not expect that civil servants would want to substitute goals of their own for those specified from above, for to do so would have been contrary to their training, their personal preferences, even their professional ethics (see also Wilson, 1887.)

The elaborate classification system envisioned by the early civil service reformers required years to evolve. The Classification Act of 1923 formally established the principle of position-classification in the federal service (Classification Act). Not until 1932, however, did full competitive standards apply to as many as 80 percent of federal career employees—and the coverage has, in fact, declined as a percentage of the total workforce during the years since. Nevertheless, the spirit of the original ideals—merit appointment, political neutrality, standardized position classification—survives in the broad structure of today's federal service.

The workhorses in this structure fill slots known as General Schedule (GS) grades. Career officials in grades GS-9 through GS-15 are usually referred to as professionals to distinguish them from the clerical and custodial personnel further down in the hierarchy (grades GS-1 through GS-8). These professionals, constituting about 48 percent of the total civilian classified service, are the degree-holding accountants, civil engineers, economists, lawyers, soil conservationists, and so on through the almost 450 separate occupational series in today's federal bureaucracy (Hartman, 1983). Once appointed, the classified civil servant enjoys the promise of steady work with regular salary increases and the eventual vesting of a right not to be fired except for cause—all of which is as the original reformers would apparently have wanted it.

Public Administration as Apolitical and Scientific

The progressives' limiting idea was that of a space segregated from the dirty processes of political deal making. Job security would encourage the nation's bureaucrats to execute their offices faithfully and without fear of reprisals. In the independent commissions, the separation of appointees from the presidential chain of command was intended to provide an extra layer of insulation against partisan intervention. Ideally, then, decision making would be rule-bound ("discretionless"), neither tainted by external special interests nor moved by political ambitions.

Widespread acceptance of a gap between policy and administration lent credibility to the belief that civil servants could be immunized against the political virus. In the year that Congress set up the first federal regulatory agency, the Interstate Commerce Commission, Woodrow Wilson (1887) published one of the most influential papers in the literature of political science, and one that did much to promote acceptance of a policy-administration gap.

According to Wilson (1887, pp. 210–211), politics "sets the tasks for administration" but refrains from interfering with the "detailed and systematic execution of public law." Wilson said that decision making involves two degrees of choice—choice as to goals and as to means. Wilson reserved the choice of the broad line of policy for political actors and, specifically, for legislators. But administrators had to decide how a given policy should be executed. Once elected representatives had set the policy goals, the experts should be trusted to find the best way to reach them (Doig, 1983).

Subsequent developments in progressive thought, however, gave a new twist to Wilson's justification for bureaucratic latitude. Early in the twentieth century, Frederick Winslow Taylor ([1911] 1947) and his followers spread the idea that careful, scientific study of any production process would yield increasingly efficient techniques. Precise rules for the execution of any task could then be formulated and taught to workers. Taylor's sometime disciple Frank Gilbreth popularized the notion that administrators and planners should be able to discover the one best way to do any job (Gilbreth and Gilbreth, 1953; Haber, 1964).

If one best way could eventually be found for any job of work, then a laborer or planner—or bureaucrat—would have to exercise intuition or judgment only during the infancy of the field of endeavor. Legislators might continue to pass vague laws that ostensibly required administrators to exercise discretion, but the administrators would actually become less and less free to use any latitude that the statutes seemed to allow. The proof that the administrators really were experts would lie in their mastery of the one best way that the science of the subject would have revealed. Conscientious administrators would end up with no real choice as to the method that they should apply in pursuit of the statutory objective. As specialized knowledge within the field became increasingly sophisticated, discretion would be squeezed out of the decision-making process by legislative specification of ends and scientific determination of means.

The idea of the policy-administration gap, when combined with one-best-way thinking, seemingly solved the progressives' problem of administrative discretion. The resulting image of administration that is not only virtually discretionless but also frictionless is still referred to as the "machine model of organization" (Simon and March, 1958; Frug, 1984).

Well into the twentieth century, the Old Theory could be invoked to justify bureaucrats' exercises of power pursuant to relatively broad grants of authority from legislators. The important distinction here is between delegations of power and exercises of discretion. The theory of expertise implied that power, though vast and virtually undefined when created by statute, could nevertheless be applied to concrete problems in a relatively discretionless fashion. Indeed, it was this very belief, fostered by one-best-way thinking, that largely justified the delegations of power that progressives such as Wilson (1887) were so remarkably willing to make. Robert Reich (1988) dates the reaction against broad grants of discretionary authority to the post–World War II period—in other words, after the Progressive Era had ended. By then, however, it had become impossible to continue believing that power and its mode of exercise were neatly separable.

The Progressive Legacy

Did the progressives succeed? Their institution-building legacy is impressive, to be sure. The bureaus that they established have proved their staying power, if in no other way than simply by sur-

viving to become today's old-line agencies. Nevertheless, a rueful
sense of doubt today surrounds the bureaucratic enterprise.

The reformers who designed the major portion of today's
federal bureaucracy believed that they could solve three interrelated
problems: the problem of *interests* (keeping self-serving special interests out of public-interested decision making), the problem of
efficiency (ensuring relatively frictionless movement of the governmental machine toward its goals), and the problem of *discretion*
(confining public officials within relatively narrow, legally defined
limits). But the record suggests that the progressives fell short on all
counts.

Certainly, the problem of interests remains as vexing as it
was in the progressives' day and arguably has gotten worse. In the
midst of the New Deal, E. Pendleton Herring (1936) introduced the
now familiar view of administrative agencies as forums in which
interest groups compete for favor in a process that is essentially
legislative in substance even when it is judicial in form. The old
image of completely rationalized, superefficient organizations is difficult to reconcile with the bargaining and jostling that are known
to occur day in, day out within the bureaucracy. Political scientists
call it "bureaucratic coalition building" or "bureaucratic politics"
(Allison, 1971; Halperin, 1974; Cook, 1989). Scholars debate the
degree of latitude that bureaucrats enjoy as they adjust to competing
interests, and they differ in their beliefs as to the degree of penetration that private lobbies have achieved into public agencies. But one
variant or another of Herring's model is accepted today by almost
all observers of the administrative process.

Efficiency, the second vital concern of the progressives, is
probably the last quality that most observers of bureaucracy expect
from large public organizations. The administrative controls under
which civil servants labor today neutralize much of the advantage
that their commitment and expertise were supposed to confer.
Furthermore, there are many (especially among the New Theorists)
who believe that civil servants themselves are incompetents or in-
veterate shirkers and, as such, parties to a kind of conspiracy of
inefficiency in contemporary governance.

One still sees references to the so-called transmission belt
theory of administration (Stewart, 1975; Byner, 1987; Calvert,

McCubbins, and Weingast, 1989; Seidenfeld, 1992). Under this theory, bureaucrats merely work out the unfinished details of the statutes that specify their goals. But "discretionless administration" in anything approaching the literal sense is generally appreciated to be a chimera. Today, the transmission belt theory tends to be cited only as an analytical foil for some more realistically drawn image of discretionary decision making. We can also note the Sisyphean, and ultimately unsuccessful, attempts that Congress and the courts have made to control the administrative discretion that, according to the progressives, was never supposed to have appeared in the first place.

Principles of the New Theory

Dissatisfaction with the Old Theory has given rise to a variety of alternative approaches. All of the alternatives have in common a determination to view bureaucracy from a more realistic perspective than the progressives' strongly ethical outlook embodied. To combine various of the critics' contributions into a coherent New Theory is the explicit aspiration of some contemporary writers (Moe, 1984; see, however, Moe, 1990. And see Brandl's concise survey, 1989, which also contains the first apparent use of the term "new theory").

Transaction Costs and the Emergence of Organizations

The New Theorists emphasize the effort to reduce transaction costs, especially the costs of gathering and processing information, as the driving factor in rational human beings' never-ending quest for efficiency. This emphasis makes the distinction between hierarchical organizations and markets more basic in the New Theory than is the one between the public and the private sectors.

The New Theorists envision society in its natural state as a free market. Only when certain inconveniences of free-market buying and selling reach a critical limit will individuals forgo the freedom of the market to join firms (thereby binding themselves to obey bosses) or form governments (thereby subjecting themselves to the regulatory authority of public officials, including bureaucrats). In the New Theory, as in the Old, therefore, hierarchy and authority relationships remain essential characteristics of bureaucracy. But students of bureaucracy today, following the work pioneered by Coase (1937, 1960), increasingly view hierarchical organization in a very different way than the progressives did—not as the most efficient pattern for transmitting orders from top to bottom but rather as a special kind of contractual relationship between superiors and subordinates.

In the free market, individuals will try to advance their interests in whatever ways give them the best returns for the costs that they have to incur. The prices of goods and services represent one category of costs. Those prices are the ones that sellers actually mark on the items that they offer for sale. But transaction costs—for example, the cost in time and effort to find out who is selling what and for how much—represent an additional cost of acquiring goods or services in a market. Thus the real cost of a traded item is its market price *plus* any external costs of the product in question, such as the costs of any pollution that the makers of the product generate in the course of producing it, *plus* the transaction costs of the exchange.

Goods that involve relatively low transaction costs (so that little incentive exists to economize on the transaction costs of exchanging them) will be traded item by item in free markets. Item-by-item trading based on prices posted in markets dominates the textbook picture of a free economy. However, for many items, transaction costs are large. Specialized technical information may be needed to evaluate certain products. Such information is costly to acquire. Furthermore, the value of certain products, such as labor, may change over time, as when a worker's skill improves with experience on the job. Employers and employees alike may dread the hassle of constantly renegotiating contracts to reflect the workers' improving performance in rising pay levels. To reduce the costs of locating and evaluating items with high transaction costs and then negotiating separate terms of exchange for every item or product traded, individuals may lump a whole series of agreements into a single macrocontract.

The Employment Macrocontract. The classic example of a macrocontract is the one that employees negotiate with an employer. Instead of renegotiating their terms of employment for every hour of work or for each separate service that is to be performed, would-be employees may agree to work for an indefinite term into the future on a graduated scale of wages. Raises will be automatic with seniority on the job.

The negotiation of an employment macrocontract establishes a hierarchy with an employer, manager, or foreman in the position of the superior and the employee in the subordinate's role. Within reason, the employees must do as they are told when on the job. As Coase (1960, p. 16) once expressed it, "Individual bargains between the various co-operating factors of production are eliminated and for a market transaction is substituted an administrative decision."

According to the New Theorists, the term "firm" is shorthand for the organization that is created when individuals decide to forgo market transactions and agree instead that a certain range of their activities will henceforth be governed by a macrocontract. A government bureau is a special kind of firm, one set up to provide collective goods such as management of public resources (national forests, the open range), pollution control, or price setting for industries that are deemed to be "affected with a public interest" under the rule that the Supreme Court adopted in 1877 in the landmark Progressive Era case of *Munn* v. *Illinois* (see Lerner, 1972). Similarly, the civil service classification scheme is just a special case of that exceedingly common type of agreement, the employment macrocontract.

Note that when a firm or bureau is created, transaction costs are reduced only internally. A newly formed firm will continue to trade with other firms and, of course, with individuals (for example, with its customers). Sometimes, the behavior of a firm increases the transaction costs of its external trades. Then the internal efficiencies that were achieved by forming the organization may be offset through higher costs encountered externally.

This line of analysis bears directly on the problems of management in old-line agencies, since the phenomenon of institutional aging can itself become a cause of higher and higher external transaction costs. The initial macrocontract might have been worthwhile, but gradually increasing external transaction costs may eventually make it desirable to disband the organization and revert to item-by-item dealing. As we will see in Chapter Eight, changes in age-related transaction costs may explain the rise and fall of special projects within established organizations.

Ouchi's Amplification of the New Theory. Although the foregoing kind of direct application of what Oliver Williamson (1985) has called the transaction-cost framework seems to be the most popular mode of explanation for the organizing process, William Ouchi (1981a) has expanded on Williamson's analysis to present a somewhat more nuanced theory of bureaucratic origins.

Like the other New Theorists, Ouchi has stressed that vast ranges of decisions in a society such as ours occur under circumstances of information costliness. As we have seen, markets often fail in such circumstances. Market failure or no, however, it remains a fact of life that exceedingly large numbers of transacters still have to interact. Ouchi points out that human beings simply cannot sustain frequent interactions unless they can take for granted a variety of shared capabilities and values. Traders for example need a common language, even if it is a sign language, and they need some minimal level of mutual trust that agreements will be enforced.

In primitive clans, intense socialization, resulting in a virtual homogenization of attitudes among all members of the group, ensures the sharing of needed skills and values. Clanlike socialization is impossible in a mass industrial society, though division of labor continues to make transactions the basic requisite of all members' lives. So in Ouchi's model, the impersonal bureaucracy based on a hierarchy of authorities—in which administrative orders substitute for freely negotiated exchange agreements—emerges as the compromise solution. Bureaucracy occupies an intermediate position between market (because it retains the market value of rationality) and clan (because it involves a more or less coherent system of attitudes, expectations, and values). The manager's fairness, instead of individual self-seeking in a context of openly posted prices, must be counted on to ensure a just apportionment of rewards within the bureaucratic organization.

Ouchi's approach is a significant departure from that of most New Theorists in that it complements rational analysis with explicit attention to the cultural dimensions of organization.

Firms, Bureaus, and the Principal-Agent Problem

Whether in a private firm or a public bureau, and whether in the models of Coase, Williamson, or Ouchi, an employment macrocontract defines a hierarchy of authorities and broadly defines reciprocal duties and restrictions for those who occupy the different rungs on the ladder. (The employer must provide certain fringe benefits, safe working conditions, and so forth; employees may have to punch in and out at specified times, observe a dress code, and so forth.)

New Theorists like to analyze relationships within such a hierarchy using the principal-agent model. In fact, the principal-agent formulation is probably second in importance only to the notion of transaction costs in the list of New Theory concepts (Pratt and Zeckhauser, 1985; Donahue, 1989).

The New Theorists stress that employees are agents of the owners of a firm and as such are legally and morally obliged to work the will of their principals. Similarly, civil servants may be considered as agents of their superiors, at least in the sense that they are expected to follow their superiors' legal orders and faithfully execute their agency's policies. The New Theorists, however, reject the progressives' belief that ethical strictures can ensure the dutiful behavior that the principal-agent relationship requires.

Drawing their premises primarily from the economic theory of the market, the New Theorists emphasize individual self-interest, not group goals. The appeal to an internalized sense of public trust may work partially or temporarily, but human egoism will eventually challenge the pattern of strict accountability that the machine model of bureaucracy implies. Bureaucratic actors have interests of their own to advance. Inevitably, these interests will come into conflict, at least to some degree, with the goals of the organization. The temptation of a conflicted employee to sacrifice the group goal for the personal one is likely to be irresistible. Thus, the New Theorists reason, if subordinates have any latitude for discretion, they will sooner or later abuse it.

Asymmetric Information, Adverse Selection, and Moral Hazard. Some New Theorists believe that asymmetric information is the source of most principal-agent problems. A condition of asymmetric information exists whenever the principal in the relationship knows less than the agent does about any aspect of the employment situation, for example, about the technical requirements of a particular job or about the employee's diligence in performance. As Mathew McCubbins and his collaborators (1987, p. 247) cleverly expressed it, "The crime of runaway bureaucracy requires opportunity as well as motive, and this is supplied by asymmetric information."

Asymmetric information tends to become an acute problem in organizations such as public bureaucracies, which often exist to process large volumes of technical data. The employees in such organizations can—if they have the incentive that self-interest may supply—bamboozle their bosses while they shirk or subvert pretty much without fear of discovery. *Shirking* refers to laziness or malingering, *subverting* to behavior that actively undercuts the policies that the higher-ups in the organization intend to advance (Alchian and Demsetz, 1972; Wilson, 1989).

Some New Theorists argue that the organization of work by classification (as in the federal civil service) invites two additional difficulties—adverse selection and moral hazard—both of which are arguably endemic in old-line bureaucracies (see Veljanovski, 1982, and sources cited there).

Those who recruit for organizations in which work is ordered by classification cannot possibly know, merely on the basis of qualifying exams and employment interviews, how an employee will perform over a long-term career. The applicant, by contrast, has a better sense of his or her real interests, real abilities, and above all, real reason for preferring a job in the civil service. The reason might be to serve, but it might also be the attractiveness of a job with virtual immunity from firing unless underperformance becomes flagrant.

The idea here is that jobs in which the pay level and the employment security are tied to performance (instead of to seniority) will select well. They will select for the "hard chargers"—the more able and aggressive. By contrast, jobs that carry the protection of a classification schedule will select adversely—for those workers who seek career cushions rather than challenges.

Once workers have been taken into the classified service, their assurance of employment, even at substandard levels of performance, will (again, given the ever-present factor of self-interest) lead them to take advantage of the situation. They will display moral hazard, a term coined in the insurance industry to describe an individual's tendency to exercise less care if he or she knows that an insurer will indemnify negligent behavior (Arrow, 1963; Pauly, 1968). Under the civil service classification scheme, the government must pay employees at least at the seniority graduated pay levels almost irrespective of their diligence. One could scarcely imagine a situation more conducive to shirking and subverting, given the New Theorists' assumption that bureaucrats, simply because they are human, will sometimes work toward goals other than those the bureau's leaders specify—including the goal of less work for the same pay.

Thus the New Theorists turn the progressive model upside down, for by way of their concept of asymmetric information, they make the expertise of career employees not a guarantee of competence and impartiality but an invitation to malingering or self-aggrandizement within an organization. To similar effect, they invoke the concepts of adverse selection and moral hazard to suggest that bureaucracy under a classification system does not solve the problem of efficiency, as the progressives expected, but actually worsens it.

Bounded Rationality, Satisficing, and Incrementalism

Distinct from the concept of asymmetric information but closely related to it is Simon's seminal concept of bounded rationality (1947). Like the problem of asymmetric information, the problems that bounded rationality generate ultimately derive from human beings' inherently limited ability to acquire and interpret information. Specifically, bounded rationality refers to the inability of humans to fulfill the exceedingly stringent theoretical requirements for rational behavior as set forth in traditional neoclassical microeconomic theory.

Neoclassical theory posits that maximization of one's satisfaction is the objective of rational choice. The New Theorists concede that most people *want* to maximize satisfaction; they *try* to choose calculatedly, rationally. But Simon and his followers argue that actual decision making can never be as calculatingly complete as the more ardent rationalists assume. In fact, bounded rationality makes it impossible for a decision maker even to know all of the alternatives that really exist, since beyond some threshold of knowledge, the information costs of acquiring additional data on possible options becomes prohibitive. In circumstances of any complexity, therefore, a real decision maker must forgo maximizing in favor of "satisficing." The same limited cognitive abilities that lead to satisficing—that is, trying to get along as well as inadequate information and limited information-processing capabilities will permit— also help to explain why change must frequently be undertaken incrementally.

The various theorists of incrementalism have put their distinctive twists on the concept, and some have been more explicit than others in spelling out the links between their own work and the seminal ideas of Simon (Lindblom, 1959; Braybrooke and Lindblom, 1963; Wildavsky, 1964; Behn, 1988). But all incrementalists argue that change should be undertaken through step-by-step moves from an existing position. The existing position in turn will have been reached through a series of prior "experiments" with altered organizational forms and policies. Overly ambitious moves by a decision maker, or moves that are taken too quickly, carry excessive risks. Such moves tend either to introduce errors in policy that will offset any expected gains from change or else simply to overburden the ability of affected workers to absorb the new rules and work effectively within new structures.

Workers, who also, of course, are constrained by bounded rationality, have limited abilities to absorb new instructions and accommodate to new structures. Typically, therefore, the employees in any large organization try to cope by devising rules of thumb and standard operating procedures (Simon, 1947; Cyert and March, 1963). These procedures "conserve on bounded rationality" by making it unnecessary to rethink every problem anew. Standard operating procedures are conservative in a second sense as well: they reflect the bureaucratic instinct to play it safe—that is, to satisfice for a time-tested acceptable outcome rather than to take risks even when an extremely high payoff could result. The members of an organization gradually fall into "grooves," or conservative patterns of routine. Thus from a general theory of human cognition, Simon and his followers derived an explanation for the traits of stodginess and routinization that are widely taken to be characteristics of bureaucracy.

(As will be seen, the urge to routinize suggests why "special" projects within organizations often cease over time to be special, and eventually even cease to be projects as they are slowly absorbed into the rhythms of the organization.)

Bureaucratic Discretion and Agency Capture

Using the concepts of self-interest, adverse selection, asymmetric information, satisficing, and incrementalism, the New Theorists present a theory of the process by which discretion evolves in old-line agencies.

The logic behind the conclusion that workers will shirk or subvert if they can do so with impunity also implies that workers will try to create the conditions in which they *are able to* shirk or subvert. It is discretion that gives employees those conditions. Executing an incremental process of their own, workers can quietly generate discretion by minutely modifying agency rules in the very acts of applying them. Because of asymmetric information, the boss will never know. And because the boss is probably a satisficer, he or she might not even care whether procedures are being followed as long as overall performance appears to exceed some minimum threshold. Shortcuts and exceptions to the rules gradually accumulate, in the end conferring on employees the freedom to do much as they wish.

According to some critics of government agencies, what public bureaucrats mostly want to do is use the discretionary powers that they confer on themselves to advance the interests of the very private actors—mostly the stockholders and managers of counterpart industries—whom the bureaucrats were originally appointed to regulate (Kolko, 1965; see also Quirk, 1981). This extreme version of the New Theory contradicts the progressive vision in the profoundest possible way: in it, discretion, instead of being minimized, is consciously and cynically expanded so that bureaucrats will have the freedom to serve not the public's interests but their own or those of counterpart industries.

Proponents of the extreme version—in one common form, it is known as the agency capture theory—sometimes suggest that members of an industry who desire to form a cartel but realize that direct collusion may expose them to prosecution under the antitrust laws, lobby for the creation of a governmental agency to "regulate" them (see, for example, Jaffee, 1954; Kolko, 1965.). Allegedly, the private decision makers know that they will be able to capture the public agency and determine its policies. In effect, they conspire to use the government as a tool of their own self-serving intentions. The effect of this view—the ultimate rationale for bureaucracy bashing—has been to cast suspicion on the institution of public service itself.

I not only reject the contention that our public bureaucracy is tainted by conspiracy, irredeemably inefficient, and out-of-control, but think that this view is as wrongheaded today as the Old Theory in its time was naive. Still, the fact that terms such as "iron triangle" and "agency capture" could have attained currency at all suggests how far the actual experience of the New American State has taken us from the progressive vision.

Indeed, in their idealism, the progressives were much too sanguine. We know today that neither higher education nor professional expertise can guarantee nonpartisan, disinterested, or incorruptible conduct by civil servants. It is also evident that neither formal rules nor technical knowledge can compel a decision maker to apply "accepted accounting principles" or the "best engineering practice." Because the nature of industrial society itself, not merely the self-interest of lobbyists and influence-peddlers, necessitates the blurring of the boundary between public and private, any attempt to banish current patterns of interpenetration by returning to the progressives' favored structural solution to the problem of governance—a strict adversarial separation of the two sectors—would be unrealistic.

But for all that the Old Theorists made mistakes, their vision of public service was edifying and ennobling. Alas, the same cannot always be said of the New Theorists' approach. Nor is the extreme form of the contemporary critique of bureaucracy consistent with the actual experiences of most of our civil servants.

The concepts of the iron triangle and agency capture, then, can be considered as wrong answers. But they were answers to some right questions, questions such as: If we cannot think of bureaucracy today in the way that the progressives would have hoped, how should we think of it? And if bureaucracy does not work in the apolitical, frictionless, and rule-bound way that the Old Theorists hoped it would, how does it work? To these questions we now turn.

chapter 2

The Bureaucracy:
What It Is
and How It Works

Although the excitement of the agency-building process—and indeed the initial attractiveness of the bureaucratic idea itself—made the formal bureaucracy a temporary magnet for top-quality employees, the gradual slippage of many Progressive Era bureaus into old-line status has made it increasingly difficult to attract these candidates into the classified service. The progressives rightly foresaw a need for specialized knowledge to deal with the problems of an industrial economy, but they failed to create institutions that, over the long haul, would be capable of handling the work that the government would have to perform.

The uncompetitive salaries that many civil service jobs pay exacerbate the problems of adverse selection and moral hazard. Many employees in the civil service today take it for granted that they cannot, or need not and should not, be expected to perform certain of the ordinary functions of our government, let alone all the highly skilled functions that the Old Theory would have presumed that they should handle. Hence the tendency to contract for experts by going to where the experts increasingly are: outside of the formal bureaucracy.

What a rigid formal bureaucracy could not supply in the way of needed expertise and talent, a "shadow bureaucracy" has duly appeared to provide—for a price. Together, the formal bureaucracy and the shadow bureaucracy constitute what might be called Washington's effective bureaucracy.

The Shadow Bureaucracy

Every employee in the formal classified service has a match in at least one member of the shadow bureaucracy, that is, a private sector worker whose full-time job depends directly on governmental grants or contracts. Of course, ripple effects through the economy magnify the actual impact of a dollar's worth of federal procurement actions, so the number of nongovernment employees who are actually supported by government contracts may considerably exceed the one-to-one ratio (Fritschler and Ross, 1980; Sharkansky, 1980; Rehfuss, 1989).

Although private contractors are outside of the classified service, they often become insiders in the conduct of the day-to-day work of the government. Contractors frequently spend most of their days in government buildings, working as fully integrated participants in project teams. Their fellow team members may include civil servants on the federal payroll and even contractors from competing consulting firms. Practically speaking, many members of the shadow bureaucracy function as full members of federal officialdom.

But because contractors' terms of employment are not covered by the civil service General Schedule, contractors may negotiate fees outside of the classified pay scales (though all fees ultimately come from tax funds by way of the government's contracting process). Private contractors are also free to sell their services to different agencies in turn or even simultaneously, a situation that can lead to conflict-of-interest problems. Batteries of federal inspectors and watchdogs are needed to prevent consultants from playing sponsors off against one another. And, of course, private contractors are free to hang their shingles anywhere they wish—in universities, in the Washington branches of leading law or accounting firms, in prestigious think tanks, and, especially, in the specialized service companies that have grown up on diets of government contracts.

Beltway bandit firms (as the Washington-based business-service firms are called) have proliferated, driving real estate prices out of sight in the stylish industrial parks around the Washington circumferential highway. Under the stimulus of federal spending, think tanks have also multiplied along a corridor from the North Carolina research triangle (Durham–Raleigh–Chapel Hill) up to Boston.

The Beltway Bandits

Washington-based firms with names that sound like anagrams of one another (Computer Data Services, System Automation Corporation, Scientific Advisory Information Services) fill a critical niche in the effective bureaucracy by supplying high-skill services that federal career officials often have not developed the competence to provide themselves. Other companies with more familiar titles— big, prestigious outfits like the California-based Rand Corporation, the Stanford Research Institute, and the Mitre Corporation (which originated as a spin-off company organized by M.I.T. scientists)— also maintain active Washington offices to service federal agencies.

Over the years, the pattern of dependency has intensified. Today, many beltway bandits offer far more than high-powered research or expert inquiry into specialized technical topics. Does the secretary of Agriculture (or Education, or Treasury) want to hold a conference of academic and other professional experts? A dozen beltway bandit firms are experienced in organizing these meetings. Does the secretary of Commerce (or Labor, or Energy) want a management study done or a big computer model built? Other Washington firms specialize in such jobs. The federal government generates enough work for these firms to keep their staffs employed full time, year round.

More and more of the work that these firms perform is rather routine and intellectually undemanding—garden-variety business services. For example, many federal buildings have long had security and custodial services provided by contractors instead of by lower-rank members of the career civil service. Beltway bandits also account for a larger and larger share of the ordinary office work of the federal government: file management, computer and copier maintenance, routine installation of commercially purchased software, and the like.

Today, the shadow bureaucracy consists of a stable enough community so that track records of typical billing costs and performance portfolios are readily available. The shadow bureaucracy is also large enough so that no federal agency is hostage to only one or two firms that are the sole sellers of needed services. If only a few potential sellers of highly specialized know-how existed, they would be able to extract monopoly profits from those who needed to contract for outside experts. New Theorists call this the "small numbers problem" (Williamson, 1975). The steps that have been taken to solve the small numbers problem, that is, active federal support for a large community of contractors and consultants, all of whom vie for government business, help us understand why the shadow bureaucracy is not only specialized but also as large as it is is.

Task Order Contracting. Much of the work of the beltway bandits is organized under a special kind of contract, known as a task order contract. A task order contract arranges in advance for a firm (called the incumbent) to complete a number of individual jobs over a number of years. In a task order contract, however, the specific jobs do *not* need to be spelled out in advance, and the incumbent does *not* need to compete against other consulting firms to get the individual jobs once it has won the major competition to get the task order contract in the first place.

Suppose that agency X lets a multimillion-dollar contract to a particular incumbent, and the agency's staff members later develop a need for specialized work that no one initially anticipated. A series of more specific assignments, called task orders, can then be interpolated into the original broadly worded contract. So without opening the work to new competitions, agency X's procurement officials can keep amending the contract with new task orders as long as any of the initial multimillion dollar amount remains.

In a typical year, federal procurement officers will take more than 21 million separate contract actions that affect some $200 billion in taxpayers' monies, which is about one-fifth of the entire federal budget (Kettl, 1988; U.S. Office of Management and Budget, 1989). Most of this money gets disbursed under one form or another of task order contracting, from service contracts with Washington-based suppliers of day-to-day business services to mammoth Defense Department prime contracts that will eventually support elaborate hierarchies of subcontracts.

One point of a task order contract is to avoid the hassle and waste—in short, the transaction costs—of individual contract competitions for each separate item on which the agency staff members need outside help (Kelman, 1990). In effect, the intent is to bring the outsiders "into the agency" but under an employment macrocontract whose terms differ from those of the civil service classification schedule. Indeed, the description of the employment macrocontract given years ago by Coase (1937, pp. 391–392) can be taken today as a perfectly accurate description of a task order contract: "The service which is being provided is expressed in general terms, the exact details being left until a later date. . . . The details of what the supplier is expected to do are not stated in the contract but are decided later by the purchaser."

The task order contract offers a middle way between the rigid, encompassing civil service classification schedule and the myriads of separate job-by-job contracts that strict competitive bidding would require. For most practical purposes, the employees of the incumbent firm join the agency's hierarchy; they submit to authoritative direction from the officials of the contracting organization (as civil servants do), although a task order contract does not guarantee them lifetime job security (as the federal macrocontract does civil servants). On the other hand, the government pays a premium for the freedom that it retains to "fire" the incumbent firm when the macrocontract expires, since the remuneration demanded by outside contractors is usually higher than that commanded by career civil servants with comparable skills.

Layered Subcontracting. Another way around the competitive intent of federal procurement regulations is layered subcontracting. Assume that agency X has let one of those multimillion-dollar open-ended contracts to company Y. Then, a new problem appears in the agency, and freelance consultant Z has just the expertise (or the old school tie or the connections on Capitol Hill) needed to solve it. Unfortunately, though, Z has no contract with the agency. Technically, agency X's procurement specialists should let anyone who wants to, including all of consultant Z's competitors, bid for the work. But an enterprising contract specialist is more likely just to phone Z, arrange terms for the job, and then amend the incumbent company Y's contract with a new task order on the understanding that Z will be hired to do the work as a subcontractor. Thus, a multimillion-dollar task order contract may end up generating many layers of smaller subcontracts to beltway bandit firms or freelance consultants. The scenario ends with the award of a contract to a consultant who never had to compete for the job. Notably too, the practices of task order contracting and layered subcontracting show that the existence of a shadow bureaucracy does not by itself ensure that employment decisions will be made through job-by-job contracting in free-labor markets—ostensibly, an objective of the New Theorists.

Federal agencies with the most funds to administer, such as the Department of Defense, support the most elaborately layered subcontracting networks. Often, the prime contractor will arrange the network to reach far beyond the Washington-based community of firms, sometimes to cover the map of the country. This approach is called "the Rockwell technique," after the incumbent company on the Pentagon's B-1 bomber project. Rockwell procurement specialists spread subcontract funds from Maine to California. Members of Congress from almost every state and district ended up with pieces of the B-1 action, and hence with financial incentives to continue support for the project when the military need for the plane became controversial (see, however, Mayer, 1991).

The Day-Trippers

The foregoing layered subcontracting scenario introduced another major figure in the shadow bureaucracy, the freelance adviser who consults to government officials, often on a part-time basis—the day-tripper. Most day-trippers (there are literally thousands of them) work out of locations along the North Carolina–Boston axis.

All points along this corridor are close enough to Washington for regular commuting by air shuttle or the Amtrak Metroliner.

It is not a coincidence that the corridor from the North Carolina research triangle up to Boston contains some of the nation's best-known universities. Nor is it coincidental that part-time moonlighting stints are relatively common among faculty members from many of these institutions. Professors by no means account for a majority of the expert advisers, inside dopesters, and influence peddlers who work the Washington consultants' market. But they are important and sometimes influential participants.

The crowd from Harvard, at the Boston end of the major air shuttles, perhaps represents the elite of America's action intellectuals. From Harvard's law school, business school, and Kennedy School of Government they come. At the Washington end of the shuttle, they disgorge to a variety of assignments: on advisory panels of the National Academy of Sciences, in workshops on acid rain control or antitrust reform, as counselors to bureau chiefs or even cabinet officers. They will be on the 5:00 or 6:00 P.M. northbound plane from National Airport and home for supper.

Although Harvard sets the pattern, most of the other high-visibility eastern schools also send contingents of day-trippers to Washington. The Metroliner that collects professors from Yale at Amtrak's New Haven station may on-load some Columbia faculty members in New York, add a professor or two from Princeton at its stop in Trenton, a few more from Penn in Philadelphia, and round out its complement of academic day-trippers with the Johns Hopkins contingent waiting to get on at Baltimore.

In a somewhat different category from the typical day-trippers are advisers and researchers from leading study centers that are not on the Washington corridor. The University of West Virginia has long been a magnet for regional development scholars and for transportation engineers; the University of Oklahoma has a record of excellence in technology assessment. The "ag schools" of the nation's land-grant universities are traditional sources of expertise (and personnel) in the service of U.S. agriculture. Dozens of other academic institutions are similarly well regarded within their particular specializations. Although distance from Washington may preclude literal day-tripping, the modern jetliner permits researchers from these centers to participate actively and regularly as advisers to government officials in the Commerce Department, the Department of Transportation, the Congressional Office of Technology Assessment, and so forth.

Despite the familiar tag phrase "high-priced consultant," the range of variation makes it difficult to generalize about day-tripping consultants' remuneration. The spread for an established Washington consultant in the mid 1980s was probably between $500 and $1000 per day, plus expenses. But even that estimate may be misleading because day-trippers can compute their overhead expenses, as opposed to direct travel expenses and fees for actual consultation, in any of a hundred different ways. It may take a skilled accountant to tell how much of a consultant's U.S. Treasury check goes for out-of-pocket expenses directly associated with the job (such as Metroliner tickets), how much for legitimate overhead (office rental and supplies), and how much for actual take-home pay.

Procurement regulations set guidelines for a given consultant's allowable fee, based on factors such as the individual's experience, publications, and documented record of fees paid for prior consulting jobs. Faculty members at research universities obviously have an advantage since their professorships require them to compile publication lists that then increase their ability to win private contracts and command higher fees. A large envelope of discretion surrounds the applicable federal guidelines for consultants' payment arrangements. And procurement regulations, like all other bureaucratic rules, contain loopholes. Frequently, the consultant and the federal procurement official who negotiated a particular contract will be the only ones who really know just what the government is paying for what.

The New Theory and the Rise of the Shadow Bureaucracy

The one generalization that can be made about *all* beltway bandits and *all* part-time consultants is that their employment must be arranged by contract. The importance of beltway bandits and day-trippers in the effective bureaucracy, combined with the salience of the contracting process in the organization of their work, makes the classification schedule—a centerpiece of the progressives' public sector personnel system—relatively less important with each passing year. The tendency to organize the work of the federal government by contract rather than by classification represents a significant change in the way that the public business is conducted, and the New Theory proves to be a good deal more helpful than is the Old Theory in explaining this change.

The gist of the New Theory, as we have seen, is that decision makers in a free-market system will prefer to order their relations with others through a large number of separate contracts *except* when transaction costs make it preferable to bundle a given set of agreements into a single macrocontract. Such a macrocontract establishes a business firm, an agency of government, or even—in the case of a task order contract—a kind of quasi-firm within a federal agency. The relative advantages of macrocontracts and free-market competitive contracts help to explain both the rise of the shadow bureaucracy and the interdependent relationship that it bears to the formal bureaucracy.

At any instant, the balance between activities that are conducted within organizations and those that are market based will be set by the relative transaction costs of the two kinds of activities. Because relative transaction costs may change over time, the system of firms, bureaus, and individuals will often be straining to shift from the old equilibrium to a new.

The New Theorists argue that if transaction costs on average fall throughout the economy, the relative rigidity of long-term macrocontracts, which have the purpose of avoiding transaction costs, might seem unnecessarily confining. A shift will then occur toward greater reliance on free-market exchanges, with an increase in bargaining and item-by-item contracting. If, however, transaction costs seem on the whole to be rising, decision makers will organize more of their activities in firms and bureaus. One would then expect to find more intensive use of authority relationships and hierarchies. As Terry Moe (1984, p. 743) has put it, decision makers will increase their reliance on organizations "up to the point where the cost of an additional transaction within the firm [or bureau] begins to exceed the cost of the same transaction in the market. In equilibrium, some transactions will therefore be internalized within firms of various kinds and sizes, and some will be left to the market."

Implicit in Moe's summary statement is the requirement that the total costs of a particular kind of activity be weighed against the total gains. Although transaction costs may be increasing, factors such as technological improvements may permit the organization to produce extra output that more than compensates for transaction costs. A shift in transaction costs relative to an associated shift in production possibilities is the crucial point. If the *ratio* of costs to possible gains shifts in a way that is adverse to organization, so will the equilibrium shift toward increased reliance on markets, and vice versa.

According to the New Theory, then, at any moment a balance will exist within the effective bureaucracy between the ordering of work by classification and its ordering by contract. This balance will correspond to the balance between reliance on career civil servants in formal government bureaus and reliance on consultants and contractors from the shadow bureaucracy. Since World War II, the balance has shifted inexorably in the direction of increased influence by members of the shadow bureaucracy. As the disparity has increased between the government's demand for expertise and our civil servants' ability to supply it, the trend toward contracting with outsiders has increased apace.

A vast literature has also appeared to document the gradual shifting of the equilibrium—a process variously known as contracting out, privatization, third-party government, or movement toward what Donald Kettl (1988) has aptly termed a system of "government by proxy." The tendency to organize work by contract rather than by civil service classification yields undeniable benefits, such as added flexibility in the personnel system and an increased ability to hire specialized experts who would never even think of tying themselves to the civil service structure. But whatever the competitive contracting system's other merits might be, the organization of work by contract has not prevented a gradual inflation of consulting costs.

Rising Costs in the Procurement Community

In response to the buildup of procurement staffs in the formal bureaucracy, beltway bandits and other would-be bidders for government work have built up special staffs of their own. There are experts at reading between the lines of government advertisements for contractor services, experts at writing proposals, experts at jiggling the firm's figures and administering the government contracts that fellow experts have helped the firm win. As members of the "procurement community," these private sector experts must use their contacts and know-how to prep their companies for any upcoming contract competitions. Inside dope passed over a lunch or simply picked up in gossip may enable a professional proposal writer to tell some agency proposal reader just what he or she wants to hear.

A bid for a federal contract has to contain detailed financial data. The successful firm has to make frequent financial reports and subject its books to audits by federal investigators. The bookkeepers of a beltway bandit firm must meet intricate federal cost-allocation requirements while avoiding accounting anomalies such as those that produced the $200 hammers and $600 toilet seats of the 1980s' defense industry contracting scandals.

Every new proposal writer or accountant that a beltway bandit firm hires adds to the company's overhead costs. The company must recover those added costs. This it can do only if its accountants spread the rising overhead charges across all the contracts that the firm manages to win. Since the sole client of most beltway bandit firms is the federal government, taxpayers end up paying not only for the specialized service, such as computer programming, that the agency staff members wanted in the first place but also for the proposal writers, bookkeepers, and contract administrators who help the firm compete for new work.

Whether the gains of relying on shadow bureaucrats exceed the costs is, and will doubtless remain, arguable. It should be noted, for example, that increasing contracting costs in absolute terms can be consistent with the claim of analysts such as Stephen Moore (1987) that contracting out is frequently economical when gains in efficiency as well as incremental costs are fully considered. Although Moore, writing from the strongly promarket viewpoint of a Heritage Foundation researcher, perhaps overstates the case for organizing more of our government's work by contract, his argument is in line with the logic of the New Theory.

What does not seem disputable is that the progressives' barrier between public and private has been breached, apparently permanently. What is more, the trend toward the organization of the work in our federal government by contract (especially by task order macrocontracts and spinoff subcontracts) bodes to intensify as action leads to reaction in a self-perpetuating cycle. The contradictory internal dynamic of this cycle is discussed in some detail in Chapter Nine.

The public is no longer shocked when members of Congress announce yet another investigation of spiraling contracting costs. Each year, legislators and judges add to the layers of administrative controls under which members of the contracting community must work. Federal procurement czars press for additional auditors and investigators. But every new layer of watchdogs, overseers, and controllers adds to the cost of government and, ironically, becomes itself a bureaucracy that is liable to abuse and inefficiency. *The New York Times*, for example, reported the results of a five-month Senate inquiry into the workings of the inspector generals' offices (Tolchin, 1990). The "investigation of the investigators" disclosed systematic patterns of cover-up, foot-dragging, and whitewashing by inspector generals' agents in at least ten executive departments and subcabinet executive agencies.

Trade Associations, Lobbyists, and Other Industry Representatives: The Adversarial Model

Beyond the effective bureaucracy lies a vast population of special-interest representatives—all those Washington-based trade associations, lobbying organizations, and law and public relations firms whose employees earn their livings by lobbying legislators, arguing before commissioners and judges, and cultivating the bureaucrats who regulate the industries that they represent.

In the early 1980s, almost 100,000 full-time special-interest representatives concentrated on the Washington regulatory process alone, in other words, on a decidedly small fraction of the total federal bureaucracy. According to Reich (1981), who compiled this estimate, the figure included 12,000 lawyers in active regulatory practice, 9,000 lobbyists, 42,000 trade association employees (many of whom also functioned as lobbyists), more than 10,000 specialized

journalists and public affairs/public relations experts, 1,200 consultants in advisory capacities to the regulatory-agencies themselves,
and more than 15,000 professionals carrying out an oddment of
regulation-related jobs either in agencies or in private corporations.

    Federal bureaucrats often become bound by relationships of
accommodation and cooperation, if not collusion, with the accountants, lawyers, lobbyists, and publicists who make regular appearances in federal agencies on behalf of their private business clients.
The institutionalization of these influence patterns represents not
only a breaching of the progressives' public-private distinction but
arguably a clearer threat than does the shadow bureaucracy to the
public interestedness of the civil service.

    In a regulated economy, the actors in public agencies and
their counterpart industries have no choice but to do business with
one another. Hence from the very beginning of regulation, there has
been no question of the need for some kind of interaction across the
public-private boundary. The sole question has been about the
proper nature of this interaction. The architects of regulation, with
their good guys/bad guys view of public administration and private
interests, saw the interaction as inherently adversarial. This view
contributed to the adoption of that prototype of the adversarial
process, the trial, as the controlling form for regulatory decision
making. The eminent legal scholar and judge Thomas M. Cooley
became the first chairman of the first federal regulatory agency, the
Interstate Commerce Commission. Cooley fleshed out the vague
statutory mandate of the ICC by transferring the evidentiary and
procedural practices of court trials to the regulatory realm (see
Jones, 1987). Ever since, the regulatory agencies have functioned as
quasi-judicial institutions, powerfully influenced—and usually
run—by lawyers.

    The representative of a regulated industry usually wants to
reduce the weight of the regulatory yoke on the firms that he or she
represents. To this extent, the industry's interest is opposed to that
of the regulatory agency.

    Regulators, for their parts, also tend to view the situation
primarily in adversarial terms. What is more, in my experience, they
normally take their obligation to protect consumers seriously—very
seriously. The FERC civil servants who were principal players in

the story to be recounted in Part Two used to describe themselves—
and really seemed to think of themselves—as "hardnosed," ever on
the lookout for the sharp practice of the natural gas industry accountants whose work they audited. To the extent that their self-
image was accurate, the pattern of behavior at least among FERC's
civil servants was close to the one that the progressives expected. It
no doubt remains so today, at FERC and throughout the federal
establishment. In other words, the Old Theorists' ethic of service,
though too optimistic, was by no means as wildly unrealistic as
some cynics claim.

The Pattern of Continuing Consultation

Public servants and their counterpart private representatives meet in
many forums other than courtrooms, where elaborate rules for the
admission of evidence ritualize their interactions. All parties to the
industry-agency relationship learn that moderation and reasonable-
ness can serve everyone's interests. Hence, even when they are formally adversarial, day-to-day interactions are more likely to be
cooperative in spirit than confrontational.

Both within an industry and among those who are responsible for regulating it, changing patterns in technology, corporate
structures, and market conditions require continuing efforts to upgrade knowledge and skills. To this degree at least, the progressives
were right that high levels of technical expertise would be needed
for effective industrial regulation. Civil servants must plug themselves into the information circuits. There are trade journals to be
read, refresher courses to be taken. (Bulletin boards in federal buildings often have sign-up lists for seminars to upgrade employees'
data processing, managerial, or professional skills.) There are frequent conferences for exchanges of information about coming technical breakthroughs, rumors of company buy-outs, personnel
shake-ups in the counterpart industry. It is a perquisite of office
even for lower-level civil servants to have time and funding for an
occasional trip on the industry-agency conference circuit.

The circuit consists of trade conventions, government-
sponsored study groups, congressional hearings, agency advisory
panel meetings. Representatives of both government agencies and

private industries regularly participate in all of these events. Viewed in the broadest perspective, the circuit exists to reduce transaction costs. Specifically, it is a means to reduce the costs of disseminating the rapidly changing information that thousands of public servants and private employees need if they are to interact constructively in the context of a complex industrial economy.

Some participants in the circuit spend much of their lives on the road: at convention hotels and in university classrooms (for example, at executive-training programs for civil servants, such as those taught every year at Harvard's Kennedy School or Princeton's Woodrow Wilson School), in the seminar rooms of Washington think tanks, or in federal agency auditoriums. The circuit brings regulators into regular contact with industry representatives in forums that promote easy exchanges of personal as well as professional views. As a result, industry conventions also serve as bazaars at which deals of all sorts can be done. A public official's specialized knowledge of the industry is itself an asset with a market value. It is even whispered that conversations at some conventions have led to offers of high-paying jobs on the other side of the famous Washington revolving door.

The Revolving Door

In the early 1980s, professional and technical federal employees (such as chemists and computer specialists) were at a 15 to 40 percent pay scale disadvantage compared to their opposite numbers in private companies. A move from the public sector to the private can, therefore, yield a substantial increase in take-home pay for the typical high-skill federal civil servant. Incidentally, however, the *higher* relative salaries that are commanded by the large population of federal clerical and secretarial workers yield an overall pay scale disadvantage to civil servants that is much less extreme than the disadvantage in the high-skill civil service positions, taken by itself, would imply (Hartman, 1983).

The career profile has become familiar: Work a few years in government. Learn the ways of the regulators. Equipped with special expertise and a Rollodex of federal contacts' telephone numbers, join one of Washington's prestigious K Street law offices, trade associations, or management advisory firms—maybe in a position advising executives how to deal with the regulators back in the agency.

A study by Linda Demkovich (1978) supports the imagery of a tightly circulating set of influence wielders. Focusing on the career patterns of twenty-one legislative staff workers from a single congressional committee, the Senate Commerce Committee, Demkovich found that eight left their jobs on Capitol Hill to become federal commissioners, agency administrators, or political appointees to other agencies under the Commerce Committee's jurisdiction; and four went on to become Washington lawyer-lobbyists. In other words, more than half of those surveyed moved from a congressional post to a position either in the related private sector industry or in an agency with which they had sustained dealings.

Of course, the door revolves in both directions. Government recruiters may be as desirous of acquiring private sector know-how as industry recruiters are to tap potentially influential bureaucrats. The headhunters of a presidential administration are always keen to find industry officials who might be suitable appointees to the top federal posts.

The in-and-out employment pattern is especially pronounced in the regulatory agencies, where the highest rates of business-government exchange have traditionally occurred. A Common Cause survey found that more than 50 percent of federal regulatory commissioners who had been appointed in the first half of the 1970s had come either from the industry that they would help regulate or from law firms with practices (and therefore clients) in that field (Quirk, 1981).

A 1978 statute, the Ethics in Government Act, severely limits the ability of officials in the executive branch to move directly from a government post to positions in a client industry. This law has therefore slowed the rate of movement across the public-private interface and will continue to do so. But few laws are without ambiguities or loopholes—although it may take some time to find them. Among the most sought-after bureaucrats are those who have proved their adroitness in the exploitation of any gaps that may exist in the federal statutes and regulations that are meant to control movement through the revolving door.

Iron Triangles, Adhocracies, and Issue Networks

In the foregoing paragraphs, I have described the typical pattern of
industry-agency contacts, based on my own observations as an
agency official (I headed the planning office at the Federal Power
Commission for a while in the 1960s) and as a regular consultant
to the FPC's successor agency, FERC (I day-tripped over six years
or so from my faculty position at Princeton University). The picture
that I have sketched may seem a simple tracing of the iron triangle
model.

In practice, however, disagreements within the industry-
regulatory complex usually can be counted on to prevent the kind
of unbroken identity of bureaucratic, industry, and legislative interests that "iron triangle" and "agency capture" imply. The monolith
fragments before it can form. So the decision making that actually
goes on in our public bureaucracies occurs, for the most part, in a
zone somewhere between the constant conflict of the extreme adversarial model and the complete, virtually conspiratorial, agency-
industry consensus of the iron triangle. A more nuanced, more sup-
ple concept than that of the iron triangle is therefore needed.

Mutual Adjustment of Public and Private Actors

Borrowing some terms and concepts introduced by James Thompson (1967) and Ellis Hawley (1974), Henry Mintzberg, a leading
organizational theorist, has developed the concept of an "adhocracy" as the preferred structure for dealing with the kinds of coordination problems that players in today's game of governance have
to solve. Mintzberg (1983) identified five key organizational relationships, beginning with mutual adjustment (that is, coordination
of related programs) and running though direct supervision of subordinates by organizational superiors and standardization of work
processes, outputs, and workers' skills. As the growing complexity
of modern society has generated more issues that need adjustment,
and also more programs that require coordination with one
another, mutual adjustment has become increasingly important.
Much of modern organization can be seen as an apparatus of interrelated structures and processes set up to perform the critical

adjustment function. It is this apparatus that Mintzberg calls an adhocracy.

Mintzberg's emphasis on the imperative of adjustment more accurately describes relationships across the public-private interface than does the conspiracy theorists' emphasis on capture. The adhocracy concept, as we will see, also helps explain the prevalence in contemporary organizations of special task forces—that is, organizations within organizations set up to facilitate mutual adjustment, reduce transaction costs, and help direct processes of change.

Also more suggestive of the true nature of public-private interaction than is the iron triangle imagery is Hugh Heclo's concept of an issue network (1978). Again, the emphasis is on adjustments and information flows; an issue network is a more loosely constructed and much less conspiratorial artifice than is the iron triangle of traditional political science. Membership in a network is not formal and it is not fixed. Players move in and out, easily forming and defecting from coalitions. A network enables regulatory officials and industry representatives to reconcile adversarial positions because its existence implies that its members recognize certain rules of acceptable behavior. The bargaining that constantly goes on encourages "splitting of differences"—quite the opposite of the strict pursuit of the one best way.

Reduction of Information Costs

Ironically, networks have arisen for the same reason that the effective bureaucracy has evolved—to mitigate certain inefficiencies in the workings of the formal bureaucracy.

Networks, like Mintzberg's adhocracies, are kinds of organizations. According to the New Theory, organizations represent efforts to arrange relationships in ways that reduce transaction costs. The elaborate routines for presenting evidence in the regulatory process are designed to ensure the fair and orderly introduction of data. But these same procedures can also prevent the easy or nuanced exchanges of all the information that may be required to resolve a dispute or advance a common enterprise. In the regulatory field, the process of gaining all the pertinent technical, financial, and legal information is itself costly. The regulatory process would, in fact, choke on its own information costs if ways could not be found to help its participants digest relevant facts and understand one another's interests.

Politicians, stockholders of affected companies, regulatory officials, consumer groups—all have access to the industry issue network, and all command different kinds of information. All participants, moreover, bring distinctive biases to their meetings. But in a continuing forum filled with familiar faces, all players can also come to learn one another's negotiating idiosyncrasies and emotional flash points.

The idea of an issue network was not altogether new when Heclo introduced it. Scholars of international relations had been developing the idea of "regimes" for some time, a regime being a kind of network writ large within the international arena that is set up to deal with an interrelated cluster of issues, such as issues in arms control or global trade policy (Nye and Keohane, 1977; Keohane, 1984).

The regimes theorists have emphasized that the diplomats who specialize in a particular issue-area will try to create a continuing forum for communication, for example, the SALT and START series of arms limitation talks or the successive rounds of trade negotiations that have been held under the General Agreement on Tariffs and Trade. To facilitate communication and understanding among all participants, a set of working principles—common norms—will be hammered out to govern the players' conduct. Whether these norms are written or merely customary, their existence establishes expectations: even when two participants find themselves in clearly adversarial positions over a specific question, they both recognize a higher shared interest in give-and-take and in obeying the rules of the game.

The participants in a regime will eventually even work out a specialized vocabulary, which makes it easier and cheaper for them to communicate with one another but harder for outsiders to understand what is going on inside the regime (an example of reduced internal transaction costs associated with rising external ones). The insiders' familiarity with one another, together with the agreed-upon principles for resolving disputes, can be thought of as a kind of capital asset. Once understandings are in place, it is unnecessary to renegotiate every point from scratch. In this way, too, a major benefit of a regime is a reduction in the players' transaction and information costs.

The Effective Bureaucracy

Bureaucracy today not only works differently from the way that the progressives expected it to but is also a basically different kind of entity from the one that the reformers thought they had built on the blueprint of the Old Theory. Relationships across the public-private interface, though adversarial, are less confrontational and far more intimate than the Old Theorists would have thought acceptable. In fact, we should begin to think of "the bureaucracy" not as a formal structure of civil servants whose work is undertaken in the name of some generalized public interest and organized by the famous civil service classification schedule, but rather as a more encompassing structure—the effective bureaucracy—in which much of the work is organized by contract.

Today the formal and shadow bureaucracies have reached such a degree of interdependency—government officials rely on contractors for services ranging from computer maintenance to political advice; consultants depend on the government to keep the contract money flowing—that they should really be thought of as parts of a single system. The emergence of this system has made the progressives' distinction between the public sector and the private all but irrelevant to much of the work of our government.

The notion of a formal bureaucracy in symbiosis with a shadow bureaucracy would have seemed absurd to the original architects of the civil service. The progressives thought that the recruitment of experts to the public sector and the organization of work by classification were requisites of reform. Had the idea of a shadow bureaucracy of superexperts and supplementary experts occurred to them at all, it would have been recognized as a contradiction of what their efforts were all about. Equally offensive would have been the idea of public-private accommodation through continuing consultation and movements through the revolving door. Given the progressives' view of the public-private relationship as inherently—and, for the most part, antagonistically—adversarial, it was natural for some bureaucracy watchers to react with chagrin over the gradual emergence of issue networks, let alone of iron triangles.

One of the most influential historians of public administration, Grant McConnell, exemplified this reaction. McConnell (1966) authored what many scholars regard as the classic critique of the progressives' theory of bureaucracy. But his outrage over the interpenetrant relationships that had developed between government agencies and their counterpart industries displayed an underlying acceptance of the progressive vision of two hermetic sectors in a strictly adversarial relationship with each other.

The absorption of our public agencies in issue networks means that public and private sector actors alike may function as much as members of informal organizations as they do in their official roles. Where a participant stands on a given issue does not necessarily depend on where he or she sits within the formal structure. Those whom the progressives cast as adversaries may cooperate, while superiors and subordinates within an agency may find themselves in conflict. In both respects, the Old Theorists would have had it the other way round—partly because they overestimated the practical possibilities of the public-private separation and partly because they underestimated the self-regarding motivations to which civil servants are liable.

The concepts of adhocracies, issue networks, and iron triangles all underscore the importance of the informal associations that bureau officials develop, especially with their opposite numbers in counterpart industries. Through continuous give-and-take within a network, the interested parties gradually develop a less brittle, less mechanical kind of organization than the old-line bureaucracy was originally intended to be—one better able to focus expertise on problems that civil servants are unable to solve without outside help and to deploy information using means that cut down on transaction costs.

Obviously, a regime does not replace politics with a purer or more neutral process, as the progressives hoped that their creation, the formal bureaucracy, would do. Instead, the regime only facilitates a process that remains essentially political by creating a forum in which bargaining and negotiation can occur more smoothly than would otherwise be possible.

It is time now to begin illustrating certain principles of the New Theory with a concrete case. The organization: FERC. The time: early 1981. The presidency of Ronald Reagan was just getting under way, and with it, Reagan's program for a revamping of the entire U.S. regulatory regime.

□ **part II**

A Case Study
in Organizational Innovation

□   chapter 3

New President, New Policy, New Chairman at the Federal Energy Regulatory Commission

Five presidentially appointed commissioners sit at the top of the Federal Energy Regulatory Commission. The president designates one commissioner as chairperson.

President Reagan's chair at FERC, a Texan named C. M. "Mike" Butler, had grown up in Midland, Texas, during the post–World War II oil boom and later got a law degree from the University of Texas. Though Butler retained his Texas connections, he had become a creature of the Capitol scene. He had practiced in two prestigious Washington law firms, spent almost four years as an executive with American National Service Company (an energy development corporation), and served twice as a legislative assistant to Senator John Tower of Texas.

Butler had developed a special interest in federal administrative practice. By every accepted standard, he was unusually well qualified for a post high in the energy policy field. Moreover, Butler's most recent Republican service, on the party's 1980 presidential campaign staff and then on President-elect Reagan's transition team, assured the White House faithful of Butler's ideological reliability.

Butler would need all the smarts and political skills that he could bring to the FERC chairmanship. He assumed the leadership of an agency with the normal problems of an industrial counterpart organization (including a reputation in some quarters for agency capture), to which were added the difficulties of a complicated new federal law that the FERC commissioners had to administer.

The Federal Energy Regulatory Commission

The agency that eventually became FERC had been created in 1920, when progressives in Congress, fearful that the country's hydroelectric resources were being wasted, fought for the establishment of a Federal Power Commission (Federal Power Act). Soon thereafter came the pell-mell construction of gas pipelines and a corresponding concern that the major new natural gas industry would become a source of abuse, either through monopolistic pricing or cutthroat competition. So in 1938 Congress added regulatory jurisdiction over natural gas transportation to the duties of the already existing FPC (Natural Gas Act).

Today, some 30 percent of all the energy consumed in the United States comes from natural gas. In turn, 70 percent of the nation's gas comes from Texas, Louisiana, and the other oil-patch states, most of it carried by long-haul pipelines to the major consuming areas up north or on the West Coast. The pipelines resell the gas to industrial users along their rights-of-way or to local utility companies who retail it to businesses and residential customers in the area.

In the 1954 case of *Phillips Petroleum* v. *Wisconsin*, the Supreme Court reinterpreted the Natural Gas Act. The Court ordered the FPC to regulate the prices that natural gas producers charge for their product as it comes out of the ground as well as the prices that the pipeline companies charge for moving gas from producing to consuming areas. In response to the 1954 decision, the bureau of natural gas in the FPC was divided into several divisions—among them, a new division to set rates for gas producers and a separate

rate-setting unit for the long-haul-pipeline companies. In 1978, through the Department of Energy Organization Act, the Federal Power Commission was given further jurisdiction over the nation's oil pipelines and was renamed the Federal Energy Regulatory Commission.

The creation of a separate bureau to regulate the nation's gas pipelines gave the representatives of that industry a single point of contact within the government and a unified staff of federal officials to cultivate. Reciprocally, the civil servants who staffed the agency's Pipeline Rates Division had a single industry to worry about. They could eat, work, and sleep pipelines—it was not a situation likely to attract Renaissance men or women. Pipeline industry representatives and FERC staffers inhabited a limited official universe. They frequently interacted with one another, but rarely had reason to deal with anyone else.

This arrangement eliminated any institutional pressure on FERC's pipeline specialists to put "their" industry in a broader context, one that included sustained attention to other energy-industry (coal, electric, oil) problems. Given the pattern of continuing consultation that counterpart organization encourages, it was natural for a common outlook on pipeline industry problems to emerge among the regulated and their regulators.

The 1978 Policy Act

In fairness to all participants in the gas industry network, there was much to occupy their problem-solving talents and much to require intense, continuing interaction across the public-private interface. The years of Mike Butler's tenure at FERC were challenging ones, owing mainly to complications following the 1978 passage by Congress of the Natural Gas Policy Act.

The issues addressed by this legislation had been years in the making. During the 1960s, a decade of widespread antibusiness feeling, Kennedy-Johnson appointees to energy regulatory posts held gas prices to very low levels. Consumers, tantalized by cheap rates, used lots of gas. But drillers, deterred by low prices (and hence low profits), began cutting back on their exploration budgets. Less and less new gas was found to replace the reserves that were being con-

sumed. Shortages loomed. Analysts began to argue that the ar-
tifically inflated demand for gas could be brought back into line
only if all the major forms of fuel—coal, gas, oil, and nuclear-
generated and hydroelectric power—were priced by a free market
(Breyer and MacAvoy, 1974). This line of thought gave rise to the
compromise solution of partial, phased deregulation in the gas
industry.

Partial, Phased Deregulation: An Accounting Nightmare

It has been said that the 1978 Natural Gas Policy Act consumed
more floor hours, more committee hours, more conference hours,
and more task force hours than any other issue before the 95th
Congress (*Congressional Record,* 1978, pp. 38349, 38360–38361). Almost two years of haggling had been required for the representatives
of producing and consuming regions to agree on a schedule for
deregulation. Under the 1978 act, a well-owner could sell his gas for
whatever the market would bear, provided that the well in question
qualified for deregulation under a complicated phasing schedule.
Newly discovered gas immediately qualified for free-market treatment. Other categories, or "vintages," of gas were to be exempted
from federal price setting on a phased basis.

The act's phasing schedule, complicated as it was, made
some sense for producers. Gas wells numbered in the thousands, so
the removal of FERC's price-setting jurisdiction would gradually
free multitudes of producers to compete with one another. In
numbers there would be safety—a free-market check against price
gouging.

But the long-haul pipelines presented a very different kind
of problem. Because few areas of the country are served by more
than three or four pipelines at the most, competitive forces are weak.
Congress thought that continued federal rate setting was necessary
to keep pipeline owners from colluding and jacking up the prices
they charged for transporting gas. The result was a hybrid and
exceedingly complicated new regulatory regime, a regime that industry planners in the early 1980s were still trying to understand
and that Mike Butler as the new FERC chairman now had to
administer.

A billion cubic feet of gas that moved through a given pipeline from Texas to, say, Massachusetts might contain some newly discovered gas plus many other volumes of different vintages bought from dozens of different well-owners. Under the 1978 act, each volume in the total could have its own price tag. Moreover, because of the act's phasing provisions, the prices would constantly change. On a given day, literally hundreds of different prices might have to be "rolled in" to compute a weighted average price for the total quantity of gas that a pipeline company would sell to one of its customers.

When Mike Butler took over at FERC, three years after passage of the 1978 act, gas producers and pipeliners were scrambling to stay abreast of the changing pricing categories. Decades of federal oversight had habituated the pipeliners to relative price stability and familiar regulatory procedures. The pipeline executives were not uniformly charmed by what Congress had wrought under the rubric of deregulation.

A Reagan Man for FERC

Butler and his fellow FERC commissioners had to review the accounting methods that the pipeline companies were developing to reflect the rapidly changing prices at which they were buying gas. Within limits, the FERC commissioners also had to decide how to interpret the phasing formulas of the 1978 act. Should they take advantage of any discretion that the law allowed to advance or retard the move toward deregulation?

Butler let on that he wanted to use every bit of discretion available, that he wanted to move as quickly and as far as he could toward removal of all price controls. Throughout his first year as chairman, he took every available opportunity to talk up rapid deregulation. And he did it all in public, giving speeches around the country extolling the virtues of the free market.

It was, in a sense, exactly what one might have expected of a Reagan loyalist. But that very expectation raised certain problems. Most top-strata appointees to the federal bureaucracy serve "at the pleasure of the president." If a cabinet officer or the administrator of a subcabinet agency crosses the president, he or she can be replaced with a more tractable successor. By contrast, regulatory commissioners, though appointed by the president and confirmed by the U.S. Senate, serve guaranteed terms during good behavior. At FERC (and at most of the other independent regulatory agencies), the statutory term is five years. Although the realities of executive- and legislative-branch influences on a top appointee to an "independent" agency are a good deal more complicated than the theory might suggest, commissioners are supposed to decide cases independently of presidential or congressional interference (see Cary, 1967).

A commissioner is to perform as a judge rather than as an advocate. In a natural gas rate case, for example, lawyers for a pipeline company ask for FERC's permission to raise prices; the regulatory staffers then challenge certain of the company's claims. The commissioner is supposed to hear the evidence, impartially weigh the facts, and then set rates at "just and reasonable" levels. Even when a commissioner performs in the quasi-legislative capacity, that is, as a rule maker for the industry rather than as a resolver of disputes, he or she is required by the federal courts to follow elaborately ritualized procedures for collecting and assessing evidence, again to the end of ensuring unbiased decision making. In theory, loyalty to a president plays no role.

But notwithstanding a commissioner's formal independence, the occupant of any high federal office invariably feels some obligation to carry out the policies of the president who appointed him or her. Conversely, a president will usually try to pack even an independent regulatory agency with sympathetic appointees. President Reagan certainly did so by nominating free-market Republicans to most of the regulatory positions that came vacant during his years in the Oval Office.

So thorough and systematic were the new president's agency-packing procedures that a reporter coined the term *reaganizing* to describe them. Reaganizing referred to the overhauling of federal practices without necessarily touching the federal statutes through "the transformation of departments and agencies by appointive officials devoted to President Reagan's vow to 'curb the size and influence of the federal establishment'" (Nathan, 1983, p. 75). Fowler at the Federal Communications Commission, Miller at the Federal

Trade Commission, Butler at FERC, and all the other new chairmen of the federal regulatory agencies were expected to help get government off the back of business.

Mike Butler's loyalties transcended both the formalities of his position and the boundaries of his own agency. President Reagan's other top appointees, whether in cabinet positions or independent commissions, were members of a free-market coalition. Every major player on the president's team knew that an opposing coalition might form. In fact, it quickly became clear that Butler's fight for the new deregulatory policy could bring him into combat with congressional Democrats, with some members of the natural gas industry, and even with members of the professional staff at FERC who had a vested interest in continuing regulation of the industry.

Relations Between FERC and Congress

In any coalition affecting the working of a federal agency, the congressional players can, if they choose to assert themselves, become the decisive players. Because of the specialized concerns of most of the old-line agencies, members of Congress often prefer to remain aloof, leaving the bureaucrats and industry figures to sort the issues out themselves (always, as long as they do nothing to rile the folks back home). But whether they actually involve themselves or not, their *potential* power makes members of Congress the one set of actors whom everyone else must always try to keep in sight (Kaufman, 1982; see also Moe, 1985, and Weingast and Moran, 1983).

Certain legislators were particularly deserving of attention by Reagan's appointees. Foremost among these were members of Congress who could express their opposition to deregulation by cutting back on agency appropriations.

Often, *external events* best explain why Congress will sometimes give an agency more money than it requests. For example, because of a catastrophe at a nuclear plant, Congress might increase the appropriation for FERC so the agency can hire more natural gas experts; with additional help, FERC might be able to devise ways to increase natural gas supplies as an alternative to nuclear power. But the "external events" explanation applies less well to cutbacks in appropriations. When Congress starts chopping at an agency's budget, the reason is usually to be found in the *political ineptitude* of the agency's own leaders. Strained congressional relations are a symptom of maladroitness at the top (Fenno, 1966).

When an agency loses political support in Congress, shrinking budgets leave it less and less able to do not only what the offended legislators want to stop, but anything at all. Everyone in the agency feels the hurt. And everyone blames the boss.

A Congressman Named Dingell

In FERC's case, "political support in Congress" was a code phrase for the goodwill of a congressman named John Dingell. Dingell, a formidable spokesperson for proconsumer, proregulatory interests, headed the major committee of Congress with jurisdiction over natural gas regulation, the House Committee on Energy and Commerce. Dingell had enormous knowledge of the regulated sector of the American economy. He exercised virtually unlimited investigatory power over the federal agencies that relate to that sector. Capitol Hill mavens called Dingell "the most feared man in Washington" (Weiss, 1989, p. 41), not only for the formal power that he wielded but also for the bruising way in which he used it. His habit of publicly savaging witnesses at committee hearings had become a Washington infamy. And his "dingellgrams"—letters demanding exhaustive written defenses of policies that Dingell found questionable—absorbed much of the staff time in agencies under his jurisdiction.

Dingell's power over FERC was particularly noteworthy. In fact, Dingell had sponsored his former legislative aide, Charles Curtis, to be FERC chairman when Dingell's fellow Democrat Jimmy Carter won the White House. (Curtis had resigned from FERC in January 1981 to join the elite Washington law firm of Van Ness, Feldman, Sutcliffe & Curtis, a group with a practice heavy in the energy field, thereby vacating the chairman's post so that Senator Tower could sponsor Butler for it when Reagan won the presidency.)

As FERC's new chairman, Butler would have to go before Dingell's committee or its various subcommittees each year. It is the agency chairperson who is expected to justify agency policies in public; it is he or she who must rattle the tin cup, as the saying goes, while defending the agency's annual budgetary request. In all of his appearances, Butler would have to drag a whole lot of political baggage out in front of John Dingell. To begin with, Butler had a long association with the conservative Senator Tower from Texas, the leading gas-producing state in the Union. Texans stood to profit if gas prices went up, which is what most energy experts expected would happen under deregulation. Dingell's Michigan, on the other hand, was a major gas-consuming state, and Dingell made no secret of his desire to hold energy costs down.

Besides, Dingell no doubt thought that he had already gone about as far as he could along the road to deregulation. At President Carter's request, Dingell had checked his proregulatory bias and helped craft the Natural Gas Policy Act. Having compromised once in support of partial, phased deregulation, he was not now going to let a nonelected Republican over at FERC drag him any further than the 1978 act absolutely required.

A Coalition Against "Agency Deregulation"

FERC watchers thought that Butler might be pushing for a pace of deregulation that Congress never intended. Indeed, rumor had it that Dingell suspected Butler of trying to achieve "agency deregulation," that is, complete and speedy (instead of partial and phased) deregulation through crafty interpretations of the law. Dingell's congressional power base positioned him to become the key player in a coalition bent on blocking agency deregulation. In such an enterprise, he would be able to count on support from some natural allies—a proregulatory constituency in the gas industry and the proregulatory civil servants on Butler's own staff.

The Natural Gas Industry

There was a widespread impression after the election of 1980 that the nation's businesspeople just couldn't wait for President Reagan and his merry men to cut the federal government down to size. But the reality (as reality tends to be) was a bit more complicated.

The nation's gas *producers* favored accelerated deregulation

by any means, including "agency deregulation," since it promised
higher prices for the gas they took from the ground. The *pipeliners,*
however, were of more mixed sentiments. The pipeliners favored
free-market pricing on principle but were fearful of accounting
chaos and were emotionally unprepared for competition. Many
pipeliners thought that too dramatic a push by Butler would complete the destabilization of gas markets that the complicated 1978 act
had begun. And then there were the pipeline companies' main customers, the local gas *distributors.* The distributors, fully a third of
the industry, knew that increased prices for producers would eventually be passed through to their own retail customers. The distributors also feared that any easing of pipeline regulation could lead
to collusion and, hence, monopoly pricing among the interstate
transporters of gas.

     The distributors' interest in holding prices down made it
likely that they would use their lobbying organization, the American Gas Association, to oppose accelerated deregulation. The AGA
could contribute to sympathetic politicians' campaign chests. The
organization could also provide research support and statistical data
to any congressional staffers who might want to assemble a brief
against deregulation—a classic example of an issue network in
operation.

     Butler might have been able to move the agenda of deregu-
lation forward if only a minority of the industry, the one-third that
the AGA mainly represented, opposed him. But if the pipeline companies joined the distributors to form a blocking coalition, most of
the natural gas industry would actually be opposed to the Reagan
policy. The pipeliners had their own Washington-based trade association and lobbying organization, the Interstate Natural Gas Association of America (INGAA). It was not yet clear whether the
proponents of the free market or the go-slow claque within the
pipeline industry would determine INGAA's position on deregulation. Should INGAA make common cause with Dingell and the
American Gas Association in active opposition to deregulation,
Butler would have to spend most of his time fighting off critics and
almost none advancing any agenda of his own.

Opposition Within the Staff at FERC

Another natural ally of the proconsumer, proregulatory forces was the staff of Mike Butler's own agency. President John F. Kennedy's court historian, Arthur Schlesinger (1965, pp. 625–626), observed that career bureaucrats often appear to be "a bulwark against change . . . a force against innovation with an inexhaustible capacity to dilute, delay, and obstruct presidential purpose." Certainly that is how members of a new presidential administration typically view the cadre of civil servants that they inherit. Mike Butler was no exception, and he probably was not far wrong. The career staff members at FERC scarcely concealed their disapproval of the Reagan program. They recognized that Butler's agenda could threaten their agency's budgetary support.

Sizing Up Mike Butler

Old-timers in an agency such as FERC are peculiarly sensitive to the nuances of the congressional relationship. The senior staff members at FERC had been dealing for years with the staffers over on Capitol Hill. Long before Mike Butler ever appeared, they had been preparing testimonial statements for FERC chairpersons to read in front of John Dingell's committees. They would no doubt prepare dozens more after Butler left the agency to go on to better things. (Everyone thought that Butler would, in the way of all political appointees, soon leave FERC for bigger, and certainly more lucrative, callings. Butler in fact moved through the revolving door in late 1983 to join the natural gas division of the Wall Street investment banking firm Kidder, Peabody.)

None of the FERC old-timers wanted their agency to be trashed because Butler's haste to deregulate brought a comeuppance from Congressman Dingell. If Butler "lost political support in Congress," the quality of life for everyone at FERC—except a short-timer like Butler—would suffer for years.

Nor could all that Reaganite talk about dismantling the bureaucracy be expected to comfort career officials. Even before Ronald Reagan took office in early 1981, Washington was awash in rumors of reductions in force (RIFs), or in plain language, layoffs from the career civil service. RIFs are rare and extremely difficult to bring about. But even the protections of the classification system are not absolute. Airline deregulation had been initiated by an act of Congress in 1978. Stories abounded of Civil Aeronautics Board staff members who were out of work and padding the halls of other agencies, seeking jobs to replace the ones that were disappearing at their agency.

Shirking and Subversion as Tactics of Opposition

The staff members at FERC generally opposed the agenda that their new boss wanted to push. Because their inclination was to resist rather than advance the chairman's agenda, their ability to shirk or subvert was not a mere academic possibility.

Bureaucrats can be masters of the delaying game. An underbrush of procedural rules covers every square inch of the bureaucratic terrain. A visitor to the professionals' home ground can easily trip in the thicket, especially if he or she cannot count on the services of guides familiar with the territory. And, after all, a new chairperson is exactly that—a visitor to the agency, certain soon to be gone, who will leave it to the permanent staffers to clean up any mess left behind. The rigidities of the bureaucratic structure, with prescribed job descriptions for every box in the organization chart, afford innumerable reasons why "we can't do that with our staff" or "with our table of organization" or "with our existing job descriptions" or whatever.

Nor is it unusual for career civil servants to make end runs around their own their agency leaders so that they can feed sensitive information to contacts on Capitol Hill and in industry. In the words of Francis E. Rourke (1976, p. 112), "Career officials will confide their doubts regarding the wisdom of the policies being followed by their superiors to friendly congressman or reporters, or they may alert pressure groups with which they have an intimate relationship to the fact that steps being undertaken are adverse to their interests. They thus convert disputes with political executives into conflicts between their superiors and outside organizations." It is a classic way to build a blocking coalition, one that cuts across the formal bureaucracy, the legislature, the shadow bureaucracy, and the counterpart industry.

It was in this not very friendly environment that Mike Butler, upon taking office, had to make his first major decisions, not about congressional diplomacy or pipeline rate cases but about the senior aides that he wanted on his top management team. Butler's mix-and-match job—some outsiders who shared his ideology, some seasoned insiders who would know how to control the career civil servants—was typical of the kind of management team that the head of a major federal agency usually tries to assemble.

The Outsiders: The Texans

Butler recruited two hard-charging Texans to fill the top staff posts at FERC. The Texans brought Butler's own kind of oil-patch background to FERC, along with firsthand experience with energy decision makers and energy issues.

For the position of general counsel, Butler hired one of the bright young men of the Houston bar, a brilliant thirty-two-year-old attorney named Charlie Moore. In the lawyer-dominated FERC, the general counsel's job is normally considered the most important staff post in the agency. (Moore resigned from FERC in late 1983 to take a partnership in a major Houston law firm, Akin, Gump, Strauss, Hauer & Feld. In his private practice, Moore represents some of the major natural gas interests in FERC regulatory cases.)

To be director of regulatory analysis—essentially, FERC's chief economist—Butler appointed a specialist in energy policy, a lawyer-economist named Bob Means who, at the time of his appointment to the FERC post, was teaching at the University of Texas Law School. Means was an analyst of uncommon balance and perspective. Yet he had more than a bit of the academic economist's uncritical faith in the efficiency promoting nature of free markets. Means left FERC about a year after Moore did and joined the Washington staff of a Boston-based think tank, Swanson Associates, to specialize in energy and regulatory consulting.

Charlie Moore and Bob Means represented two of the most prominent and powerful constituencies behind deregulation—the oil-patch constituency and the free-market ideologues. All in all,

FERC watchers had good reason to strap in and expect the new Butler-Moore-Means team to accelerate the deregulatory machine.

The Insiders

Because Butler foresaw that his agenda would rankle the careerists, however, he knew that he also needed a few FERC regulars on his top staff along with the Texans, if only to help him keep his own staff members in line. The professionals who are most valuable, and hence most in demand, for the kinds of responsibilities that Butler had in mind come from the elite civil service ranks known as the Senior Executive Service.

"SESers" are professionals who have worked their way up to the top career posts. Evaluators from the federal Office of Personnel Management thoroughly vet an applicant's credentials and qualifications before granting the SES designation. Most knowledgeable observers of the Washington scene seem to regard the review process as a serious one rather than a mere formality. And, though acceptance in the SES ranks is fairly common for most highly experienced civil servants, it is properly regarded as a recognition of managerial skill and an appointment of genuine honor.

The approximately ten thousand federal SESers possess both the broad managerial experience and the specialized technical expertise that are needed to make government work. Presidents, cabinet officers, chairpersons of regulatory agencies come and go. But the career bureaucrats are *forever*. Among these careerists, the so-called supergrades are expected to translate policy directives from above into workaday programs for the midlevel and lower-level civil servants to implement. Technically, a supergrade is anyone in the General Schedule rank of GS-16, GS-17, or GS-18. Almost all supergrade careerists accepted SES appointments when the Civil Service Reform Act of 1978, which created the Senior Executive Service, gave them the opportunity to do so.

Incidentally, supergrade pay levels start at about $85,000 per year and run to something well above $100,000 for those at the peak of the career structure. Under the Reform Act of 1978, SESers were also made eligible to collect special lump-sum awards, often in the range of $10,000, for meritorious performance. Under the mounting federal budget deficits of the 1980s, however, Congress reduced the dollar pool for bonus awards, which added to morale problems within a senior civil service cadre already alarmed by the Reaganites' determination to crimp bureaucratic power (Gormley, 1989).

Ken Williams, Chief of Natural Gas Regulation

First to be chosen for reappointment from those already filling FERC supergrade ranks was a taciturn southerner named Ken Williams. Williams had entered the federal civil service in the early 1960s with a background as a high school social science teacher; he sometimes described himself as an economist. Over the years, he had worked his way up through most of the specializations within FERC's natural gas bureau. It was this bureau and its one thousand or so staff members that Ken Williams headed when Butler became chairman.

Williams was tough and honest and, if neither imaginative nor colorful, undeniably expert in every aspect of gas regulation. I don't know if Williams knew more about the natural gas industry than did anyone else in the country. I do know that most of his staffers thought so. And I, at least, never saw anyone challenge Williams within his field of expertise. That expertise consisted in equal parts of technical knowledge and deep sensitivity to industry concerns. Williams knew the psychology as well as the physics of the business. Nor was it surprising that detractors accused him of selling out to the very gas companies that his bureau existed to regulate. The critics nodded knowingly when Williams retired from FERC in 1985 and moved through the revolving door to a senior post at one of the nation's leading natural gas consulting firms, Brown, Williams, Quinn & Chinn.

Nevertheless, Williams's reputation alone made him a reasonable selection for the top natural gas job. Given the anxieties that hints of agency deregulation were generating among pipeliners and distributors, Williams's sensitivity to industry concerns made him, on political grounds, the candidate of choice. He was a known commodity within the issue network and, from the industry perspective, a trusted administrator. Never mind all those unsettling speeches by Butler. Williams would stay right where he'd been in the past—perfectly positioned to fine tune any harmful directives that might come from the feisty Butler.

Ironically, therefore, Butler kept Williams on in part because Williams's continuing incumbency would limit the threat of damage posed by Butler himself to the counterpart industry. The new chairman seemed personally and ideologically uncomfortable with his own top natural gas adviser. But Butler's reappointment of Williams reduced the incentive that key potential opponents might otherwise have felt to assemble an aggressive blocking coalition.

Bill McDonald, Executive Director

Williams's popularity with the muckety-mucks of the gas industry always irritated the other old hand that Butler kept on, Executive Director William G. McDonald. More than once, I heard McDonald suggest that the esteem in which businesspeople held Williams resulted from the latter's too-accommodating attitude toward gas industry and oil-patch interests.

Williams's laconic and rather awkward way with people (except with the technicians on his staff and industry executives who shared his intense interest in gas issues) was in starkest contrast with McDonald's blathering, amiably profane swagger. Moreover, if Williams exemplified one of two classic patterns of ascent in the civil service, McDonald exemplified the other. Williams had made the slow climb up without ever leaving his home agency. McDonald was a relative newcomer at FERC but had brought with him an enormous range of experiences in government employment. Between them, in fact, Williams and McDonald's combined years in the bureaucratic harness exceeded Mike Butler's actual age.

The Making of an Organizational Entrepreneur. A scholarship to the University of Tulsa and then military service in World War II had offered Bill McDonald the way out of blue-collar life in his hometown of Providence, Rhode Island. As an air force officer, he had done graduate work in economics at Columbia, taught at West Point, and gone on to the Pentagon. In the 1960s, he had helped institute Secretary of Defense Robert McNamara's management reforms.

McNamara also had been an air force officer in World War II, one of an elite cadre on whom Air Force Chief of Staff Henry "Hap" Arnold had relied to apply statistical techniques in the strategic planning process. Following the war, McNamara went as one of the original "whiz kids" who sold themselves as a team to manage the Ford Motor Company. McNamara rose to the presidency of Ford, from which position President Kennedy recruited him to head the Pentagon. By 1961, when McNamara went to Defense, researchers at the Rand Corporation and similar institutions had developed an array of formal management techniques, such as program budgeting, statistical decision making, and computer-assisted data processing (Kaufmann, 1964). McNamara stamped his commitment to these modern techniques on dozens of Pentagon disciples, including Bill McDonald. McNamara's lingering influence helped to explain certain of McDonald's actions when opportunities to upgrade management practices at FERC offered themselves.

McDonald retired from the air force in 1968 as a colonel and joined the civil service. His flair took him rapidly up through a series of assignments in the Office of Management and Budget, several presidential commission staffs, the U.S. Nuclear Regulatory Commission, and finally to the top administrative post at FERC. There he set to assembling his own praetorian guard. With every month, it seemed, the executive director's office grew in size. By surrounding himself with loyalists, McDonald ensured himself a staff cadre committed to his own management goals.

The Rainbow Books. McDonald brought the whole McNamara bag with him to FERC. His and his staff's obsession with work-load statistics earned him the title "chief bean counter." The old-timers grumbled over the management reports that McDonald demanded. They laughed at the monthly data summaries that were published in volumes known as McDonald's "rainbow books."

McDonald's analysts divided the work of the agency into 116 task categories. They then assigned milestones to mark the progress of every case (and there were thousands of cases in the works at any moment) through every category. They further grouped the 116 categories into eight "functional classes" and regularly reported progress within each class in a separate book. McDonald had followed the work of the Federal Reserve Board from his days as a graduate student in economics. Taking a cue from the Fed's publication procedures, McDonald ordered that a different color be used for the cover of each monthly report. He let a contract for a beltway bandit printing firm to do the actual composition and publication. I recall how struck I was when one of McDonald's aides explained the design of these rainbow books:

"The staff guys," the aide said, "think the books are just show. But Bill's really thought it through. That's why the books are different colors, so people'll notice: something new's happening at stodgy old FERC!

"That's also why the rainbow books are the size they are." McDonald had specified that each report be specially printed on nonstandard 14 1/2- by 21-inch paper. "A rainbow book won't fit in the government issue in-out basket. Bill wants lots of copies distributed, but he doesn't want them thrown in mail trays and ignored. He wants those books out on the workers' desks, where they'll get in the way, where people might flip them open and learn something."

During McDonald's stewardship at FERC, the agency's budget increased at one of the highest rates in the federal government. Chairman Butler, I know, attributed much of the agency's success to the image that McDonald fostered: that of an agency with highly systematic and carefully tracked flows of work, as demonstrated in the rainbow books that McDonald sent to members of FERC's congressional oversight committees and their staffers.

Line-Staff Distinctions at FERC. To understand why the tension between Williams and McDonald went a good deal deeper than mere differences in personalities or management objectives (the bean counter slur), it is necessary to know something of their positions in the line-staff structure that is common in large organizations.

The structure of FERC strictly separates "line" from "staff" functions. Under the line-staff distinction, the officials who are responsible for an agency's substantive work (the line functions) have to rely on separate units to provide them with personnel, legal advice, supplies, data processing services, and all other administrative supports (the staff functions) that they need to do their jobs.

As the head of FERC's most important line office, Ken Williams had responsibility for gas industry regulation, a job with a multi-multi-billion dollar annual impact on the nation's economy. Nevertheless, Williams had no authority to buy a single one of the $150 desk calculators that his rate makers used when reviewing pipeline companies' cost records. He had to turn to the agency's chief housekeeper, Executive Director McDonald on the staff side. McDonald's job was to supply the line workers with janitorial services, parking spots, promotions, safe elevators, and suchlike.

The line-staff separation institutionalizes the distinction between the professional and the administrative points of view (Rourke, 1976). Increasingly in governmental agencies, the substantive work—such as rate making, with its requirements for accounting, economic, and, often, engineering skills—calls for experts in particular professional disciplines. The professionals' emphasis on the skills and standards of their specialities often brings them into conflict with the demands of administrators such as McDonald for economy and efficiency.

A Matter of Style. McDonald was sought after throughout the federal service because of his record as an expediter, a cost cutter, an organizational entrepreneur. Only an operator with the ability to see the angles—and the nerve to play them—can compile this kind of record. In the line-staff context, however, opportunistic management by a staff-side official often requires pushing onto another's turf. McDonald was always ready, when opportunity presented itself, to push onto Ken Williams's line operations.

McDonald looked, talked, even moved the way Victor McLaglen did in those hard-drinking, hard-fighting cavalry sergeant roles in old John Ford movies. A FERC employee once told me, "Bill McDonald reminds me of a story: There's this Irishman who sees a brawl break out. The fellow jumps from his carriage, shillelagh waving, and shouts: 'May God lead me to the right side, but right or wrong, I've *got* to get into the fight.'"

Scholars of the Irish-American subculture have stressed the value that Irish politicians have traditionally placed on loyalty to benefactors and to "one's own kind" (Rakove, 1975). That sense of loyalty helps explain why McDonald so selflessly served Mike Butler after the new chairman decided to keep him on as executive director. And loyalty to one's own kind may partly explain why McDonald sometimes threw chances for consulting jobs in the way of another Irish-Catholic, named Garvey, who had also made the trip to Washington by way of the U.S. military.

Milton Rakove (1975, p. 60, citing Levine, 1966) has written that the Irish political style implies a broad tolerance for "the moral and situational shortcomings of others." The morally unassuming mayoral styles of Jimmy Walker in New York, James Michael Curley in Boston, and Ed Kelly in the Chicago of my own youth all exemplified the politics of the easy conscience. It is a style suitable to milieus other than that of the city. The impersonal relationships and procedures of a bureaucracy can be made a bit more human with a willingness to forgive the inevitable venial sin here and there.

McDonald had spent a career in the military and then in the civil service watching others gain certain preferments to which he could not realistically aspire. A promotion to general, for instance: his Pentagon co-workers who wore West Point rings got most of those. Or a presidential promotion to a political job: as a military officer and then a federal civil servant, McDonald had been legally prohibited under the Hatch Act from cultivating the kind of political sponsorship that can lead to an assistant secretaryship or a full U.S. commissioner's appointment. It must have been as plain to McDonald as it was to most of his associates that he was abler than most of those in the superior posts whom he had served.

For years, McDonald had been an illusionless witness of the general officers' privileges and the political appointees' hypocrisies. Though he never reached the pinnacle of the nation's power structure, he played by the rules that the peak players seemed willing to use when it suited them. McDonald sometimes rushed the writing of contracts (how else would anything get done?). He cut deals at lunches when procedure might have required negotiations on the record; he often phoned instructions to subordinates or contractors when a more cautious administrator would have put it in writing. Nor did he hesitate to reward deserving retainers—a promotion out of time for a loyal aide; an extra trip on the conference circuit for a tired worker.

I have heard it said that the Irish find endless fascination in the manipulation of forms (never mind if the forms are political or poetic). I don't think that McDonald gave a damn one way or the other about deregulation as a substantive policy—leave substance to brainy theorists like Bob Means or dutiful technicians like Ken Williams. But McDonald reveled in the process. He loved the angling, the battling, the wheeling and dealing. In short, he loved the politics.

Bill McDonald was, in fact, the compleat bureaucratic counterpart of the machine politician who uses blarney and bravado to distract and disarm, while carefully counting the votes. In one sense, the story I have to tell really begins with an incident that illustrates McDonald's defensive political sense.

chapter 4

Regulation and Discretion: "Are We in Trouble?"

Seasoned bureaucrats ceaselessly demand information, especially information about potential threats to their positions. The most senior members of the career civil service spend more than 50 percent of their working time receiving and reviewing data. Herbert Kaufman (1982, p. 87) has likened these senior bureaucrats to animated intelligence-gathering installations, bionically equipped with "radar and sonar transmitters constantly sweeping 360 degrees to call their attention by return signals to things they might otherwise have missed."

It was Bill McDonald, antennae always out, who first sensed that Butler's espousal of accelerated deregulation might invite an anti-FERC backlash in Congress. Butler's speeches were as taunts challenging the proregulatory constituencies to combine against him. Politically, it would have been most unwise for Butler to continue testing John Dingell's reputation for vindictiveness. Legally, if agency deregulation really was what the chairman had in mind,

Butler was opening himself to a serious charge of abuse of administrative discretion.

McDonald saw a classic principal-agent problem in the making. He sensed the increasing anxiety of congressional leaders—Butler's principals—over the chairman's speechifying on behalf of rapid deregulation. Was Butler promising what the law prohibited? If so, it would be in almost everyone's interest at FERC if Butler were reminded that his duty was to administer, not rewrite, the law. McDonald, therefore, wanted someone to review Butler's speeches, research the pertinent laws and legislative histories, evaluate how the speeches related to the laws, and then write a confidential memorandum of findings.

McDonald's "Are We in Trouble?" Study

Such a study—McDonald referred to it as the "are we in trouble?" study—called for exactly the kinds of skills that members of the formal bureaucracy are expected to possess as a matter of course. The lawyers on FERC's own staff were certainly practiced in legal research and memo writing. But the study might raise some eyebrows, and that argued against entrusting it to someone in the agency's Office of General Counsel. What if John Dingell, who displayed a curmudgeonly mien on his best days, learned that the executive director of FERC had commissioned "apolitical" civil servants to assess Mike Butler's vulnerability to reprisals from Congress? McDonald might not only fail to get Butler out of trouble but could end up getting himself into a whole lot of it.

McDonald wanted a researcher on whom he could rely—someone from outside of FERC, whose activities would not even become known (let alone a subject of gossip) within the agency, someone who would limit the flow of any information that might turn up in the course of the study.

I had worked for McDonald in the 1960s while we were both air force officers in the Pentagon. In 1968, the same year that McDonald had resigned from the air force to begin his rise to the top of the federal civil service, I had left my planning job at the Federal Power Commission to join the Princeton faculty—and the shadow bureaucracy. McDonald had hired me for editing jobs or research assignments during several of his civil service stints.

FERC's agency funds could not legally be spent if the "are we in trouble?" study would actually be only a political assessment. Any contract for the study, therefore, had to be carefully phrased to stress technical interpretation of Butler's announced intentions at FERC as compared with Congress's legislated policy for the agency. Otherwise, someone might argue that it was a disingenuous cover for the real purpose of the study—in other words, that it was a fraud.

McDonald's decision to commission me to do his study, instead of giving the task to someone in the classified civil service, seemed well within the customs of the effective bureaucracy. Nevertheless, questions about the assignment surfaced years later when McDonald's contracting procedures came under the gaze of the inspector general of the Department of Energy. But the inspector general's investigation still lay well in the future. In 1982, McDonald was concerned only with the problem of Butler's speeches. Notwithstanding any allegations of impropriety that the study might later elicit, McDonald decided that immediate concerns over FERC's "political support in Congress" justified a special assignment to someone who would do what he wanted, and in the way that he wanted it done.

I hauled copies of Butler's speeches and congressional statements to Princeton. The university library contained all the materials (such as congressional committee reports detailing the legislative intent of the 1978 Policy Act) that I needed for line-by-line comparisons between what Congress had ordered and what Butler proposed. *Was* Butler in trouble?

Was Mike Butler in Trouble?

The short answer was no. At least not in serious trouble, and he could probably keep out of it entirely if he toned down his rhetoric in future speeches. Butler had repeatedly rebuked President Carter for "reneging" on promised support for a faster deregulatory schedule than the 1978 act mandated—language that Democrats in Congress found offensive and inappropriately partisan coming from the chairman of an independent regulatory agency.

On October 3, 1982, I wrote a memo suggesting a tempering of Butler's rhetoric. I added some "DRAFT REMARKS FOR CHAIRMAN BUTLER," with the suggestion that they be inserted in Butler's remarks the next time he testified before Dingell. The idea was for Butler to soften his tone and explicitly disavow any intent to engage in agency deregulation.

The truth was, Butler was not going to be able to speed the deregulatory process, no matter how ingenious his reading of the 1978 act. Dingell and the other potential members of a proregulatory coalition were watching too closely. Yet if Butler refused to moderate his language, he'd probably end up doing a slipshod job of administering the existing law because his opponents would feel goaded into an open confrontation. Butler would then have to exhaust himself in political battling. By adopting a less aggressive stance, Butler could remove himself as a target of the proregulatory forces in Congress. If the proregulatory legislators wanted a showdown with someone, let them shift their aim from Butler to one of the others in "the Reagan crowd."

In fact, they did so. By mid 1983, the Reagan regulatory appointee who had managed to create the most aggressive image, and hence the most exposed situation, for herself, was Anne Gorsuch-Burford of the Environmental Protection Agency. Her apparent determination to reduce the toughness of environmental enforcement made her a lightning rod for congressional attacks. Gorsuch-Burford gained a reputation for political ineptitude and was eventually driven from office. By contrast, Butler left FERC for the kind of high-powered Wall Street job that is reserved for those who demonstrate a combination of smarts, toughness, and finesse. Dingell never actually had to exercise the awesome sanctions that were his to administer, should he have felt driven to take reprisals against FERC.

A Politics of Caution and Circumspection

In a variety of ways, Butler's allies (I among them) tried to caution him. In various ways as well, members of the potential countercoalition also expressed their demands to Butler, who, happily, responded satisfactorily. At one point, he did try to enact a rule at

FERC that would have speeded deregulation (U.S. Federal Energy Regulatory Commission, 1982). He thus at least made his intention explicit, disarming the charge that he intended to advance the Reagan agenda by cunning and guile. Even so, however, Butler had to withdraw his proposal after both formal (U.S. Congress, 1982) and informal messages from Congress made it clear that FERC's adoption of any rule speeding deregulation would start a war that the agency could not win.

One of the foremost students of post–World War II administrative law, Jerre Williams (1987), has observed that the independent regulatory agencies function as buffers among the three branches. Officials must simultaneously try to carry out "the broad, general, and usually disputed delegations of power from the Congress . . . satisfy the executive branch of the government on budgetary and legislative proposals, and satisfy the courts as to the scope of its activities and the fidelity with which they are carried out" (p. 34). Much of the energy in a typical federal agency is dissipated in absorbing the tensions that are generated in the competition among the branches. Administrative agencies cannot, in this context, generally be expected to function as initiators or creators. They cannot even be expected to optimize their established programs, let alone to proceed with creativity and vigor once plans have been set; too many compromises are inevitable, too much "feeling of the way" rather than bold initiation is required.

Butler could push for accelerated deregulation because the statutory mandate seemingly left the FERC commissioners with a measure of discretion to speed or slow the pace of gas-price decontrol. The Supreme Court has validated the right of an official in Butler's position to exercise administrative discretion to advance a sitting president's policy so long as the letter of the law does not inarguably exclude the preferred line of movement (see *Chevron* v. *NRDC*, 1974). However, when Butler sensed the gathering of a proregulatory coalition and responded with discretion, he displayed the political sensitivity that was the first requisite of his position.

Chairman Butler proved to be adept indeed at feeling his way through the Washington fog. Butler needed political acumen to decide how the opposing force fields delimited his own area of action. When Butler sensed the gathering of a proregulatory coalition within the issue network and responded with a more modest deregulatory agenda, he displayed the political, not the mere technical, skills that are always in play at the top reaches of the bureaucracy.

Had a citizen dropped in on one of the commission's public meetings, he or she would have seen Chairman Butler engaging in the technical discussions that are the traditional stuff of industrial regulation. But just as the placid surface of a pond belies the unseen drama of predator and prey beneath, the appearance of technical decision making free of "mere politics" belies the issues with which presidential appointees are mainly concerned.

Butler's retention of the reliable Ken Williams had surely done more to relieve fears of intemperate action by the Butler-Moore-Means gang than did any advice of mine. The chairman's adoption of a more circumspect public posture on deregulation also helped ease the strain in the situation by removing the provocation that might have induced Dingell to organize a coalition to dismantle the Reagan program at FERC (as the proregulatory forces eventually did at Gorsuch-Burford's EPA). In the end, all parties concerned were able to husband their energies for other battles on other fields since prudence and discretion—as well as skills in giving and reading hints—made it possible to avoid fighting an open battle of agency deregulation.

Butler's "Are We In Trouble?" Study

I had not yet met the new chairman but got the chance to do so shortly after McDonald passed my cautionary memo on to him. Butler took me to lunch at The Broker, a "power restaurant" near Capitol Hill. The Broker is the kind of place that businesspeople use to impress clients or clients use to repay patrons for special kindnesses.

Butler had the look and style of a middleweight boxer: quick, ringwise, disposed to force the fight. Ostensibly, the lunch invitation was Butler's way to thank me for alerting him to a potential problem and suggesting a way to handle it. But it soon appeared that Butler had more than an expression of thanks in mind. He had a little "are we in trouble?" study of his own to commission.

The Broker lunch marked the end, as far as I could see, of Butler's flirtation with a policy of agency deregulation. This abnegation was prudent, since agency deregulation could have cast him as an agent acting in violation of his principals' wishes. Butler refocused on a rather different version of the principal-agent problem. Indeed, Butler had decided to face up to a variant of this problem that many high federal appointees prefer to ignore.

A Principal-Agent Problem at FERC?

In our system of government, citizens confer lawmaking power on their agents, the elected representatives. The lawmakers, in turn, are principals with respect to those next lower down in the hierarchy, the top bureaucratic appointees—cabinet officers, agency chairpersons, and so forth. These officials are principals with respect to the career civil servants who carry the load of day-to-day administration (Moe, 1984).

Certain disciplines apply to the top levels in this principal-agent hierarchy. For example, the periodic nature of elections and the appointive nature of most top agency positions confer marketlike characteristics on the jobs of legislators and senior administrators. Citizens can refuse to renew an unresponsive politician's contract by "throwing the rascal out" in the next election. And although substantial opportunity exists for determined agency heads to exercise discretion, they operate for the most part under close and knowledgeable scrutiny by members of the issue networks. Should agents appear to violate their duties to their principals, watchful opponents may challenge them in court. Of course, the politicians who appointed them may also replace high-level administrative appointees if the latter get out of line (McCubbins, Noll, and Weingast, 1987; Calvert, McCubbins, and Weingast, 1989).

The formally independent status of commissioners makes them the significant exception to the rule of replacement. A president can move to impeach a commissioner only for cause. However, in most cases, a president can demote an ideologically unsympathetic commission chairman to the level of an ordinary commissioner. The demoted chairman may then serve out the remainder of his or her statutory term without administrative responsibilities (Schwartz, 1982; for a somewhat more conservative interpretation of the control that a president has over a commission chairperson, see Cary, 1967).

What if lower-level functionaries, those beneath the levels of elected representatives and top appointees, prove recalcitrant? Unfortunately, the chain of principal-agent accountability often breaks down within the ranks of the agency careerists. Civil service tenure makes it difficult to fire uncooperative or even incompetent employees. Furthermore, although the impact of a top administrator's or commissioner's ruling on an important matter (such as accelerated deregulation) will attract immediate attention, the mid- or lower-level bureaucrat typically works on a minute and detailed aspect of a particular problem. The "faceless bureaucrat" is faceless not only because he or she works impersonally but also because the impact of his or her work is often simply beneath notice.

The Parable of the Engine Room

A kind of parable has made the rounds in Washington. Over the years I've heard several versions of this parable, which puts the mid- and lower-level bureaucrats' version of the principal-agent problem in vivid terms

> The U.S. sailors who manned the gunboats on the rivers of China in the 1920s found the dirty details of engine room work to be beneath them. So they began to hire local coolies to do the scutwork. Over time, pipes began to break, and the Chinese laborers jury-rigged substitutes. Gauges gradually slipped out of calibration, but only the Chinese knew how to interpret them. Eventually the engine room became not only the workplace of the hired Chinese but—in a curious reversal—their fiefdom, since they alone knew how to keep the vessel at steam. Ominously, the Chinese workers who had gradually redesigned the ship's power plant could also, with impunity, sabotage its smooth operation or even shut it down entirely.

As FERC's chairman, Butler was captain of the ship. But he feared that FERC too had its version of the gunboat engine room, the Pipeline Rates Division. He thought that he might have reason to doubt the integrity of the chain of accountability in the mid- and lower-level professional ranks.

The New Theorists stress that asymmetric information within any large organization often enables agents to bamboozle their principals. The complexity of rate-making computations all but invited the career civil servants at FERC to twiddle and tweak billion-dollar calculations in ways that their principals might never suspect.

Unsupervised twiddling and tweaking can spell big trouble in an administrative agency. The regulatory process touches the property rights both of pipeline stockholders (who reap the profits when FERC permits pipelines companies to raise their rates) and natural gas consumers (who pay the prices that produce the profits). Under the constitutional guarantee that no person will be deprived of property without due process of law, rate-making procedures are supposed to follow strictly prescribed legal forms. These forms are complicated and cumbersome; they greatly increase the transaction costs of public administration. Moreover, they require more than merely the absence of arbitrariness or corruption. The due process requirement also guarantees standard treatment under the law. All pipeline companies should have their rates set on the basis of well-understood rules that FERC's staff members apply identically across the entire industry.

Butler wasn't certain that due process requirements were being met. When determining whether or not the prices that pipeline companies charge for gas were "just and reasonable," he and his fellow FERC commissioners had to rely for analysis and advice on the workers in the rates division. Several of the commissioners, like Butler, had come from backgrounds in energy policy. But none had anything approaching the expertise of the staff technicians at FERC. So Butler had no way of knowing if the career staff members had gradually altered the rate-making procedures that were prescribed by law.

Though Butler was legally responsible for smooth sailing at FERC, he could not actually be sure what "tubes" or "gauges" might have burst over the years, let alone what jury-rigged solutions might have been worked out to keep the engine running. Butler's chairmanship could explode in a scandal. Or it could be disabled by a series of embarrassing judicial reversals if the courts found inadequacies in the way that Butler's employees did their work. "There's no such thing as a good surprise" is an axiom of the politically astute. Butler wanted to find out if problems were lurking in the rate-making process instead of waiting for any overpressured steam mains to start popping.

The Rate-Making Process at FERC

What eventually became an enterprise of organizational change—the modernization of FERC's rate-making procedures through computerization—originated as a much less ambitious (but arguably a more important) project. During our lunch at The Broker, Butler made it clear that his primary worry centered on possible abuses of bureaucratic discretion by the workers in his engine room. He was much less interested in dramatic organizational change than he was in simply ensuring obedience to the existing laws and regulations.

To describe the content of those laws and regulations is a formidable task. Nevertheless, an attempt to provide at least a broadbrush picture of the rate-making process seems justified for several reasons. Primary among them is the ubiquity of administrative price setting in the American system, which makes it important for citizens to know the basics of the process (Garvey and Garvey, 1990).

The essentials of administrative rate making are not difficult to master. But this is not to say that a reader should expect to find the lesson engrossing or even pleasant: it is hard to make a page-turner out of an account of the rate-making process. This disclaimer hints at the kind of unglamorous but necessary work that someone somewhere has to do if the gears in a complex industrial society are to be kept synchronized. In our system, it is "faceless bureaucrats" who do the needed work, and the venues of their activity are regulatory agencies such as FERC. The inescapable tedium, the legal requirements for regulators to follow precise procedures, and the specialized knowledge that these regulators need are key factors in the story of the automation project at FERC.

Some Rudiments of the Rate-making Process

Rate-making principles are applied at the federal, state, and municipal levels of government across the entire U.S. economy in the regulation of electric, garbage disposal, telephone, water and sewer, and many transportation services. Private companies in these industries have traditionally been permitted to operate as natural monopolies or near monopolies. Electric companies that supply all of their respective cities' power are true natural monopolies. The long-distance pipeline companies are near monopolies. There are some 135 of these firms nationally, but fewer than 4 of them normally supply all of the gas within a particular geographic area (called a load area). To ensure that they do not abuse their monopoly or near monopoly positions, these companies must periodically submit their costs and prices to governmental review. Federal law requires FERC to approve the rates that a pipeline company can charge for transporting energy from, say, the gas fields of Texas to the big energy-consuming areas of the northern and western states.

A pipeline company may petition FERC for permission to raise its prices whenever its currently approved rates fail to cover its cost of service. Price setting or rate making (the terms are more or less interchangeable) is therefore really a process of rate reviewing, in which private companies take the initiative and government officials react. For decades, the pipeline companies' bookkeepers had been submitting voluminous amounts of statistical data to support their requests for rate increases. FERC accountants had to check these submissions number by number, using pencil, paper, and desk calculators. The FERC staff members evoked a scene out of Dickens: clerks on stools wearing green eyeshades. They didn't use quill pens, but somehow quill pens might have served as metaphors for the process.

Computing the Cost of Service

Cost of service is a technical term that refers to the costs incurred by a pipeline company, including a fair return on its investment.

have accumulated since Congress first mandated pipeline regulation in 1938—adds to the complexity of the rate-making process.

In theory, the proper technique for allocating costs to different classes of customers should have been spelled out in prior rulings by the FERC commissioners and in court opinions reviewing commissioners' rulings. But when, as often occurs, the existing case law yields no definitive answer, the rate designers must make personal judgments. The illustration in the upper portion of Figure 4.1 suggests the kinds of judgments that the bureaucrats have to make.

Suppose that a company is entitled to a cost-of-service recovery of a billion dollars—actually, a much more representative figure than the million dollars used in the "pyramid of aggregation" illustration. The rate designers estimate that the company will sell a trillion cubic feet of gas to each of the four customer types that are shown in Figure 4.2: two heavy-industry complexes (load areas one and three) and two residential centers (areas two and four).

One of the industrial centers and its associated residential area is three times farther from the source of the gas than the other complex. The rate designers must develop equations that will tilt the cost burden against industry and in favor of residential

Figure 4.2. Four Load Areas for Distribution of Natural Gas.

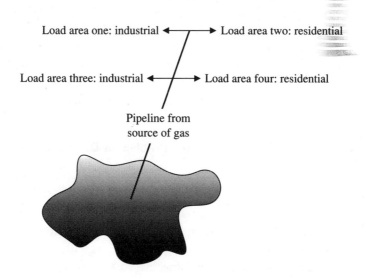

Load area one: industrial ◄———► Load area two: residential

Load area three: industrial ◄——► Load area four: residential

Pipeline from
source of gas

consumers—say, by a ratio of three-to-two—but that also reflect the three-to-one distance premium that customers in the farther industrial-residential combination should pay. These ratios are reflected in multiplicative coefficients, shown as the numbers in the parentheses of the following sample equations:

$1 billion × (0.75) × (0.6) = $0.45 billion, burden to area one
$1 billion × (0.75) × (0.4) = 0.30 billion, burden to area two
$1 billion × (0.25) × (0.6) = 0.15 billion, burden to area three
$1 billion × (0.25) × (0.4) = 0.10 billion, burden to area four
                                           ———
Sum of cost burdens: $1.00 billion

The rate designers have to adjust the coefficients in parentheses to ensure that the sum of the equations—the total of the cost burdens separately assigned to the four load areas—will equal the cost-of-service level of a billion dollars.

This example has shown only two types of tilting categories (residential versus industrial, and close-by versus distant load centers). In actuality, dozens if not hundreds of individual judgments may be needed to design rates for one of the big pipeline companies. Such a company may engage in four kinds of service (gas production, long-distance transportation, storage of excess gas in underground tanks or caves, and local distribution) at dozens of different rates (for factories, hospitals and schools, residential customers, and so forth) to many different load areas at increasing distances along pipeline systems that cross ten or more state lines. Every service category calls for its own set of coefficients, and many categories call for discretionary judgments as well as objective expertise by the rate designers.

Issue Networks and the Problem of Discretion

Enough has perhaps now been presented to give a feel for the texture of administrative rate making. Theoretically, it is a straightforward if tedious computational process, for the most part bound by rules—just as the Old Theorists envisioned that it would be. Actually, however, rate making is a process laced throughout with judgments regarding allowable versus disallowable costs, cost categorizations, tilting principles, and accounting methodologies. The need to make judgments implies the existence of bureaucratic discretion, which in turn invites the exercise of influence. Herein lies much of the significance of Heclo's (1978) issue-network model of the public bureaucracy.

Our civil servants do not make their judgments in the hermetic, apolitical space that the progressives envisioned but rather in an environment of constant interchange of information (and career opportunities) across the public-private interface. All participants in the gas industry issue network have a degree of access both to the private accountants who prepare the companies' cases and to the public servants who prepare the recommendations on which the commissioners will act. To provide that access is a primary function of the issue network—and, indeed, a reason for relying on networks rather than merely on units of the formal bureaucracy as the effective decision-making arenas in our system.

The penetration of day-to-day administrative processes by private interests does not necessarily imply venality or corruption, although these, of course, are possibilities. Because rate-making computations are frequently complicated and involve many steps interspersed with judgment calls, actors on either side of the boundary may confer with their counterparts on the other side for no other purpose than to clarify, or even teach, a difficult accounting procedure. Interchanges of information often occur merely because public administrators find their opposite numbers in the private sector to be the best sources of needed specialized data. FERC rate makers frequently made decisions about disallowances or allocations during telephone conversations with their contacts in the company's headquarters. It was my observation that the rate makers often took the telephone "testimony" of their counterparts in the companies on faith.

Still, it would be naive to deny that interests as well as information are involved in virtually all of the contacts that are made across the public-private interface. Whether one accepts or rejects discretionless administration as an ideal, the care with which private parties cultivate contacts in the bureaus suggests how rarely it is attained in fact.

For years, "understandings" between FERC staff members

and company negotiators had been the custom, not the exception. I never uncovered an "understanding" that clearly had been motivated by a FERC staff member's desire to increase a pipeline company's profits. These understandings were usually in the nature of agreements (whether tacit or explicit, and made without much apparent thought for their *indirect* effects on the company's finances) about the accounting methodologies that the staffers would permit the pipeline people to employ. But irrespective of the motivation behind an "understanding," every time FERC rate makers split the difference with company negotiators or customized their tilting principles in a particular case, they were in effect rewriting the rules, not neutrally applying them.

Enter Mike Butler.

Chairman Butler knew that "understandings" across the public-private interface could easily have been hidden in a process of labyrinthine complexity, one that he did not begin to understand and certainly didn't control. He was aware that in the worst-case scenario, the complexity of the rate-making process could actually have been used to hide outright corruption. Butler didn't have the time to learn all the technicalities of rate making himself. But he thought that Princeton's teaching schedule might leave me enough leeway to investigate the fairness of FERC's rate-making process in his place. Mike Butler wanted to know, as had McDonald before him, "are we in trouble?" Neither he nor I could have anticipated the turns in the lives of FERC officials to which Butler's question would lead.

□   chapter 5

Launching a Project
of Organizational Change

I was visiting in Bill McDonald's office when Butler phoned with instructions. McDonald hung up to announce: "Mike wants you to come down to Washington and be his special assistant. He wants you to 'investigate' gas rate making."

To become Butler's special assistant, I would have had to join the federal civil service, at least for a temporary hitch. "You're on sabbatical from Princeton this year, aren't you?" McDonald asked. Thinking that I was at complete liberty from my duties at the university, McDonald saw no reason why a special civil service appointment couldn't be zipped through. Butler would get a quick clearance from his White House pals to appoint me to a special, quasi-political civil service position known as a Schedule C post.

Appointing a "Political" Civil Servant

Schedule C jobs represent an exception to the relatively rigid classification procedures that must be followed when making appointments to most posts in the federal government. Schedule C jobs are formally in the official civil service, normally at the highest General Schedule ranks (GS-16, GS-17, or GS-18). But they are political in the sense that their incumbents must pass a personnel screening by White House officials as a precondition for appointment. Jobs that carry a Schedule C rating may be filled either by senior career civil servants or by appointees specially brought in from outside of the agency—what McDonald had in mind for me. These jobs involve duties that may significantly affect the implementation of the policies of the current presidential administration. For this reason, the White House watchdogs get to review Schedule C appointments. For the same reason, the "investigation" that the chairman of the Federal Energy Regulatory Commission wanted might naturally call for a Schedule C rating.

A Schedule C incumbent, whether a career bureaucrat or an outsider, can normally expect to be removed at the point of transition from one presidential administration to another. Thus members of the new team of leaders can fill policy-sensitive posts with employees of their own choice. However, the tenure protections of the classified service continue to operate while a career staffer is in a Schedule C job. Although a career civil servant who has occupied a Schedule C post during one administration may be removed when a new president takes office, that incumbent cannot be summarily fired from federal employment. Instead, the incumbent will normally return to something like the job that he or she held before the Schedule C stint began, that is, to some less politically nuanced slot within the same agency.

My appointment to a Schedule C position was blocked by a peculiarity of a different bureaucratic system, the one to which I remained subject as long as I stayed on the faculty at Princeton. I was not, as McDonald had thought, "on sabbatical" and hence available for an interim government appointment. I was instead on academic leave. McDonald seemed puzzled by the distinction.

A sabbatical is a fully paid year off from academic duties, normally granted on a seven-year cycle so that a professor can recharge the intellectual batteries. By contrast, academic leave is typically granted at a research university after three or four years of teaching. But leave time is not made available merely for intellectual refreshment. One's faculty peers expect a colleague to use any time released from teaching to conduct publishable research. Nor is academic leave time off with full pay. I was on full academic leave but with only half pay from the university—the standard arrangement at Princeton. I had to raise the remaining 50 percent of my salary somewhere. Working as a consultant for FERC seemed as good a way as any to do so.

"I could come down to Washington a couple of days each week," I offered. A day-tripping arrangement from Princeton would certainly not be unusual and would leave me enough time to turn out some publishable writing (see Garvey, 1983).

Unfortunately, though, it would not be as easy for McDonald to arrange an outside consultancy for me as it would have been for Butler to clear a full-time Schedule C appointment with his White House sponsors. The consultancy would require a special government contract; it would require activation of the Rube Goldberg contraption known as the procurement process.

The Procurement Process as a Transaction Cost

More than 4,000 separate provisions of federal law cover the procurement process, not to mention shelves full of implementing regulations and an additional half dozen or so specialized statutes. Thus a thicket of rules covers the legal terrain, terrain that seemingly quakes and re-forms almost constantly. The Small Business Act of 1953 illustrates the impact of special statutes that bear on thousands of procurement actions each year. This act alone was amended almost eighty times between the date of its passage and 1990, which suggests something of the complexity of federal procurement law (U.S. Office of Management and Budget, 1989).

The cumbersomeness of the federal contracting process creates high—in some cases, enormous—transaction costs, costs that obviously can be bypassed whenever work can be performed by permanent civil service employees. Therefore, the fact that agency decision makers are willing to absorb the transaction costs of negotiating contracts for outside help tells us something about the capabilities of our government's classified employees. The prosperity of the shadow bureaucracy rests on the judgment that outside contractors are not only better able to do certain jobs than permanent civil servants are but also better enough at these jobs to justify the substantial extra transaction costs that the procurement process imposes.

So many and so severe are federal procurement rules that they are often observed in the breach. Contracting procedures have become Byzantine, with innumerable opportunities for finagling. It should surprise no one that the rules sometimes get folded, bent, or mutilated. Nevertheless, violations are not to be undertaken casually since every step of the contracting process must be documented. The documentation requirements generate elaborate paper trails. Although violations of procedures rarely lead to prosecution, the paper trails can be made to yield evidence of wrongdoing, if wrongdoing indeed occurred, should a watchdog or whistle-blower pursue a suspected violation.

Taxpayers' money is supposed to be spent only for necessary work by the best-qualified contractor. Those requirements presented a bit of a problem if McDonald were to hire me as a consultant to conduct an "investigation" of the rate making process. As the executive director at FERC, McDonald was also the agency's chief procurement officer. His name would be on any contract for my work. Though he was my personal friend, he had to justify in writing the claim that I was the best-qualified person in the country to do a necessary job at the agency.

A time-consuming open competition is normally required to decide who is best-qualified to do a particular job. Butler's desire for quick answers, however, made it preferable to get me immediately to the task. There was no time to "compete the contract."

Competing a Contract

For an understanding of what eventually followed, it is necessary to appreciate the importance of competition in the contracting procedure. In theory, "competing a contract" performs much the same function for beltway bandits and day-trippers that the merit provisions of the classification system do for career civil servants. Competitive procedures are intended to ensure that the contractor who gets a given job is the most qualified applicant.

If the agency's higher-ups approve the hiring of outsiders, the procurement specialists in the agency announce a competition, using either a formal "invitation to bid" or—when they want bidders to detail *how* they would do the work as well as how *much* they propose to charge—a document known as a "request for proposal" (RFP). A ritual then must be followed in which an evaluation panel reviews and grades every bid for the work. Six to eight months may be needed for all parties to complete the paperwork for an award of a relatively small contract, say, one in the range of $100,000.

The RFP usually specifies the basis that will be used to grade proposals from would-be contractors. For example, if each bidder will be graded on a 100–point scale, then each bidder's formal qualifications (such as educational degrees) may count for 10 percent of the final grade; the bidder's "understanding of the tasks," as shown in the write-up that he or she submits in response to the RFP, for 15 percent; and so forth. The contract must go to whoever gets the most points. This kind of formalism invites bidders to play games. An applicant for government work once asked me to serve as a consultant in a competition mainly because he wanted to get my resume into the submission; my Ph.D. would have inflated the point score.

The evaluators of bids are often required to award extra points to a "small business," a "minority-owned company," or a "women-owned company." More game-playing. Stories are told of consulting firms that are controlled by white males but that are nominally directed by African-Americans or by women for the precise purpose of enabling them to claim preferences when they submit bids in contract competitions.

Or suppose that Congresswoman Jones, who serves on the oversight committee of a given agency, comes from a state with lots of minority citizens and a high unemployment rate. Procurement officials can influence the list of bidders and the probable winners. Procurement specialist Smith from the agency in question just might be tempted to treat a new project as a small business set-aside, so as to cut out the big Washington-based consulting firms and give an edge to upstart minority or women bidders from the congress-

woman's district. Congresswoman Jones would be likely to remember the gesture at appropriations time.

The Sole Source Alternative

Just as my Princeton appointment prevented McDonald from re-
cruiting me as a special Schedule C employee, Butler's demand that
I, not someone else who might submit the low bid for the job, get
to work *immediately* prevented McDonald from posting the investigatory assignment for open competition. The remaining feasible
option was the sometimes dangerous (and always touchy) alternative of a sole-source contract.

For more than a dozen years, I had been consulting on energy
matters to clients ranging from the president's science adviser to the
director of the Oak Ridge National Laboratory. McDonald studied
my resume and convinced himself that he could safely shortcut the
process by declaring me, simply on the basis of credentials, qualified to receive a noncompetitive award of work. McDonald reached
for the phone and instructed a FERC contract specialist to expedite
the cutting of my contract.

A government contract for an outsider's services must contain an explicit list of tasks—"deliverables"—to be furnished on
specified dates called "milestones." Without a list of deliverables, it
would be impossible for an auditor to assess whether each requirement was met and whether the quality of the work justified the
amount that the government paid. In an apparent answer to a question from the contract specialist about deliverables, McDonald
simply said, "Just be straight when you word Garvey's contract . . .
a study of rate-making procedures, and underline that it's for the
chairman of the commission."

McDonald hung up, then almost immediately redialed the
contract specialist. "When you write up Garvey's contract," he ordered, "add a deliverable—a plan to automate pipeline regulation."

"A Plan to Automate"

Automate? As far as I knew, the study that Butler wanted, an investigation of rate making, had nothing to do with automation.

On the other hand, what Butler really wanted would be tricky for a federal contract specialist to write up. An outside consultant to "investigate" Butler's staff? That wouldn't play very well with the Department of Energy inspector general, who had the official investigative responsibility for FERC, let alone with Butler's own employees. So maybe "a plan to automate" was a sensible way to go after all.

The Case for Automation

The government had been sluggish to the point of negligence in adapting to the computer age. When McDonald initiated the automation project at FERC, the average age of the federal government's computer inventory was twice that of private industry's automated data processing equipment (U.S. Office of Management and Budget, 1989). Given the situation, both throughout the federal bureaucracy and at FERC in particular, no auditor was likely to quarrel with McDonald's decision to improve efficiency by computerizing the regulatory process.

Furthermore, the auditing procedures of FERC staff members—number-by-number reviews of company rate filings using only pencil, paper, and desk calculators—were as antiquated as the agency's hardware was inadequate. McDonald thought that all of the 135 or so interstate pipeline companies should be required to submit their rate requests in a standardized machine-readable form. A specially programmed computer could then speedily process each company's filing. One did not need to be a data processing whiz to know that a computer could check the millions of bits of accounting data in a big rate filing more reliably and quickly than civil servants cranking desk calculators could. FERC was infamous for "regulatory lag," but computerization could cut the red tape, thus saving consumers hundreds of millions of dollars every year by increasing the speed and accuracy of regulatory decision making.

McDonald's plan, so attractive in view of the facts at FERC, seemed altogether consistent with traditional administrative theory as well. The progressives' doctrine of public administration evoked the metaphor of a well-designed mechanism. As has already been noted, the progressives' theory is still sometimes referred to as the machine model of bureaucracy. The mechanical image ran through the literature of the Old Theory, from the writings of Woodrow Wilson (1887) to those of the German sociologist who gave classic expression to the theory of bureaucracy as rational organization, Max Weber. In Weber's oft-quoted words ([1910] 1946a, pp. 214, 216): "The decisive reason for the advance of bureaucratic organization has always been its purely technical superiority over any other form of organization. The fully developed bureaucratic mechanism compares with other organizations exactly as does the machine with the non-mechanical modes of production. . . . Its specific nature, which is welcomed by capitalism, develops the more perfectly the more the bureaucracy is 'dehumanized,' the more completely it succeeds in eliminating from official business love, hatred, and all purely personal, irrational, and emotional elements which escape calculation."

But why settle for bureaus patterned on Weber's metaphor of a machine, once an actual machine—the mainframe computer—had been invented to store the data, plug inputs into formulas, and compute solutions with impartiality and breathtaking speed? When viewed in this way, the process of automation seems the logical means of realizing the Old Theory values of efficiency, impersonality, and emotion-free calculation—and this to a degree that unassisted humans could never hope to achieve. Unlike fallible analysts with their eyeshades and quill pens, computers can function as flawless calculating machines and perfect file clerks in one.

Finally—and probably in the end most importantly—automation arguably offered the best way of getting at the deeper problems that were worrying Butler. At an early opportunity after he decided to add the automation deliverable to my contract, McDonald pointed out to the chairman that computerization would force uniformity and standardization onto the rate-making process. In other words, computerization offered an excellent way to reimpose orderliness and predictability on procedures at FERC.

Automation as a general idea, then, was eminently defensible. But McDonald's choice of me as the best-qualified outside expert to manage the job might not be. Although McDonald had no choice but to find a way for me to complete the investigation that Butler wanted, a hyperscrupulous critic could have questioned his decision to put me in charge of the automation portion of the project. I had published a fair amount on energy policy but knew relatively little about rate making as a process. And I was almost an innocent in the computer field.

But my ignorance of the art of automation was of no interest to Bill McDonald. To McDonald, it was enough that he had figured out a way to write a legal contract. At least the contract would be legal if I could quickly learn enough about computers to write a competent "plan to automate." Nothing less would justify the deliverable on which the propriety of the whole arrangement would depend.

McDonald's Strategy of Indirection

Was McDonald's automation deliverable a ploy, a way to give the appearance of validity to an otherwise questionable government contract? Maybe so. But it was also something more. Ever since he had arrived at FERC, McDonald—still imbued with a faith in rationalization as one of McNamara's acolytes—had wanted to computerize the agency. He just hadn't found a way to get an automation project started. Butler's phone call gave him the idea. McDonald's decision to tack a computerization deliverable onto an investigative effort mandated by the chairman illustrated the indirect way—often the only way—that things get started in the federal bureaucracy.

Heclo (1977) has emphasized the prevalence in the federal bureaucracy of goal-seeking by indirection. So filled is the bureaucratic landscape with pitfalls and mantraps that the executive who marches frontally toward an objective is likely to be ambushed, forcefully diverted and delayed, or otherwise blocked before the journey is hardly begun. The way of the skilled operative is the way of stealth, opportunism, and indirection.

McDonald, on the administrative or staff side of the agency, had no direct way to force computerization on agency professionals such as Ken Williams's rate makers on the line side. The executive director's job, as mentioned earlier, was to support the line workers logistically, not to tell them how to discharge their technical responsibilities. It was out of character, however, for McDonald to reserve action—even on someone else's official territory—when he saw an opportunity to push a project of his own. The automation deliverable trespassed on ground that Ken Williams and his rate makers would fight to defend. If the assault on their ground was by way of the flank rather than the front, their determination to resist might be reduced. McDonald therefore decided on the special-project approach to computerization. The FERC automation effort originated in his judgment that the agency's traditional ways of conducting business should be attacked selectively, rather than through an across-the-board attempt to modernize the regulatory process.

Apart from any fears that they would have of eventually being displaced by computers, Williams's rate makers could be expected to see automation as newfangled and a bit scary. Computer buffs refer to this response as "technophobia." Given that the professional rate makers' aversion to change was predictable, as would also be their reaction to a head-on effort at computerizing their work, McDonald used the indirect tactic to get an automation project started—not as the agencywide initiative that he would have preferred but seemingly as an afterthought in the boilerplate prose of a contract ordered by the chairman. McDonald hoped that some momentum might be generated which could propel the project to completion before it succumbed to the forces of bureaucratic entropy and resistance.

Lessons from the Pentagon

In the bureaucratic context that McDonald had to deal with at FERC, the likelihood of opposition from the old hands in the agency argued against an effort at across-the-board change. Within an organization that has been in existence for any period of time, habituated routines and vested interests may present nearly insurmountable bars to radical transformation. This realization can give rise to an instinctive acceptance, even by an ambitious bureaucratic entrepreneur (such as McDonald), of the teachings of Simon (1947) and his incrementalist disciples (Lindblom, 1959; Behn, 1988). Instead of aspiring to bring about change across the breadth of an agency's well-established procedures, incrementalists prefer to focus an effort at change on a critical subunit of the organization. Mc-

Donald's acumen, sharpened by recollections from his days at the Pentagon of the rancor that a revolutionary organizational shake-up can cause, told him that selective, targeted computerization was the way to proceed at FERC.

In an important sense, the FERC automation project was inspired by the reforms of McNamara at Defense. McNamara had shown that a herculean effort at thoroughgoing change can succeed *if* the conditions are right. Radical change in the Defense Department succeeded in the early 1960s because of unwavering support from the very peak of governmental power. As a cabinet officer, McNamara enjoyed direct legal responsibility to the man in the Oval Office; McNamara never had reasons to doubt that he would receive unequivocal political support from President Kennedy.

McDonald had brought McNamara's objectives with him to FERC, but he could not duplicate the conditions that had favored across-the-board procedural changes in the Pentagon. McNamara's direct legal and political relationships with Kennedy differed from Butler's situation as a legally "independent" official. Furthermore, whatever stakes might have justified McNamara's bold project at Defense, no such stakes seemed to be at play in the regulatory agencies of the early Reagan years. President Reagan, having come to Washington in January 1981 as a committed deregulator, had had to invest most of his political capital in the fight for tax reduction. FERC had to be reckoned of secondary importance to President Reagan. Where political support must be husbanded, the prudent course is likely to be the more modest one. There were limits to the internal turmoil and possible bad press that the Butler-McDonald team could afford to generate at FERC (just as there were limits over at EPA, as Anne Gorsuch-Burford learned when her attempt at radical change in environmental policies and enforcement standards led her to overstep the political tolerances).

At Defense, the steely McNamara persevered in his entrepreneurial purpose despite enormous organizational turmoil and in the face of bureaucratic resistance worthy of the Masada heroes. McDonald never forgot the bitterness that the changes of the early 1960s had engendered among military men used to having their own way with civilian superiors. McDonald's decision in favor of selective computerization was motivated in part by a desire to avoid the kind of agencywide resentment at FERC that McNamara's revolution had occasioned within the uniformed services.

The need for constructive change in the pipeline rate-making process was recognized by almost all knowledgeable observers. And whereas Butler could not count on President Reagan for complete backing in advancing the deregulatory policy agenda, McDonald had every reason to hope for sustained support from Butler in changing the rate-making process, based on the chairman's special interest in the due process aspects of natural gas regulation.

Getting Started

A task force can be used as the organizational expression of the decision for selectivity. The task-force approach permits a leader to focus energies on a critical subunit in the hope that benefits will eventually accrue to the institution as a whole. McDonald trusted that the example of selective renewal in the form of efficient, computerized rate making would spread to other subunits of FERC. Unfortunately, though, McDonald knew just about as much as I did about rate making—damned little. He couldn't even begin to appreciate how big and complex a rate-making computer program would actually have to be. Neither he nor I, in fact, had a clue to the obstacles that lay in the way of automation.

Mike Butler had asked only for a confidential study, an inquiry into possible rate-making tricks or due process violations within the FERC staff. In principle, the "investigation" that Butler wanted might have been conducted by a lone researcher. There was no apparent reason why the kind of one-man research effort that had produced a reassuring answer to McDonald's "are we in trouble?" question couldn't produce a satisfactory response to Butler's inquiry as well. But by tacking the automation deliverable onto my consulting contract, McDonald had amplified his boss's idea into a major project, one that would require a cast of supporting players. Computer automation obviously requires programmers, who in turn need computers if they are to test and debug their programs. Good programmers are in scarce supply; there seemed to be none available on FERC's staff. Nor had funds been explicitly earmarked in the current FERC budget to rent or buy the computers that McDonald's project would require.

I admired the skills that McDonald displayed in overcoming these start-up problems.

McDonald carried in his head detailed ledgers of favors and IOUs ("chits"). Who owed what to whom? How much was each of his innumerable creditors' and debtors' chits really worth in the coin of bureaucratic exchange? The postings covered years of trading across a dozen federal agencies. One of McDonald's old and close friends was another former air force officer, a computer specialist named Al Linden, who, as it happened, owed McDonald a favor.

Who Was Al Linden and What Could He Do for McDonald?

Like McDonald, Al Linden had become a double-dipper following his retirement from military service. (A "double dipper" is a former military person who continues in federal service after retirement, and therefore draws two government checks each pay period, one for military retirement and one for the civil service job.) Also like McDonald, Linden had risen to a post of great responsibility in the civil service. As Number Two at the Energy Information Administration, the official data-gathering office of the U. S. Department of Energy, Linden oversaw millions of dollars worth of government contracts with beltway bandit data processing firms. He eventually resigned from the civil service and took a senior job in one of the most active and prestigious of these companies, the Orkand Corporation of Silver Spring, Maryland.

Linden was also in charge of the gigantic IBM computer— known as "Linden's toy"—in the basement of the Energy Department's Forrestal Building. McDonald wanted to use this computer, accessed via telephone lines, to automate FERC's rate-making process.

McDonald and Linden were not only personal friends but also were in regular touch professionally as a result of an arrangement that Congress had specified when it created the Department of Energy. Congress had set up the Energy Information Administration as a clearinghouse for energy data throughout the federal government. Officials from FERC and other federal agencies, therefore, had the right to "task" the Energy Information Administration for various data processing chores. Congress even appropriated a kind of scrip, that is, "funny money" that FERC officials could spend only at the Energy Information Administration to pay for data processing jobs. Technically, such an arrangement is known as a common support agreement, whereby a central federal agency—in this case, Al Linden's Energy Information Administration—must furnish a specified level of support to entitled customers. As FERC's executive director, McDonald could spend his scrip to buy time on Linden's toy, to pay Linden's staff members for processing FERC data-collection forms, and so forth.

Negotiating the Data Processing Schedule

About halfway between FERC headquarters on North Capitol Street and the Forrestal Building in southwest Washington is an Irish pub named The Dubliner. The word among their subordinates was that McDonald and Linden met periodically at The Dubliner to trade lunches and negotiate the forthcoming schedule of data-processing services. During any fiscal year, McDonald was supposed to use his current allotment of scrip to buy the data processing services that he wanted from Linden. But FERC's actual appropriation rarely fit its needs exactly during a given year. So McDonald reportedly "loaned" funding to Linden when there was a surplus of scrip at FERC and counted on Linden to repay him with computer time when the FERC budget fell short.

McDonald now needed more than computer time. To automate the review process for pipeline rate filings, special rate-making programs would have to be written. Fortunately, McDonald held a chit or two, accrued on past favors that he had done for Linden. He could use one of these chits to prevail on Linden for the needed support.

Linden's procurement people had recently let a big task order contract to a beltway bandit firm named Computer Data Services, Inc. (CDSI). Linden could write a new task order mandating CDSI to provide the data processing experts that the FERC automation project needed to get started. McDonald and Linden could sort out the cost accounting and tidy up the paperwork at their leisure. McDonald thus expanded the scope of the investigative effort, started the contracting process, and—with a little help from his friend Linden—arranged by task order for a team of high-quality computer programmers from CDSI to work full time under my direction.

Completing the Team

The start-up of the automation effort seemed auspicious. But the project would have quickly self-destructed if the team consisted only of me and the programmers from CDSI. Such a team would have contained only members of the shadow bureaucracy: outside consultants and contractors. The effective bureaucracy works through an interpenetration of the formal and the shadow bureaucracies. In the case of the FERC automation project, active participation by agency civil servants was crucial since only they had the specialized, nuanced knowledge that would be needed for computerization.

Penetrating the Mysteries of Rate Making

A vast store of specialized knowledge had to be made available to the programmers, who were then supposed to convert it into a software package that would run on Linden's computer. I couldn't do the necessary homework all by myself. Even if I had been able to find my way through the published materials (as I had done for McDonald's "are we in trouble?" study), the literature on administrative rate making was inadequate. Academics had written widely on the administrative process during the 1930s and 1940s, while the excitement of New Deal–era agency creation still fired the scholarly imagination (Frankfurter, 1935; Herring, 1936; Landis, 1938; Gellhorn, 1941). But few books were available in the early 1980s to guide a learner through the thickets of the administrative process.

An upsurge of interest in the administrative process has, more recently, produced some excellent studies (Frug, 1984; Byner, 1987; Gruber, 1987; Shapiro, 1988; Gormley, 1989). And, of course, the rise of the New Theory itself attests to a reawakening of interest in the bureaucratic phenomenon. FERC staff members have published some rate-making guides (Rogers, 1982; U.S. Federal Energy Regulatory Commission, 1983); however, agency procedures tend to change much more rapidly than the manuals do, so a handbook that purports to describe current procedures might be, in actuality, a book of past history.

The upshot was that, at the time Butler commissioned his "investigation" of rate-making methodology, published materials could be used to develop no more than a generalized, overall picture—the kind of schematic view shown in Figure 4.1—but not the detailed model on which a computer program has to be built.

Involving the Professional Rate Makers

What Ken Williams's professional rate makers really did when they reviewed pipeline company filings remained pretty much mysterious to all but the members of the small circle of gas company accountants, regulatory lawyers, legislative specialists, and FERC civil servants who had made careers of the process. No "investigation," and certainly no automation project, would succeed without some direct involvement of the rate-making experts.

Just as McDonald had already had to go (by way of Al Linden) to a beltway bandit firm for the data processing skills that computerization would require, he would have to go to the line side of the FERC organization for the special knowledge that Williams's professional rate makers possessed. Ironically, Linden—who worked for a different agency—was McDonald's friend and long-time bureaucratic trading partner, but Williams—who as a FERC veteran worked in the same agency—had strained relations at best with McDonald. There seemed to be little chance that Williams would cooperate, particularly when he and his staffers thought through the implications of McDonald's project. They would foresee a diversion of FERC funds from travel allowances and promotions to repay Linden for the services of the CDSI computer programmers. If the automation project succeeded, jobs might eventually be cut within the Pipeline Rates Division because Linden's computer would be able to do rate-making calculations more efficiently than the quill-pen wielders could. Williams's rate makers were hardly likely to help McDonald abolish their own jobs.

The nudge for Williams to cooperate had to come from Mike Butler, who alone in the agency had authority over both Williams on the line side and McDonald on the staff side. But before Butler could be expected to order Williams on board the automation effort, he had to be fully convinced of the value of computerization.

Again, McDonald knew how to do it.

McDonald told me to make a rapid study of the relevant portions of the *Code of Federal Regulations* and assorted FERC rate-making manuals. These documents specified a "uniform system of accounts" for use by pipeline company bookkeepers and purported to describe gas rate-making procedures as they were executed by the FERC analysts. I translated the bureaucratic gobbledygook as best I could into algebraic formulas, called algorithms. These algorithms summarized the mathematics of FERC's cost-of-service and rate design computations. Once algorithms have been written, a software specialist can transform them into a language that a computer understands, that is, a program.

A computer programmed from my algorithms might not have been able to do what the professional rate makers actually did. But such a program would have been able to do what federal law, federal rules of procedure, and FERC's own public pronouncements said rate makers did when a pipeline company submitted a filing. If the algorithms were correct, they would match the published descriptions, and the program could take over the rate-making computations directly. If the program didn't work, it would be because the published descriptions failed to reflect what the rate makers were really doing. Thus automation could be used to test for exactly the kinds of due process issues, such as departures from the established procedures, that had worried Butler to begin with.

Butler reviewed my mathematics (or at least looked with bemused fascination at my equations) and bought the idea of using the algorithms for a double purpose—as the template for a computer program and as a vehicle for smoking out any idiosyncracies in FERC's rate-making procedures. He sent a curt note to all FERC office heads on October 4, 1982, announcing his decision adopting McDonald's strategy. Williams, getting the message from Butler himself, had no choice but to assign a half-dozen experienced rate makers to the newly-formed automation team.

With Ken Williams's somewhat reluctant assignment of the professional rate makers to the computerization task force, the automation project, described by some as the project to "drag FERC kicking and screaming into the twentieth [sic] century," actually seemed to be under way.

Coalitional Politics and Compromise

Would the rate makers really cooperate, or would they just sit on their hands waiting for the CDSI programmers and me to fall on our faces? What if the algebra that I had shown Butler was faulty? Butler discounted this possibility because he had too much confidence in me and too little knowledge of algebra. But I had no illusions of infallibility, and I knew that Williams's professionals would find any mistakes in my algorithms before I did.

In effect, McDonald headed a coalition within FERC bent on computerizing the agency. Ken Williams headed a countercoalition whose members were wary of automation if not downright hostile to it. For McDonald to succeed, he needed to find a way to detach key players from Williams's blocking coalition and induce them to join the automation effort in spirit instead of just in terms of formal assignment to the project team. It would be embarrassing for Butler if the rate-making professionals let me, a drop-in from academia, mess up the rate-making process with a program that they knew contained errors. Merely formal participation by the professional rate makers wouldn't do. The professionals had to sign on emotionally, had to be co-opted into the effort.

Coalitions to advance or contest particular policy initiatives constantly form and re-form within organizations. Chits and compromises, as we have seen, are the very stuff of the coalition-building process. The recognition of the need for coalition building as an inherent feature of public administration is inconsistent with the picture of bureaucracy as a machine that moves directly and without internal friction toward whatever goal the higher-ups set. The goals of an organization should instead be viewed as a kind of resultant drawn by compromise from multiple individual objectives. To draw that resultant is a task of management, a fact underscored in the professional literature by recent writings on "management as negotiation" (Lax and Sebenius, 1986).

As the nominal leader of the automation effort, I had to deal with the fact that the workers—the professional rate makers—would ultimately decide much of what would get done. Their decisions in turn would reflect not only technical expertise but also any biases that they had developed over the years as they negotiated "understandings" with their counterparts in the natural gas industry.

The professionals had to be convinced that by helping me, they wouldn't be hurting themselves. Only then would the automation project be brought within what management theorists call the workers' "zone of acceptance."

The Zone of Acceptance

The zone of acceptance is a range of demands that subordinates will treat as legitimate because they seem consistent with the understandings—often, only implicit understandings—in the employment macrocontract of the firm or bureau.

When workers accept the employment contract, they forgo the right to disobey orders from the employer to the extent that they see those orders as lying within their zone of acceptance. If an order outside of this zone is obeyed at all, it will be obeyed grudgingly— in a context of resentment, malingering, and possible sabotage. Barnard, the seminal contributor to contemporary organizational thinking, drew the striking conclusion that because subordinates gradually develop a kind of common law among themselves to define their zone of acceptance, it is the agents lower down in a hierarchy, not the superiors, who decide what *can* be done and largely what *will* be done as well. (Barnard actually used "zone of indifference," but Simon's substitution of "zone of acceptance" seems better to communicate the basic idea. See Barnard, 1938; Simon, 1947; and Moe, 1984.)

The New Theorists stress that the actual objectives of an organization are not handed down by principals and pursued unquestioningly by agents but also reflect the demands of subordinates within the organization. Therefore, organizational change is most likely to be attainable when the goals of the involved individuals can simultaneously be brought within a common zone of acceptance *and* aligned with the direction of change desired by the organization's leaders. Because individuals' goals are often disparate (or in the lingo of the New Theory, "incongruent"), it may be difficult to meet either of these criteria, let alone to satisfy them both at the same time.

When goal incongruity is a major factor, as certainly was the case at FERC, the critical managerial task is to modify significant actors' objectives so as to bring them within a single zone in which a tolerable degree of coordination can be achieved for the conduct of all actors. Contrary to the teachings of the Old Theorists, who posited that the authorized decision makers at the top of a Weberian hierarchy would specify organizational goals for their agents, the group goal that emerges from the compromising process is likely to differ from the goal of any one participant—even the boss. It is also likely to differ from what anyone might have foreseen when the process of compromising began.

Butler's goal was to defuse any time bombs in the rate-making process. McDonald's goal was rather different—to expedite the regulatory process by computerizing it. The other participants in the automation effort also had objectives of their own. None of these objectives could have been considered to be the true goal of the project. In any project of change, it may, in the end, be necessary to bargain out team goals from the cross-tugging preferences of all the members of the relevant issue network. The aim, then, is to identify those members who can be induced to join a coalition in support of . . . well, in support of whatever goals have to be promised in order to form a successful coalition.

At FERC, much learning and sensitization had to occur within the automation team before the real goals of the project could be brought within the professional rate makers' zone of acceptance. For this reason, the computer program that finally emerged didn't look very much like the procedural mishmash that (it turned out) the rate makers had developed over the years. But neither did it look like the original algebraic description that I derived from the *Code of Federal Regulations* or, for that matter, like the kind of technically elegant program that CDSI's high-powered computer programmers would have preferred to write. Compromise was necessary all around.

Negotiation and compromise proved, in fact, to be at the center of virtually every significant process at FERC. They were central to the workings of the automation task force. They were equally critical in the overall rate-making process, which typically involved not only the development of informal "understandings" between Ken Williams's technicians and their counterparts in private industry but also formalized processes of bargaining and compromising in the early phases of rate-making litigation. The day-to-day workings of the automation task force and the broader litigative process—the latter touches all other aspects of regulatory politics—are the subjects of the next two chapters.

chapter 6

The Task Force
as an Engine for Innovation

A sidebar story about the role of the outside consultants on the automation task force illustrates the relationship between coalitional politics and technical expertise at FERC. This sidebar story also bears on McDonald's task, that of detaching key players from Williams's coalition of individuals hostile to (or at least suspicious of) computerization.

Over the years, Ken Williams had built up his own little empire within FERC. To his ranks of gas industry experts exercising line responsibilities, he had added an entourage of staff advisers, including some computer specialists under a branch chief named John Moriarty. Williams may initially have resisted McDonald's automation plan partly because he had himself been trying for some time to computerize portions of the rate-making process. However, Moriarty had apparently tried to automate the rate-makers' procedures without developing a general model of the underlying accounting procedures. As a result, his team had produced a rather

disjointed series of programs, one for each separate pipeline company, instead of a single rate-making program applicable to them
all. From Chairman Butler's perspective, this approach could only
intensify any idiosyncrasies that had already found their way into
FERC's rate-making procedures. From the perspective of Williams's
own professional rate makers, Moriarty's ignorance of the underlying theory made his team's work suspect on technical grounds.

The more foresighted members of Williams's technical staff
saw that computerization was inevitable in one way or another. In
fact, as we will see, they eventually concluded that computerization
was desirable, even necessary. Moriarty offered little help. The professionals' desire to break contact with Moriarty made them much
more willing to detach from the Williams coalition than they otherwise would have been, even if the price of detachment would have to
be an alliance with an outsider from the shadow bureaucracy—me.

The rate makers eventually prodded Williams to back Mc-
Donald's project team in an active way and abandon the effort of
his own man, Moriarty. In the course of the later formal investigation of McDonald's procurement practices at FERC, questions were
raised about the need to hire "high-priced outside consultants" for
the computerization project. But the record of Moriarty's group left
little doubt that an unsuccessful try at automation within FERC's
own staff had made outside help necessary.

The defection of the professional rate makers from the line
of official loyalty that the formal FERC table of organization would
have required, and their gradual switching of support to the project
team that McDonald had set up, helped establish the legitimacy of
the automation task force. As noted, the rate-makers' decision to
sign on resulted, in the main, from their own hardheaded calculations of the best way to sharpen the tools that they needed in their
day-to-day work. But there was also a psychological dimension to
the professionals' transference of loyalty from the Williams-Mori-
arty effort to the one that McDonald had launched.

The Psychology of a Special Project

Though the rate-making specialists were at first skeptical about
automation, those from Williams's staff who were selected for ser-

vice on the team apparently sensed that they were involved, willy-nilly, in a meritorious enterprise. The very fact that a task force had been brought into existence generated a sense of possibility, a certain élan among those assigned to participate. That spirit gave us all the sense that we were on the cusp of something important and promising at FERC.

As we have seen, McDonald's first problem was not mobilizing political support from above but overcoming resistance to change from below. In part, this resistance reflected the initial perception of career officials at FERC that their own interests were at odds with the interests of the new agency leaders. Furthermore, a kind of lassitude, engendered by the FERC veterans' comfort with their "grooved" ways of working, had become the norm in the agency staff. Discussion of the torpor that sometimes afflicts long-established bureaucracies perhaps gives the best lead-in to a consideration of the task force as a vehicle of organizational adaptation, if only because the psychological hurdle often presents the most formidable barrier to change.

A Sense of Specialness

An agency such as FERC periodically needs a zap of energy to initiate change. In chemistry, such a zap refers to the heat or electricity that a reaction needs if it is to go forward—a pile of sticks needs the touch of a match for ignition to occur, and even the most powerful explosive needs a fuse (Blum, 1955). This analogy from chemistry readily carries over to organizational theory. The psychological boost that the act of forming a task force can give to those selected for membership can also provide the energy needed to spark change. A special project can be the way to jerk an aging bureaucracy from the ruts of stodginess and routine. It can be thought of as an aging agency's way of concentrating energies, at least temporarily, to overcome its own entropy and inertia.

It is doubtful that the different interests and viewpoints of the task-force members could have been reconciled with one another in the absence of the special structure that Butler's and McDonald's support made possible. Because the FERC staff members could not initially be expected to embrace automated data processing methods without some prodding from above, the effort was likely to succeed only under the official patronage of the chairman and in a project monitored personally by the executive director. Instead of simply being folded into the routine work of the existing FERC staff, the effort needed its own charter of authority and its own special staff of assigned civil servants and hired outside consultants.

The lifting of workers' spirits, of course, provides only an opportunity for more energized, innovative effort, not a guarantee that it will be forthcoming. This attitude needs to be translated into conduct; the psychology of specialness needs to be translated into improved performance. To this end, the special-project structure not only focuses the adaptive effort within the organization, as FERC's automation project focused all participants' energies on the specific area of pipeline rate making, but also focuses the leader's expectations on those who are assigned to the special task force. The boss will be watching the members of the task force in a way that will not be true for those who remain unselected. All assigned members knew that, in some sense, they had to deliver—and deliver *as a team*, for it was the team's output that the chairman and executive director kept constantly in view.

Making a Special Project Special

Men and women live by symbols as well as by bread (Arnold, 1935; Edelman, 1967). It has long been recognized that the hierarchy of offices and duties within a bureaucracy is also a hierarchy of prestige and status. Honorific perquisites of office may be as important a source of motivation to an employee as are more tangible rewards, such as the worker's salary (Barnard, 1938). The very word *special* in special project relates to workers' demands for prestige and recognition. Such a project is, by definition, a structure out of the ordinary, worthy of unusual attention. A budget of its own attests in a concrete way to the privileged position of the enterprise.

The status of the computerization project ensured that team members could get quick action on requests for tangible resources. Because of the privileged position of the project, at least in its start-up phases, we had but to declare what is called "a requirement" and we received extra funds, extra equipment, or extra training support to move the project along. (A so-called requirement can often be accurately translated as "a wish.") We frequently had to make special requests for special kinds of help, for example, requests to the budget people for funds to hire more programmers (at one point, eight full-time programmers were at work), requests that the maintenance staff wire the FERC building for more computer terminals, requests to Ken Williams's middle managers that they release staff members from assigned duties to attend computer courses at the Department of Energy.

The demonstrably privileged positions of the task-force members fed the psychology of specialness and fostered the members' striving for excellence in the eyes of many in the agency who were watching. Toward the end of the project's life cycle, the scrutiny—and jealousy—of the outsiders became a liability. But in the early days, there could have been no doubt anywhere within the agency of the priority or the position of privilege that we enjoyed.

The Task Force and the Transaction-Cost Framework

A special task force is a temporary organization within the organization. The boundary of this temporary structure is a kind of membrane. Exchanges of material resources and information can occur *within* this membrane instead of *across* it. Managers can thereby take advantage of what military tacticians call "interior lines." Transaction costs within a unit tend to be lower than across the membranes that separate units from one another. Thus a temporary restructuring of relationships, resulting in an interiorization of participants' interactions, can reduce the costs of necessary transactions—which, according to the New Theorists, is what organizing is all about.

Suppose that McDonald had tried to computerize FERC without organizing all of the resources and skills needed for automation into a single project. Suppose that he had simply given Williams's rate makers computer accounts and encouraged them, as individuals, to modify their day-to-day routines by adopting automated techniques as best they could with no supporting modification of existing organizational relationships or work-flow patterns in the agency. Each staffer would have had to coordinate his or her efforts with every other staffer in a series of separate discussions; each individual would have had to negotiate item by item with those who controlled the resources needed for computerization. The transaction costs of such individual-to-individual, item-by-item negotiation within large organizations can be high, as they often are for item-by-item market interactions. McDonald was acutely aware of this fact.

Shortly before he launched the automation project, McDonald (1980) had published a humorous article in *Fortune* magazine about the woes awaiting newcomers to the Reagan administration. The article illustrated the problem of intraorganizational transaction costs—the organization in this case being the federal bureaucracy. Addressing a fictional incoming cabinet officer, McDonald described the hassles involved in dealing with one of the least understood but most pervasively influential of federal agencies, the General Services Administration:

> You'll also contend with . . . the General Services Administration, which allocates office space, maintains buildings, and provides word-processing equipment. GSA controls the temperatures in buildings, the flow rate of hot water, and the number of usable bathrooms. Its rules specify whether employees should wear ties, who will have which parking spaces, and what the spaces will rent for.
>
> About the only thing the General Service Administration is not concerned with, it seems, is services. Many federal buildings are dirty. Furniture is often old and worn. Poor security is a constant worry. The executive time wasted in negotiations with GSA over such problems is incalculable.

Consider the natural response of a high-level appointee who tires, as he or she eventually must, of wrangling with sticklers from the GSA. Inevitably, such an official will try to cut down on the transaction costs of external negotiations with the GSA by building an internal staff to manage the physical plant.

The creation of an internal building-services staff to take on

GSA's functions may improve the transaction-cost problem (at least temporarily) but will not eliminate it. Bureau chiefs on the line side of the agency will still have to bargain for equipment and maintenance, albeit with the resource controllers in the "son of GSA" that has been set up on the staff side. The point is, from the standpoint of a typical line manager who needs supporting services, the supplier represents an external unit, whether it is entirely outside of the manager's home agency (as GSA and the Energy Information Administration are outside of FERC) or is merely a different subunit within the manager's own agency. In either case, the manager must negotiate across the membrane that separates his or her unit from the supplier.

Just as top officials—such as the cabinet and subcabinet officers to whom McDonald addressed his *Fortune* article—try to internalize services in a way that will reduce their hassles with external agents, bureau chiefs try to cut down on negotiations within the agency by hiring specialized service staffs of their own. In this way, we have seen, Ken Williams had quietly built up an internal staff of computer jocks to free him from dependence on an external supplier—Executive Director McDonald—for data processing support.

The need for members of different offices within an agency to negotiate with one another obviously presents, once again, the central problem of the New Theory, that of transaction costs. If the task in question is sufficiently important, it makes sense to form an organization within the organization, a separate unit to which certain line employees (such as the FERC rate makers) and outside consultants (the programmers) can be assigned on a semipermanent basis. For the duration of the effort, the project leader, instead of dozens of separate managers, controls the assigned employees' time. Thus, the special project format carries the effort to internalize externally supplied services a step further; a new, albeit temporary, organization is created with as many of its own line and staff capabilities as can be assigned to it. The project leader is thereby relieved of the need to negotiate item by item with external suppliers of needed support activities.

Task-Force Working Procedures

Meetings are the primary mechanisms used to adjust subunits and subprograms within an organization (Mintzberg, 1983). A task force (closely related to Mintzberg's adhocracy) can be thought of as a series of meetings that are thematically tied together by a continuing focus on a single problem. At these meetings, the same members regularly interact to exchange views and solve problems.

The compromises that were necessary to move the FERC computerization project forward occurred issue by issue at regular meetings of the project team—FERC analysts on one side of a table, I and the programmers on the other. Each week, the rate makers had to teach the programmers some new secret of their craft. The following week, the programmers had to submit their computer coding of what they were required to learn for review by the rate makers. (To his credit, Williams had played it completely straight once Chairman Butler made it clear that he wanted the computerization effort to be fully supported. Only top people were assigned to the team—though if Williams had dumped less skilled rate makers into the project as a way of crippling it, the fact would have become evident only over time, after their cumulative damage in the form of bad advice had gradually undermined the effort.)

Jane Hannaway (1989) has noted the symbolic importance of meetings, irrespective of any business that might (or might not) be transacted at them. Hannaway found that workers assign high importance to the agenda items of large meetings. Many of our task-force conferences ended up with substantial attendance: we called them "tent meetings." The entire FERC staff knew our meeting schedule, and anyone was free to attend if normal duties permitted. The regularity and openness of the project team's working sessions, plus the occasional drop-in visit by Ken Williams, Bill McDonald, or Chairman Butler himself, kept the agency spotlight on the team.

Trust Within the Team

The automation project's format of weekly meetings contributed in important ways to the work of the task force. The knowledge that one must look the same people in the eyes week after week creates powerful incentives not only to deal fairly with the other guys, but also to understand their deeper professional and personal concerns.

The professional regulators on the team and the CDSI programmers had initially seen one another as natural enemies. But the cloud of distrust gradually cleared. Had it not, Williams's rate makers certainly would not have switched their loyalties from colleagues within their permanent division—even colleagues such as Moriarty and his group, whose expertise was suspect—to the project team. Indeed, of the factors that decisively shaped the performance of the group, I would list the development of trust within the team as most important, in large part because trustful relationships were most critical to the processes of bargaining and compromising that had to occur. Without trust, there would have been no way to overcome the suspicions that members of different constituencies had brought to the project.

The dynamics of the automation project gradually came to resemble those of an issue network; frequent contacts among participants promoted attitudes of accommodation and easy exchanges of information. Co-workers started getting to know one another as persons, not just as representatives of organizations or interests. The programmers reported to their regularly assigned cubicles in the FERC office building at 8:30 A.M. along with the permanent FERC civil servants, and they left in car pools at 4:45 in the afternoon. To the proverbial observer from Mars, their work patterns would have been indistinguishable from those of the full appointees to the classified civil service. Gradually the automation project took on the aspect of a typical organization within the effective bureaucracy, with civil servants and members of the shadow bureaucracy cooperating without any notice of their formally different statuses.

Of course, more than synchronized schedules and shared locations are needed to knit individuals from diverse professions into a team. Any relationship of trust undergoes periodic strains. Tests of good faith, tests of technical competence, and tests of team loyalty are unavoidable. The relationship deepens, if at all, only if team members pass these tests in one another's eyes.

I was perhaps less able than any other member of the team to evade questions. My own loyalties and *bona fides,* my own agenda had to be established. Although my primary responsibility was to McDonald, I could serve him well only if the FERC professionals regarded me as a fair intermediary. In the late winter of 1984, an episode occurred that tested my ability to serve as the needed "honest broker" among the various factions. During a meeting with McDonald and his assistant, Eileen Mason, McDonald questioned me about the timetable for computerizing the processing of pipeline rate cases and the pace at which we would be able to start turning staffers' work over to the machine. I replied that I was trying to keep the trust of the rate makers and that I didn't think they would expect me to help McDonald plan a campaign of attrition against their jobs.

McDonald would have liked to trim FERC's table of organization, but his higher goal was to modernize the rate-making process. This higher goal seemed a good deal more likely to be achieved in an environment of implicit trust. I drafted for McDonald's approval a document we simply called "the treaty" (Garvey, 1984). This document clarified what would thenceforward be the official rationale of the automation project—not to cut costs through job phase-outs, but to equip FERC staffers to deal with "the current environment of unstable gas markets [and] the increased complexity and frequency of company filings." McDonald never again raised issues that might have affected the rate-makers' job security. And my responsibilities to McDonald were never again, even in private, made to strain the trust that I had tried to earn from Williams's rate makers.

Give-and-Take Working Relationships

The weekly meetings also facilitated the creation of an institutional memory. Assigning people to work with one another on a regular basis, instead of only when specific needs require them to interact, binds relationships over time and promotes the development of "team lore." The benefits are both technical and interpersonal.

Technical problems frequently occur in sequence. They may be separated in time by weeks, months, or even years but still occur within common formats or frameworks. The team that has learned how to solve a particular kind of problem early in the course of a common effort has built a store of technical information from which it can draw when a similar issue occurs later on. There is no need constantly to reinvent the wheel. Because they know that they will be expected to cooperate in the future (their relations are not mere isolated interactions motivated by immediate needs), the task-force members develop cooperative repertoires of problem-solving techniques.

All FERC task-force members also quickly learned that team performance would be impossible without considerable give-and-take among parties who represented different personal and organizational interests. Give-and-take is a time-binding process, one that works best when the traders know that a concession made today will earn them chits capable of being called in tomorrow. Such calculations were critical in arranging the compromises that were needed to align the positions of the rate-making experts with those of the computer programmers and of Ken Williams's line officials with those of the various members of McDonald's staff.

Compromises within the project team generally took the form of changes in the design of the computer program, almost always to make it more interactive and less automatic. Though the practices offended their professional sensibilities, the programmers wrote all sorts of options into their code. Each option let the FERC technician press a key to override the program with a computational method of his or her own choice. Dozens of points eventually existed at which the analyst could halt the machine, open a "trap-door" into the program, and modify an algorithm. These options gummed up the software package, making it more complex and less economical than it need have been. But data processing efficiency was by no means our only criterion. Our compromises with efficiency were also the compromises with one another, and especially of the professional programmers with the professional rate makers, that helped win over the potential users of the new system—users who were also the system's potential saboteurs.

In the FERC project, for example, we learned early to read signals from Williams's rate makers regarding those procedures on which they wanted to retain flexibility and those that they were willing to let the computer perform mechanically. Eventually, we were able to draw on these understandings and avoid the exhaustive negotiations that might otherwise have been needed every time a decision was needed whether to add another trapdoor to the program.

Standardization Through the Backdoor

When a technician activated one of the trapdoors in the program, the computer would remember that the standard procedure (called the "default algorithm") had been overridden and would record the alternative steps that the FERC staffer actually used to perform the particular computation. This automatic recording feature served as a protection against staffers' excessive use of trapdoors to escape the standardizing effect of the basic program.

Fortunately, the inclination to sabotage or even obstruct the drive to computerize FERC diminished over time. The staffers gradually became comfortable with the automated processing of their work loads. Reassured by the knowledge that they could intervene in the running of the rate-making program if they wanted to do so, and hence could retain control over their own computations, the technicians became less determined to exert the very control on which they had originally insisted as the implicit condition of their support for computerization. They became less and less inclined to use the options that the programmers had written into the new software package. Their increasing willingness to let the default algorithms do virtually all of the computations moved rate making, at least temporarily, toward something like the truly standardized methodology that the due process requirement implies.

Standardization of procedures and a consequent quieting of due process concerns was what Butler had really wanted from the beginning. Thanks to McDonald, an automation project that was no part of Butler's original plan became the way to standardize rate making, albeit indirectly and by the backdoor. Note, however, that standardization occurred *not* because FERC's shiny new computer program made it impossible for the regulators to continue customizing. On the contrary, standardization came about mainly because the program's default algorithms made it very, very easy for FERC staffers to avoid the bother of overriding and customizing.

In the bureaucracy-bashers' stereotype, unimaginative and

rather lazy functionaries drone away at the tedious tasks of an agency such as FERC. Although it is as unfair as it is easy to overdraw this picture, there is an element of truth in it. If automation can complement human ambition and inventiveness, it can also capitalize on laziness and timidity by relying on these qualities to deter humans from interfering with work that they know a properly programmed machine can often do more efficiently than they can.

The Task Force in the Larger Context

Actually, a funny thing happened on the way to computerization. Many of Ken Williams's professionals had resisted automation because they thought that a machine would devalue their expertise and hence reduce their prestige (see Gruber, 1987). But hands-on experience with computers helped even the most technophobic of the rate-making specialists to overcome their fears. As the professionals learned to be selective—assigning computational drudgery to the machine and thus freeing their own time for more thoughtful analysis—they actually started to compete for terminals and printers of their own. It is a familiar story in contemporary bureaucracies: the computer, initially an object of fear and loathing, ends up as a status symbol.

The factor that finally converted the FERC staff members to active support for computerization was the firehoselike pressure of an increasing work load. Without computerization, the rate makers would have been unable to keep up. Under the complex phasing schedule of the 1978 Policy Act, the big pipeline companies devised evermore imaginative new accounting formulas. At the start of each new phase in the statutory scheme, company bookkeepers recomputed their costs and often petitioned FERC for rate hikes. Thanks to the way Congress had written the law, there would be more than enough work to keep FERC's rate makers gainfully employed, even if they used computers for the more tedious calculations.

In time, it became clear that the main difficulty would not come from obstructionists on Williams's staff who were put off by a project that hadn't originated in their office (the not-invented-here syndrome). Nor would it come from timid bureaucrats who feared for their jobs. Instead, the most formidable obstacle to automation at FERC was closely related to the problem of idiosyncratic procedures that had worried Mike Butler about the rate-making process. This obstacle involved a mismatch between the underlying theoretical assumptions of *any* automation project and the actualities of the regulatory process as it had evolved at FERC.

chapter 7

Discretion, Negotiation, and Litigation

The procedures that were actually used by the FERC rate makers became evident to us outsiders only over time. Automation required that we capture, in a language that Al Linden's computer would understand, the expertise that the professional administrators were supposed to be applying when they received those periodic rate filings from the pipeline companies. What we learned in the course of capturing and translating the rate-makers' expertise did indeed, as Chairman Butler had feared, raise questions about the fairness of the regulatory process.

Again, it is necessary to develop a bit of background information, this time, about the techniques that computer experts use when they try to capture and translate a body of knowledge into a machine-readable language.

Expertise and the Process of Computerization

A rate filing can easily contain upward of a thousand pages, many of them densely filled with numbers. As experts, Williams's professional regulators knew what data to cull from those humongous pipeline company filings. The experts knew which numbers had to be added up when computing a cost of service and which others had to be multiplied by what in order to produce a rate design.

Ideally, all of the factors that a rate maker would need to consider when determining which rule to apply could be expressed in mathematical equations. As has already been indicated, in theory, fairly simple equations govern each of the thousands of summations that FERC Rates Division staffers had to review when making a cost-of-service estimate (the lower pyramid in Figure 4.1). Other equations apply to the process of disaggregating costs into the hundreds of pricing categories that a rate design might contain (the upper pyramid).

Much of the expert knowledge that the FERC staffers carried in their heads was how-to knowledge: given a filing, the staffers knew how to categorize the numbers so that the right subtotals would get added to one another. And given a decision by the commissioners favoring one class of natural gas consumers over another, they knew how to tilt a company's rates to ensure that the right customers got the intended benefits.

McDonald's basic idea was to transfer as much of this knowledge as he could from the heads of the rate makers into Al Linden's computer and then to let the machine apply the rules. For that matter, that's what most automation efforts are all about: taking what certain humans already know how to do and then teaching a machine to do it more accurately and quickly.

From Anecdotes to Algorithms

The first step in such an effort is usually to express the humans' personal expertise in mathematical language—that is, to change the form of the knowledge without changing the content. Systems analysts specialize in this kind of work. They are experts in the art of extracting how-to knowledge from so-called domain experts such as FERC's rate makers. The analysts then translate the knowledge that they have teased from the domain experts into algorithms.

But the generally unsystematic, anecdotal nature of how-to

knowledge often presents a problem. As the term implies, anecdotal knowledge usually consists of personal stories: "When ABC Company filed for a rate increase, I did *this;* when XYZ Company filed two years later, I did *that.*" There is no explicit reference to a general rule that may be applied uniformly to both ABC and XYZ companies. The formulas may exist, but the anecdotal form in which the staffer carries the knowledge in his or her head will not reveal them.

Under the due process requirement of the Constitution, there is a presumption that rate-making procedures for ABC Company will be the same as those that are applied to XYZ Company and, indeed, to all other regulated pipeline companies in the nation. The systems analyst's job is to find the general rule, assuming that it exists. It may take hundreds of hours of anecdote-collecting to piece together the underlying formula. Over a four-year period, I met with the programmers and the FERC staffers (in all, a team of perhaps a dozen individuals) virtually weekly, usually for several hours at a crack. Most of our time was spent trying to generalize "I did this/I did that" anecdotes into algebraic equations, thereby preparing the way for further translation of the rate-makers' expertise into programs that a computer can understand.

A program would have to be written to "teach" the computer to read a rate filing and store its contents in the computer's central memory bank. A second program, called an edit check, would be needed to let the machine audit the submitted data for internal consistency and for compliance with standard rate-making rules. Once it had assured itself that it was working with "clean" data, the computer would have to know how to add, subtract, and execute all the other algebraic operations that were involved in a rate review. Such algebraic rules are the algorithms to which I have referred.

Algorithms and Demystification

Because an algorithm is an unambiguous statement of some mathematical or logical procedure, an algorithmic description of a process is inherently *public.* It eliminates what the experts cultivate— mystery. Anyone who understands the algebra can immediately understand exactly how the process works. There are no leaps of intuition, no x factors. For this reason, if FERC's rate-making procedures really were deterministic and discretionless (as the Old Theory implied and due process, strictly interpreted, required), it should have been possible to derive a complete algorithmic description of the rate-makers' job.

Because an algorithmic description would have spelled out every step in the FERC computational process, it would also have given Mike Butler the assurance he sought that procedures at FERC were fair, reasonable, uniformly applied, and otherwise in accordance with due process requirements. A methodology that the professionals had spent decades converting into a mystery would thus be made accessible, through analysis, to anyone who had completed a high school algebra course. On the other hand, if the algorithms showed that the methods actually in use differed from the ones that rate-making theory required, the discrepancy would immediately become apparent and fixable.

But what gradually became evident was that in certain rate-making areas, the experts' anecdotal knowledge did not so much disguise an underlying general rule as hide the embarrassing fact that no uniform rule existed at all. At points, bureaucratic discretion appeared to have devoured standard procedures. This discovery would not have caused misgivings if the only concern were the expertise and basic fairness of FERC's regulatory officials. But inasmuch as those officials function only as agents of higher-order principals—the legislators, judges, and appointive commissioners who prescribe or approve the promulgated rules—the level of compliance as well as the level of fairness in staffers' rate decisions had to be addressed. The institution of judicial review and the pervasive threat of litigation—ultimately, an appeal to the due process clause of the Constitution—pointed up the potential seriousness of idiosyncratic decision making at FERC.

Against this background, it is possible to consider some causes and implications of the discretionary practices that the taskforce members discovered in the course of their work.

The Evolution of Discretion in the Rate-Making Process

The enormous complexity of a pipeline company's operations meant that real expertise to audit its books could be acquired only if a staff member spent years learning the peculiarities of the company's structure and accounting procedures. Among some of Ken Williams's employees, therefore, a practice had emerged of assigning the same analyst to audit the same three or four companies in successive rate reviews. Specialization was counted on to produce the necessary detailed understanding. In a curious and indirect way, specialization also contributed to an additional, wholly unexpected consequence: bureaucratic discretion.

The limited case-assignment system had predictable effects. Specialization by each staffer in a few companies indubitably made that staffer an expert on his or her own little part of the natural gas industry. But it also meant that members of the FERC rate-making staff rarely developed a detailed appreciation of what was going on in companies other than the ones that defined their regular "practices." An analyst's lack of concern with companies other than his or her own invited the gradual development of idiosyncratic auditing methods. Each analyst gradually drifted toward rate-making methodologies specific to his or her own companies. The process went pretty much unchecked, since colleagues who might have brought fresh eyes to cases had little need—or inclination—to look beyond their own companies.

The limited case-assignment system also intensified patterns of contact across the public-private interface. Filing after filing tightened the tie of the same public official to the same few regulated private companies. Over the course of a few years, a FERC staff member might repeatedly visit the headquarters of particular companies to conduct field audits. FERC's accountants looked forward to these trips; they *wanted* to spend as much time as they could away from their crowded, tacky offices conferring with their company counterparts. Such meetings also served as important learning experiences, both personally and professionally. The regulators soon came to appreciate that working relationships must outlive any bitterness that a dispute in a given case might generate. Sticking to an adamantine position in this year's review might only make it more difficult to work out agreements the next time the FERC staffer had to sit down with the same company accountants. ("Not many months from now you'll be back talking to the same fellow you're squabbling with today. Why make life difficult?")

It would have been less than human if such enduring contacts had failed to underwrite "understandings" tailored to the regulator's and regulated's joint interest in a mutually accommodative relationship. But it appeared to the outsiders on the project team that every major company seemed bent on working out its own special regulatory regime.

A Process of "Genetic Drift"

Over time, the limited case-assignment system resulted in the fragmentation of the rate-making process into a series of somewhat independent methodologies—a separate methodology customized to each rate-maker's specialized practice. The decentralized nature of the process was perhaps its critical characteristic and the one that made it almost impossible to control.

Biologists have a term, genetic drift, for the process whereby mutations gradually accumulate within different strains of a species. Eventually, the strains drift so far apart that, although they may have come from the same ancestors, they lose their ability to interbreed and finally become separate species (Wright, 1931; Dobzhansky, 1962; Kimura and Ohta, 1971). Such a process of drift had occurred at FERC. On the average, major pipeline companies filed for rate increases every eighteen months or so. More than forty years had elapsed since the passage of the Natural Gas Act, easily long enough for FERC's regulators to evolve idiosyncratic rate-making approaches. Each filing cycle brought new problems and with them opportunities for new "understandings" to be worked out with the industry people. Because of the limited case-assignment system, the "understandings" that had been worked out usually applied to specific companies rather than as uniformly across the gas industry as a whole.

Each understanding that a FERC accountant worked out with a company spokesperson was a kind of procedural mutation. Such minute deviations may seem insignificant when considered individually, but over time they build on one another. In their cumulative effects, these individually minute accounting mutations could have created significant advantages for some firms and disadvantages to others, thereby undermining the legitimacy of the rate-making process for a whole industry.

When minor exceptions and obfuscations accumulate at multiple decision points in an organization, the breakdown of control can become chronic and pervasive. (Were it acute and concentrated, the condition would be easily diagnosed and more readily cured.) The chronic version of the breakdown of control is characteristic of old-line agencies because these, the senior agencies of our government, have been around long enough for the cumulative mutational process to run its term. The computer programmers from CDSI often found it impossible to reconcile the techniques of different staff members with one another. Rate making sometimes seemed a process composed mainly of exceptions.

Automation-Augmented Discretion

A final point is worth discussing in connection with the important issue of bureaucratic discretion achieved through a process of genetic drift.

In principle, it should in many circumstances be possible to control subordinates' activities through effective use of modern data processing technologies. The work of the automation task force was initially focused on the development of the cost-of-service program for use on Al Linden's mainframe. It turned out, however, that our reliance from late summer 1985 onward on Linden's toy backfired within the FERC rate-making staff. All FERC cost-of-service analysts had to use the same program on the same IBM computer. The mainframe remembered who did what. The computer automatically recorded how much time each analyst spent working on each case, and could, with the punching of a single key by a superviser, print out a report on each rate maker's recent work profile. Understandably, the members of any staff tend to resent this kind of centralized surveillance, which is one reason why most computer users prefer the independence of unshared workstations, that is, personal computers (PCs).

It was in fact the PC that created conditions for the first major break in the momentum of the original automation project. In the early 1980s, easy-to-learn spreadsheet programs for PCs, especially the Lotus Corporation's famous 1-2-3 package, appeared on the market. One of the rate design experts found that he could tailor 1-2-3 to do his rate-tilting computations, thus freeing him from dependence on the mainframe.

To speed the adoption of automated techniques at FERC, McDonald approved the purchase of a bank of new PCs for the rate designers. But when the rate designers learned how to do all of their rate-tilting computations on PCs with software bought off the shelf, they felt no need to continue participating in the development of the mainframe program. They could just take mainframe printouts of cost-of-service computations (the lower pyramid of Figure 4.1), and retreat to their workstations. There they could input the cost-of-service information into their PCs and develop their rate-tilting recommendations (the inverted top pyramid) free of surveillance by the mainframe. Since the mid 1980s, the rate designers have used their stand-alone personal computers—and perhaps their own idiosyncratic methodologies—on the upper pyramid of the rate-making process. Because they have no need to use the mainframe to gain the benefits of computerization, the rate design experts also have no need to let the mainframe know what new variations they might be introducing into the rate-design process.

The rate designer who uses a personal computer can work with a high degree of autonomy, because of his or her personal control over the input data (which can be retained in the worker's private diskette collection rather than in central storage on the mainframe), control over the computational procedure to be used, and even control over the information that will eventually be printed. There is no easy way to find out if new sequences of evolutionary drift have begun to occur in the FERC rate-making process. Any mutations that the rate designers might have introduced would be hidden on separate computers at separate workstations.

Though mainframe-based automation had been an instrument of standardization, the introduction of PCs reintroduced personal autonomy. In an unexpected way, then, automation might have created the conditions in which unsupervised customization could reappear in a portion of the rate-making process. With this customization comes a new, electronic version of the principal-agent problem and a new cycle of due process concerns. Here we come to a major irony of the automation task force at FERC: the delivery of new opportunities for administrative discretion out of a project that had originally been conceived in concern that the coolies might have taken over the engine room. *Plus ca change* . . . !

Control of Bureaucracy Under Conditions of Asymmetric Information

The problem generated by genetic drift in the rate-making process, perhaps compounded at FERC by the rate designers' use of PCs, is, at bottom, a principal-agent problem. It raises not only due process questions but also doubts about the ability of FERC's senior bureaucrats to control their subordinates. The accumulation of mutant rate-setting methods at FERC had not been the result of the civil servants' efforts to sabotage the policies of their higher-ups, but rather of the inability of the SESers to keep track of their agents' behavior. It was the result of asymmetric information within the bureau.

In *A Government of Strangers*, Heclo (1977, p. 248) argued that bureaucrats, and they alone, are the masters of their environment; hence "only bureaucrats can control the bureaucracy." It follows that if the political appointees are to succeed as top administrators, they must somehow inspire the senior permanent officials to provide the bureaucratic services that they need. As Mike Butler concluded shortly after taking office at FERC, no service is more important than that of controlling the professionals in the engine room of the bureaucracy.

Heclo's description of the relationship between political appointees and the senior cadre of civil servants also applies to the relationship between senior civil servants and those who are below them in the hierarchy. As one works downward in an organization, the detailed knowledge of individual workers increases. The accountant who audited ABC Company's books last year may know less than his or her section chief does about the general work of the unit. But that accountant has a much better line than the chief does on the ABC bookkeepers' latest tricks. The accountant's knowledge is narrow, but dense and detailed. Using his or her informational advantage, the nonsupervisory worker can gradually modify procedures. As the density of the subordinate's knowledge increases relative to that of the superior, so does his or her ability to exercise discretion—if need be, by flimflamming a less well-informed boss. Heclo's assurances notwithstanding, therefore, sometimes not even bureaucrats can control the bureaucracy!

Principals, Agents, and the Chain of Accountability

Do principal-agent problems as between bureau heads and their subordinates allow "faceless bureaucrats" to exercise unchecked discretion? Such a finding would contradict the basic belief in the United States in the existence of a chain of political accountability (Moe, 1985). Fortunately, we are not necessarily driven to this conclusion.

The Fire-Alarm Theory

One view of the policy process implies, surprisingly, that the chain of accountability actually remains in relatively good repair as a result of surveillance by members of the relevant issue network. The New Theorists who take this line do not, as the progressives did, identify good government with decision making in an apolitical space insulated from special interests. On the contrary, the New Theorists stress the vital role of interested parties, who have both the strongest motives and the needed knowledge to check bureaucrats. According to this view, issue networks, combined with the workings of the litigative system, structure the external checks that must be relied upon to limit administrative discretion (McCubbins and Schwartz, 1984; Calvert, McCubbins, and Weingast, 1989).

Neither government investigators nor prosecutors have the resources to sniff out every area of possible abuse unless citizens alert them to probable incidents of bureaucratic malfeasance. By taking advantage of laws such as the Freedom of Information Act (FOIA), attending public hearings, and following rumors as well as official reports of agency proceedings, those who are most affected by administrators' decisions can discover how and why those decisions are made. Interested parties can sound "fire alarms" if they think something is amiss, thereby focusing the inquisitorial attention of Congress on the problem or forcing the suspected bureaucrat into litigation.

As is usual, reality may be a bit more complicated than the freedom-of-information principle suggests. A curious citizen often finds that he or she must know exactly what to ask for and then must wait interminably for agency officials to review and fill the request. Those catches may make the FOIA relatively ineffective as a means for ordinary citizens (as opposed to special interest representatives who are geared up to use all the mechanisms of the issue network) to gain information about the inner workings of federal agencies.

Why the Alarm Did Not Sound at FERC

The fire-alarm theory of the role of interested parties contains useful insights into the workings of issue networks. But it raises a question about the "understandings" that had developed across the boundary between FERC and the natural gas industry. Why did industry representatives fail to resist the discretionary rate-making practices that were developing at FERC? As members of the issue network with direct access to information about developments in cases that affected them, the accountants and lawyers of the pipeline companies surely knew what had been happening in the FERC rate-making process. They understood that some individuated treatments had evolved and that pipeline companies were not always being regulated on the basis of common, public criteria. They knew too that cumulative mutations might have violated one of the traditional canons of fairness in our constitutional system. Yet objections from the pipeline companies were relatively rare.

The companies certainly had the legal right to sound the gong. And in cases of big-stakes disagreements, they did exactly that by contesting FERC staffers' ratemaking procedures in lengthy hearings and court cases. But in the main, the representatives of the pipeline companies accepted the FERC process as it continued to evolve. The question is, why?

Part of the answer no doubt lay in the fact that, on balance, the advantages that each company gained from FERC's regulatory pattern outweighed the disadvantages of a challenge to the overall arrangement. The attitudes of agreeability and accommodation that prevailed within the network made for an environment likely to select for even more agreeability and accommodation. Why contest the fairness of a process that could be turned to one's own benefit? Through continuing consultation with FERC staff members, the company accountants and attorneys could influence the direction of the drift in procedures in their own favor.

Also, the pipeline companies could take a somewhat relaxed view of the process of evolutionary drift because the nature of the legal system permitted them to. A set of procedures known as "top sheet service" and "settlement" had evolved to ensure members of the issue network a relatively high chance of resolving disputes amicably and by informal agreement. So important are these procedures, as is the litigative framework in which they are embedded, that a few words of amplification seem in order.

Litigation and the Incentive to Settle

When FERC staffers complete their review of a pipeline company's rate submission, they list their disagreements with the company accountants in a document known as a top sheet (so called because it gets clipped to the voluminous file that the FERC clerks accumulate as the case works its way through the bureaucracy). Before the process was computerized, a top sheet would take about four months to prepare and could be a dozen pages long, one page for each major cost category in which more than a couple of disagreements had turned up between the company and the FERC reviewers. A staffer's determination to disallow a particular company-estimated expense, for example, might appear as one of many points of disagreement logged in the top sheet for the case.

FERC's accountants used to prepare their top sheets by hand, frequently turning out documents of literally calligraphic elegance. It was an eye-opener to see these belletristic documents submitted as official position papers of the U. S. government. The human touch was quaint and in a way engaging. But the handcrafting of official papers for multibillion dollar rate cases encouraged the view that FERC had a great deal to learn about business in the twentieth century. It took us almost three years to produce the first fully computerized cost-of-service top sheet (for the Texas Gas Company rate filing of 1985).

Every disagreement recorded in the top sheet has to be resolved, one way or another. The way in which most conflicts are actually reconciled, rather than the mere fact of eventual resolution, tells us the most about the workings of issue networks—and, for that matter, about bureaucracy in general.

Top sheet service occurs when the FERC staffers express-mail their listing of disagreements to the company, thereby giving formal notice of the points on which the company's claims are to be contested. Service of the top sheet marks the end of the technicians' (accountants, economists, and engineers) primacy in the rate-making process. The action then goes to the lawyers, who conduct a settlement conference, that is, a meeting of spokespersons for all interested parties to see if an informal agreement can be reached on the company's cost of service and rate design. Only when the FERC's staff members and the company's lawyers find it impossible to compose their differences in the easy give-and-take of a settlement conference will the parties move on to more formal litigation.

The Formal Litigation Process

The progressives enshrined expertise and efficiency in theory. But in practice, they delivered decision making to lawyers and judges, whose controlling professional values are often inconsistent with efficiency. Formal regulatory proceedings are conducted with excruciating attention to due process requirements. Congress and the courts have fashioned a whole new branch of public law, administrative law, which is aimed largely at limiting "arbitrary or capricious" administrative power. One scholar has traced the evolution of six separate categories of procedures under the 1946 Administrative Procedures Act (APA), the axial statute of the federal administrative process. At the relatively simple extreme of the procedural spectrum in an agency such as FERC, officials are merely required to publish their decisions in particular cases, giving reasons for their actions. More complex cases and rule makings—which naturally tend to arise over the big-stakes or extremely complex issues—

require full trial-like proceedings, with every conceivable procedural safeguard (Verkuil, 1978).

A FERC rate case that is required to run the full procedural gauntlet will first go to a hearing before an official known as an administrative law judge (ALJ), who is, however, not a judge in the usual sense but just another bureaucrat serving in a judgelike role. For years, ALJs were called hearing examiners, a title that is less honorific but perhaps more descriptive of their role in the administrative process. A pipeline rate hearing before an ALJ is an elaborate, ritualized affair. The presentation of evidence follows strict rules. Witnesses appear to support the company's positions. FERC staff attorneys then cross-examine these witnesses and present experts of their own. Almost always, these experts are the technicians from the Pipeline Rates Division who prepared the top sheet. The administrative law judge considers all of the evidence and prepares a point-by-point analysis of outstanding issues, together with decisions on all of them.

In a case of any size, six months or more may elapse between the service of the top sheet and issuance of the administrative law judge's analysis. Since FERC regulations give staffers four months to serve the top sheet after the company submits its rate filing, the ALJ may not have his or her "decisions" ready much before ten months has gone by. One way and another, that ten-month lapse often stretches into a year or more.

The ALJ's decisions, however, are really only recommendations, since the case then goes to the FERC commissioners (the "Five Great Americans," as McDonald used to call them with good-humored sarcasm). The commissioners may simply approve or modify the ALJ's recommendation or may decide to hold a formal hearing for themselves. In the latter event, the lawyers for both sides will have another chance to present essentially the same evidence that the administrative law judge has already heard. Following their hearing, the commissioners issue a final order setting the pipeline company's rates.

Even the final order often turns out not to be very final because the loser may appeal. Thus occasionally a case will go through five separate courtlike reviews: at the levels of the administrative law judge, the commission, the federal district court, the federal court of appeals, and the U.S. Supreme Court.

The Incentive to Reduce Transaction Costs

First to last in this marathon hurdle race, due process concerns are the critical factors affecting fairness and efficiency—or inefficiency—in the federal administrative process. In the words of Supreme Court Justice Byron White: "The Constitution recognizes higher values than speed and efficiency. Indeed, one might say of the Bill of Rights in general, and the Due Process Clause in particular, that they were designed to protect the fragile values of a vulnerable citizenry from the overbearing concern for efficiency and efficacy that may characterize praiseworthy government officials no less, and perhaps more, than mediocre ones" (*Stanley* v. *Illinois,* 1972, p. 656).

Nevertheless, the cumbersomeness of the formal administrative process has made the search for informal means to reduce transaction costs all but inevitable. The most important of these means is the aforementioned settlement conference, which occurs at the start of the whole process and which participants typically attend fervently hoping that the subsequent more formal stages can be avoided altogether.

A settlement conference is an official meeting between company representatives and FERC staff members. Under the guidance of their respective lawyers, spokespersons for each side test the others' negotiating skills. Each side's attorneys know exactly what game the other side's are playing, and they all understand the posturing that is normal in the process. Early in the settlement conference, each side stakes out ground that can be given away during the haggling that will follow.

All participants share the foreknowledge that every major rate case will eventually be turned over to the lawyers, probably to be decided in settlement-conference bargaining or in litigation. Any doubts that rate setting is as much a negotiating process as it is an exercise in "discretionless administration" vanish in the settlement conference. Company and FERC representatives often resolve top sheet issues by the simple expedient of trading adjustments. "We won't fight you on the deductions you want to make to our purchased gas costs," a company lawyer might offer, "if you'll drop that reduction you want to make in our depreciation expenses for last year." Splitting of differences is another way to move the process forward.

Usually, disputes *can* be resolved in settlement. My notes for a briefing presented on January 27, 1984, to then-chairman Raymond O'Connor, based on a survey of the disposition of all FERC pipeline rate cases, indicate that during the early Reagan years 80 percent of all issues were being resolved in conference. Only the 20 percent remainder therefore had to be contested in formal hearings before administrative law judges.

The dynamics of a shared industry culture help to explain the success rate that settlement-conference participants expect to achieve. All parties recognize their common interest in solutions that will contribute to the stability of "their" industry. Inasmuch as participants in these settlement conferences often know one another from prior encounters and may expect to face one another in future negotiations, the settlement process itself should be thought of as a function of the broader issue network. The same game will be played again, and by the same players, so everyone knows that fair dealing all around today will influence future attitudes in a favorable way. The fascinating work by Robert Axelrod (1984) on the impact of "the shadow of the future" on putative adversaries throws light on the incentive to cooperate that an issue network, by creating time-binding conditions, brings into existence.

Discretion, Litigation, and Negotiation

The right of losers to appeal unresolved differences up through the federal courts also encourages dispute resolution at the settlement stage. It is often better to split the difference while an issue can be absorbed into a whole set of amicable trades than to break it off from the bargaining process. When an issue becomes a sharply focused point of litigation, it tends to stimulate all parties' fighting instincts.

Litigation, although bread and butter for lawyers, adds to the cost and uncertainty of governing while often doing little to improve the quality of decisions. In an influential study, Shep Melnick (1983) documented that the federal courts have increased the costs and delays of resolving environmental policy while often contributing only marginally to the quality of decision making.

Litigation is the quintessential avoidable transaction cost in our system. The desire not to see the other guy in court explains why interested parties use all the opportunities that the issue network gives them for negotiation and consensus building. Noteworthy in this connection is the argument of the New Theorist Gordon Tullock (1980, 1986). Tullock argues that because formal litigation carries such high transaction costs, driving disputants to invest resources to forestall court proceedings, Americans have developed increasingly sophisticated and hence costly avoidance techniques. The result is a system biased toward reliance on informal dispute-resolving practices. These practices save costs relative to those that would be incurred if all issues were formally litigated. But in absolute terms, the costs of conflict resolution even through settlement are higher than they need be; an expensive litigation system breeds an unnecessarily expensive litigation-avoidance system as well.

The frequency of issue-resolution in settlement conferences gives the lie to any lingering belief in the predominance of problem solving by technical expertise. Splitting of differences in settlement conferences not only expedites the rate-making process but also ensures that factors other than economic or engineering analysis will finally decide many issues. Thus, government attorneys with no more principled a goal than that of striking a workable compromise with company lawyers, can almost always override a position that the technical experts—the professional rate makers—may have taken when they prepared their top sheets. An agreement to trade the FERC lawyers' interpretation on issue X for the company lawyers' on issue Y signifies the parties' acceptance of pragmatism or expediency as the arbiter of both issues. What such trading cannot ensure is what due process—at least in the sense of rule-bound administration—requires, namely, decision making based on general principles that were adopted and publicized before the joining of particular issues in actual cases.

Of course, technical expertise remains an important input to the process. And statutes as well as judicial opinions limit the kinds of bargains that negotiators are free to strike. Yet it remains true that rate making, like much else that goes on in today's bureaucracies, depends on bargaining and deal making as much as it does on the discovery of any one best way.

Just as issue networks have evolved to facilitate exchanges of information (including information about network-participants' interests), settlement procedures have become important because they help adversaries to substitute negotiation for litigation and thereby reduce transaction costs. At the same time, the negotiation to which the threat of costly litigation so often leads implies the existence of enormous discretion. In fact, the freedom of the negotiators to split the difference in whatever way will settle a case often swamps the discretion that the cumulative mutational process might have won for the technicians. This fact helps to explain the relative quiescence of the private industry respesentatives who surely knew what shortcuts the FERC rate makers were using.

Why should pipeline company experts fight with their FERC counterparts over modifications that the latter migiit be making in the rate-setting process when recommendations based on the experts' analysis are subject to replacement if the lawyers reach a more expedient solution based on bargains rather than on technical knowledge?

Litigation, negotiation, and discretion are thus bound up in a complicated dialectic. Litigation provides much of the incentive for negotiation, which widens the discretionary element in the administrative process. But the widening of discretion also invites more litigation lest "arbitrary and capricious" decision making overtake the administrative process. So the process goes. And goes. And goes.

chapter 8

Bureaucracy
Under Stress:
A Federal Investigation
and Its Aftermath

The most chilling legal threats are not those of litigation over the proper interpretations of laws, or even over abuses of administrative discretion—unless the alleged abuses carry the possibility of criminal punishment. The final phase of the automation effort gave way to such an ultimate threat—an extensive, enervating federal investigation across a wide-ranging field of allegations.

    Inevitably, a special project is exposed to the hostile scrutiny of those who feel left out, those whose habituated ways will have to change, and those who may for any other reason resent proponents of the project. At FERC, the diversion of agency funds into the automation effort naturally invited jealousy from those supervising officials whose budgets had to be reduced to hire outside consultants and contractors. In this way, the very existence of an automation project contributed to the eventual coalescence of forces that would eventually undermine it.

Yet the merits of budgetary allocations within FERC were the least of it. *Ad hominem* considerations proved to be more potent factors. Over the years, Bill McDonald—ever the battler, ever the bureaucratic entrepreneur—had collected quite a gallery of resenters. It was out of a context of bitterness involving personalities, not policies, that the charges of "scandal at FERC" eventually came. The susceptibility of the automation project to dissolution in the context of an investigation says much about the importance of personal differences and psychological factors in day-to-day bureaucratic life.

Gestation of a "Scandal": The Personalities

When Mike Butler left FERC to take an investment banking job on Wall Street, President Reagan picked another Wall Streeter, the aforementioned Raymond O'Connor, to succeed him. O'Connor came to FERC encumbered by political IOUs (by no means an unusual condition). Reagan's aides wanted O'Connor to appoint some reliable conservative Republicans to high Schedule C positions on his staff. When the general counsel's job opened up at FERC, O'Connor brought a lawyer named Robert Satterfield over from the Interior Department. In his turn, Satterfield brought one of his own proteges, a lawyer named Lawrence "Lonnie" Lebow, to serve as a special assistant, a title that some FERC staff members translated as "political hatchet man."

McDonald thought that Chairman O'Connor had embarrassed himself when he made Satterfield FERC's general counsel. When Satterfield promoted Lebow from special assistant to the key legal position as chief of litigation, McDonald saw a threat to the credibility of FERC proceedings. It was another case of "antennae out." No one wanted to see O'Connor's tenure at FERC marred by a string of reversible errors.

Morale plummeted in the general counsel's office. One heard grumblings and mutterings among the FERC lawyers: "While they were at Interior, Satterfield and Lebow helped Watt [James Watt, President Reagan's controversial first Secretary of the Interior] sell public lands to private interests at bargain-basement prices; now they're going to sell out gas regulation!" "Lebow's in charge of all appeals up through the federal courts, but where's his trial experience?"

A Story About Lebow

McDonald gave me his version of the origins of what would become a major agency debacle at a meeting in his office in June 1986.

McDonald told me that Vic Stello, executive director at the Nuclear Regulatory Commission (NRC), wanted him to join the NRC's Bethesda, Maryland office as deputy executive director for administration. McDonald stressed that the new job would be closer to his home in the Maryland suburbs. But if he took Stello's offer, it would be a demotion—from executive director of one federal agency to *deputy* ED of another. There had to be reasons other than the one McDonald cited for his interest in Stello's job offer. McDonald's next comment suggested what those concerns might be.

"Let me tell you a story about Lebow," McDonald said. "You know the job that Lebow's filling as chief of litigation. . . . Well, the job's an SES billet." A civil servant who is admitted to the Senior Executive Service remains on probation for twelve months; only after a formal one-year review is the SES status confirmed. "Lebow," McDonald continued, "came up for his one-year check last month." McDonald had played an active role in the review process.

Charges had been made that Lebow was guilty of sexually harrassing secretaries in the general counsel's office (Effron, 1986). In addition, there were rumors that Lebow had "conducted personal vendettas" and allegations that he was using government time and property to carry on a private law practice for personal profit (Effron, 1986). The alleged personal vendettas involved Joe Neubeiser, a McDonald protege. As the sitting deputy director of administration at FERC, Neubeiser had responsibility for the processing of senior personnel appointments and promotions. McDonald told me that Lebow, who had recently married another FERC employee, Moira Roberts, tried to pressure Neubeiser into upgrading Roberts's job.

Federal conflict-of-interest laws require all FERC SESers to report their stock holdings. In McDonald's telling of the story, Lebow had somehow managed to get his hands on FERC's financial disclosure files. Based on his research into McDonald's and the others' disclosure reports, Lebow concluded that Neubeiser owned stock in companies that were under contract to FERC. Lebow made a similar charge against yet another McDonald protege: Ken Pusateri, who became acting executive director of FERC when McDonald left the agency to take the Nuclear Regulatory Commission post. To cap it, Lebow alleged that both Neubeiser and Pusateri had helped negotiate the contracts with the firms in which they held stock (see Effron, 1986). If the charges were true, Neubeiser and Pusateri might have been liable to criminal prosecution under the conflict of interest laws. According to McDonald, Lebow had threatened to "expose" Neubeiser's stock situation if Neubeiser refused to initiate a promotion action for Lebow's new wife.

The rumors swirling about Lebow made for an unpleasant atmosphere. The SES panelists had to consider the truth or falsity of these stories when they assessed the candidate's suitability for permanent acceptance in the seniormost ranks of the federal civil service. After weighing the evidence, some of it offered directly by McDonald, the reviewers recommended that Lebow be denied a permanent SES position and dropped to a nonsupervisory job.

When he was told of the adverse decision, Lebow agreed to go quietly. In return, the review panel promised to close the book on his alleged malefactions and "shred" the derogatory evidence (Effron, 1986, citing Chief Administrative Law Judge Curtis Wagner, the chairman of the SES review panel). No one, however, could shred the rumors. Tales of Lebow's conduct were all over the agency grapevine. In due course, reporters scented the story and detailed the case against Lebow in print (Effron, 1986), although Lebow denied any wrongdoing on his part.

The Start of the Investigation

Lebow's accusers had taken their best shot. The shot had hit its mark, but not fatally. Lebow, though demoted, remained an agency employee. With the file on his alleged derelictions presumably de-

stroyed, there was little additional harm he had to fear if he decided
to get even.

To understand the next step requires some knowledge of the
recent evolution of the federal investigatory apparatus. By a series
of laws passed in the late 1970s, Congress mandated the creation of
inspectorates in the major federal agencies. All executive departments except Treasury and Justice have inspectors general to investigate reports of waste, fraud, or abuse (IG Act; Gormley, 1989).
Allegations arising within FERC lie under the purview of the Department of Energy inspector general, who was at the time of the
Lebow episode a specialist in white-collar crime named John
Layton.

Lebow wrote to Inspector General Layton accusing McDonald and the others of improper activities (Raymond Madden, conversation with author, October 21, 1986). Ken Pusateri told me in
August 1986 that Lebow next alerted the *Washington Post* to
rumors of a scandal at FERC. Before the matter ended, there was
talk of a full-scale congressional inquiry to be led by the intimidating John Dingell. From the time that the first rumors of criminal
probes began circulating until Inspector General Layton finally
closed his files on the case about a year later, the lives of most of
the leading figures in the automation story were dominated by the
investigation of Lebow's allegations.

The Next Stage in the Automation Project

Lebow's letter to the inspector general containing formal allegations of wrongdoing was dated June 29, 1986, but I didn't hear
about the inspector general's investigation until more than six
weeks later. Word of the impending inquiry reached me by a round-
about route in mid August 1986, as I was preparing for what the
team members thought would become the next stage in the automation project.

At that point, I was spending a good deal of my time stroll-
ing from office to office in the FERC building, schmoozing the
members of the automation project team. How's morale? What are
the problems? With the project team planning to move onto a new
plane of activity, it was my job to uncover any glitches that might

prevent us from meeting the next critical milestone in the project—an impending get-together with gas industry representatives.

We had finally reached the point at which it made sense to ask all interstate pipeline companies to begin submitting their rate requests in a standardized form, ready to be read by the computer. This procedure, McDonald's ultimate objective from day one of the project, would save FERC clerks the task of keypunching the data that the companies were still submitting in ledgers. If rate filings arrived at FERC in machine-readable form, the computer could speedily check submissions for internal consistency and then feed them directly into the nearly completed cost-of-service program.

FERC could mandate machine-readable filings by passing a rule. But even when they contemplate making a relatively noncontroversial rule, agency decision makers must meet the requirements of the Administrative Procedures Act: they must give notice of their proposed actions in the *Federal Register*, must allow all interested parties to submit comments, must explain the rationale for the rule they propose to pass, and must publish the new rule at least thirty days before it is to go into effect (Verkuil, 1978). It gets much more complicated if any of the interested parties object. Under the APA, those who would have to submit the data in the fully automated format would have ample opportunities to declare themselves for or against the plan. Our aim was to keep the matter as noncontroversial as we possibly could. That way, any rule-making process could be kept relatively simple, and we would avoid dragged-out litigation.

We knew that the machine-readable filing idea might turn out to be a hard sell. Gas industry executives cherish their image as frontiersmen. Spawn of the oil business, they wear three-piece suits but think of themselves as wildcatters. They were likely to oppose computerization on principle, a euphemism for sheer orneriness.

We meant to use one of the standard techniques of continuing consultation to build a favorable consensus within the issue network. The pipeline officials were more likely to cooperate—that is, more likely to refrain from using APA rule-making requirements as a stalling device—if they could see a working mock-up of the data processing program we wanted them to adopt. We hoped to show them, not just tell them, how easy it would be to submit data in computer-ready form. We also planned a full-dress briefing (called a dog-and-pony show) for industry representatives. At that briefing, we would ask for certain data that the computer programmers needed right away. If the pipeline companies refused to volunteer the information, FERC would have to order them to submit it— another potentially troublesome rulemaking. Lawyers for the companies could manipulate the process and appeal any order up through the federal courts. It might take years.

The key figure working on the mock-up for the dog-and-pony show was Jim Lighthauser, the chief of our programming staff. Jim had developed a special set of floppy disks containing all elements of a rate-making computation except the actual data. The filing company would have to furnish those. Under our plan, any pipeline company would get a set of these diskettes for the asking. A bookkeeper could insert them in a personal computer and fill in the blanks as panels flashed up on his or her computer screen. At FERC, a clerk would stick the filled-in diskettes into a specially adapted computer. FERC's computer would then evaluate whether the data justified a price increase. The company could get its answer almost by return mail.

It was up to me as project manager to preside over the dog-and-pony show and demonstrate Jim's floppy disks. The presentation was only a week off, and we were worried that there might still be bugs in the diskettes. But Jim had other matters on his mind. I date the beginning of the end of the FERC computerization project to the message that Jim gave me.

Ken Pusateri's Urgent Meeting

"Pusateri phoned," Jim said. "I don't know what his problem is, but he says it's urgent to meet with you."

In August 1986, Ken Pusateri seemed on his way to becoming the full (not merely acting) executive director at FERC. If it happened, it would be quite an achievement for someone in his mid-thirties. Alas, it was not to happen.

Pusateri handed me a letter. Its *Washington Post* letterhead was an attention grabber. The *Post* had assigned a reporter to investigate FERC.

"What's to investigate?" I asked.

"I think Lebow's behind it." That was no answer, but it gave me a hint. Lebow was now claiming a conspiracy of character assassination to distract attention from improprieties allegedly committed by the FERC officials who, he claimed, had railroaded him (see Effron, 1986). Specifically, Lebow accused McDonald, Pusateri, Neubeiser, and several others—including even the acting FERC chairman, Anthony Sousa—of multiple derelictions. Someone had leaked it to the *Post* that one of President Reagan's nominees for a judgeship, top-rank FERC civil servants, and an Ivy League professor—that was me—were guilty. I tried not to think about probable reactions at Princeton if the deans heard that one of their professors might be targeted in a criminal investigation.

Pusateri warned me that the "storm troopers," his term for special agents of the inspector general, would want to question me. "About exactly what?" I asked.

"The charges amount," Pusateri answered, "to bribery, conspiracy, and fra d on your consulting contracts."

The Beginning of the End

Pusateri shifted, signaling a change in subject. "Now, about your dog-and-pony show for the INGAA people . . ." (INGAA is the pipeline industry's trade association, the Interstate Natural Gas Association of America mentioned in Chapter Three.) I told Pusateri about Jim's diskettes, probably fishing for a compliment, since our project had recently pulled ahead of schedule. Our next milestone, the INGAA meeting in August 1986, would represent a major speedup in the computerization effort. But efficiency in the automation effort was just one more problem, not an achievement worthy of praise, as far as the beleaguered Pusateri was concerned. To understand why Pusateri took no joy from the news of our progress requires an appreciation of yet another peculiarity of the federal contracting process.

The "urgent meeting" with Ken Pusateri occurred on August 14. My consulting arrangement with FERC was scheduled to expire on September 30, 1986. But since we were now ahead of schedule, our mock-up diskettes didn't appear as a subtask on the current contract. In fact, no contract existed to authorize the dog-and-pony show that we wanted to give the INGAA people.

Earlier in the year, I had put in a bid for a follow-on contract. Under my proposal, written before the project team gained ground on its original schedule, the diskettes would be produced sometime after September 30. What if our project team completed the diskettes now, and a contract was awarded calling for those same diskettes to be finished three months later? Pusateri feared that the investigative reporter or the inspector general's storm troopers would uncover a follow-on contract entitling me to be paid during the next fiscal year for already completed work. It would be an improper contract.

It might have seemed an easy enough problem to solve: keep up the ongoing work but rewrite my bid for the follow-on contract, eliminating subtasks such as completion of the diskettes that could be done immediately. The government would get an unexpected bonus, the diskettes, under the current contract, right? Wrong. My bid for the follow-on work had been submitted four months before. Other computer consultants had been free to try for the job. The competitors could cry foul if I were now permitted to modify my own proposal by changing deliverables or milestones. The only way to modify anyone's proposal would be to invalidate the entire competition and reset the clock for everyone.

"I Want You Outta Here . . ."

In the context of an impending criminal investigation, we had to be above suspicion. Pusateri forbade me to get ahead of my milestones, since that would taint a follow-on contract. Put differently, if I wanted a follow-on contract, I had to delay the work that was under way. "I want you outta here, at least for now," Pusateri ordered. "Stop work on the diskettes and don't meet with the industry people."

After Pusateri ordered me "outta here," our chief programmer, Jim Lighthauser, went ahead and tried to convince the gas industry people that it would be in their interest to volunteer the data needed for the project to continue apace. But the INGAA executives were unwilling to commit to anything until the dust of the rumored upcoming criminal investigation had settled. Alas, long before that could occur, Pusateri concluded that he should do more than just order me to lie low until my bid for a follow-on contract had been approved. In early September, Pusateri informed me by phone that it would look better if he invalidated the entire competition (which, the investigation later revealed, I had already won, although the award was not yet announced). My consultancy at FERC thus came to an end. "Time and chance," as the wise Ecclesiastes wrote centuries ago, "happeneth to all."

The Death of a Thousand Cuts

During the period of the ensuing FERC probe, the massive insider trading scandal broke on Wall Street. The revelations of illegalities in the financial community called into question the effectiveness of the Securities and Exchange Commission, another regulatory agency under Congressman Dingell's jurisdiction. It is probable that those involved in the FERC episode were spared the threatened congressional investigation of alleged improprieties because Dingell's attention was suddenly distracted by the peculations of Ivan Boesky and other Wall Street figures.

Nor was anything ever published on the FERC "scandals" in the *Washington Post,* although it wasn't clear whether the assigned *Post* reporter simply found little that was newsworthy in the agency's files or was reassigned to juicier stories before he could uncover evidence of wrongdoing at FERC. The scandals at FERC, then, turned out not to be very scandalous at all—no one made headlines, no pictures appeared on the television news shows, no one went to jail. But everyone touched was hurt.

Acting Chairman Sousa, Ray O'Connor's successor as the nation's top energy regulator, was tarred by allegations that he had tried to cover up the abuses that Lebow claimed to have found (Effron, 1986). Sousa became an embarrassment to the Reagan administration. The Senate never confirmed him for the federal judgeship that he had long coveted and for which the President had nominated him.

McDonald, by accepting the NRC job, forwent any chance to finish the management reforms at FERC that had, even partially completed, won him admiration all over Washington. Some old hands later suggested that McDonald accepted the Nuclear Regulatory Commission demotion to leave FERC quickly, thus deserting the field of fire before his enemies could retaliate for his role in *l'affaire Lebow*. If that was McDonald's thought, he failed to appreciate the destructive power of the weapons that our investigatory laws put within easy reach of a determined revanchist.

Pusateri and Neubeiser suffered perhaps most grievously and least fairly of all. No formal actions were ever taken on the charges that they had violated federal procurement and conflict-of-interest laws. But during the investigation, Pusateri and Neubeiser necessarily turned their main energies to the tasks of self-defense. Their performances in office may have suggested that their minds were elsewhere. (Taxpayers bear the indirect as well as the direct costs of a witch-hunt.)

I am convinced that Pusateri and Neubeiser were blameless—casualties of the kind of "mindless bureaucratic process" about which we hear much from the critics of organization, but which can as easily grind up the lives of the bureaucrats who work within the system as it can the dignity of ordinary citizens. Pusateri's civil service status ensured against his being dropped to a lower pay scale, but he was moved from the prestigious acting executive director's post to positions within FERC that carried less authority and visibility. Though Neubeiser, too, was virtually immune from being fired outright, the job that he filled was suddenly declared to be unnecessary at FERC—a rare instance of the removal of a civil servant whose presence is no longer desired despite the protections of the classification system. Neubeiser's removal also illustrated the use by bureaucratic superiors of the indirect tactic: get at the man by eliminating the job.

Throughout the investigation and its aftermath, Pusateri and Neubeiser were in no-win situations. The knowledge that one is under investigation seeps out. Doubts persist in the minds of potential employers, making it difficult for the target of an investigation to move into a different job. This last wrinkle, well understood by professionals in bureaucracy, explains why FERC staff members put the interpretation that they did on Bill McDonald's sudden jump to the NRC. Had McDonald stayed at FERC until he became an official investigative target, he too would probably have been rendered ineffective in his job yet incapable of leaving it.

The investigation, once under way, slowly expanded as members of the FERC staff used it to try to settle scores of their own. Pusateri had correctly discerned that the atmosphere of doubt and fear made it unrealistic to continue the automation project in anything like the form in which McDonald had set it up. Every accusation and counteraccusation was as a knife slash. Support for the effort simply bled away, and in the end, the automation project quietly died the death of a thousand cuts.

The Psychology of an Investigation

Month after month, rumors spread about possible criminal actions against both proponents and detractors of the automation project. As the probe deepened, participants in the project who seemed to have bonded together despite differences in professional affiliation and apparent organizational interest began seeking ways to avoid one another. Almost everyone in whom the inspector general's investigators showed serious interest consulted an attorney. The lawyers uniformly counseled against any activity that could conceivably attract a potential accuser's notice, and most of them apparently also advised their clients not even to talk to others involved in the investigation if they could avoid it.

The corrosion of trust, the wondering about who's saying what to whom, the withdrawal of friends from even telephone contacts with one another—these changes occur gradually. One of the more trying aspects of the investigative process is its glacial nature—tediously slow, silent, very cold. Thus, it took almost two months from the time of my "urgent meeting" with Ken Pusateri until the inspector general's agents caught up with me for the interrogation that Pusateri had warned was coming. During this interim period, Sousa, McDonald, Pusateri, and Neubeiser fired off a series of countercharges, so Satterfield and Lebow were both drawn in as targets of investigation themselves.

Charges and Countercharges

The main charge against Satterfield was that he had repeatedly abused his office by arranging for official travel funds to subsidize private hunting trips around the country. Like McDonald, Satterfield resigned from FERC before the formal investigation got seriously under way; but, unlike McDonald, Satterfield left Washington altogether and without another job to go to (Effron, 1986). The charges against Lebow were more difficult to document since all parties were obligated by the decision of the SES review panel to close the record on which Lebow's demotion had been based. Because Lebow's accusers knew of his effective immunization from most formal charges, their main effort seems to have been simply to gossip his reputation to death.

Hundreds of hours of testimony were taken by teams of investigators. Rumor had it that everyone the inspector general's agents interviewed came up with additional charges against someone or other. For more than six months, the investigation stopped much of the work at FERC, not just on automation, but on virtually everything else as well in the area of natural gas regulation.

All rules of behavior change during an investigation. The chemistry of personal relationships alters. The official you worked with yesterday might be hauled onto a witness stand tomorrow—not as an expert in some technical area of public policy, but in a criminal proceeding. Words or conduct that may seem within the margin of acceptability during the normal course of work can appear very different when the context turns nasty. There is no nastier context than that of a federal investigation, replete as it is with opportunities for grudge holders to have their revenge.

The Inspector General's Hotline

Inspector General Layton at the Department of Energy, like other federal inspectors general, kept a twenty-four-hour telephone hot line for anyone who wanted *anonymously* to report suspected waste, fraud, or abuse. One can imagine what use might be made of such a hot line by a disgruntled employee anxious to play tit for tat with an interoffice rival or an unsympathetic boss.

Because a hot line is subject to abuse, a single derogatory report will be tape-recorded but not necessarily treated as a full-blown criminal accusation unless the charge is very grave or external evidence lends it credibility. A single triggering event, however, can prompt a whole lot of catching-up. When a special agent from the inspector general's office finally interrogated me in late 1986, he raised questions not only about my own recent contracting experiences at FERC but also about "stale" hot line charges that had been made against McDonald as much as five years previously. Given the animus that had been building over the years against McDonald and his bean counters, it was not surprising that several years' worth of anonymous charges had been taped, covering a wide variety of alleged improprieties.

I believe that those tapes might still be collecting dust if Lebow had not forced Inspector General Layton's hand by involving the *Washington Post* in the developing imbroglio. With an investigative reporter from the *Post* digging through FERC contracts for evidence of bribery, the inspector general could not appear to be lax in pursuing leads. Layton ordered that all hot line reports, whether new or old, be run down.

Investigators run down anonymous tips in the same way that they run down the kinds of formal charges and countercharges that McDonald, Satterfield, and the others were now making against one another. Special investigative agents audit all written records and conduct extensive confidential interviews. These interviews provide cover for anyone who wants to make further charges: "Why's this investigator talking to me? Did so-and-so tell him about such-and-such? Maybe I'd better lay the groundwork for a plea bargain later on." So the interviewee fesses up to the investigator about thus-and-so, adding to the list of allegations. The chain reaction runs on, involving people other than those initially named and embracing events other than those that had given rise to the investigation. Since no one knows who the accusers are, or for that matter even who the targets are, everyone avoids everyone else.

Nothing more sinister than the "avoidance syndrome," for example, accounted for the FERC budget people's refusal to pay me for completed work until three months after my check was legally due. Vouchers lay untouched in FERC in-out baskets. Officials feared any appearance of approving the work of someone who, rumor had it, might be handed over to the Justice Department for prosecution.

An Interview with a Special Agent

In late October of 1986, I got the call from Special Agent Ray Madden of the Department of Energy. Investigators such as Madden earn their living ferreting out criminal activity. They can make their reputations by making out sinister cases, that is, by scrutinizing masses of evidence and fitting the separate pieces into a pattern of corruption. I, and presumably everyone else involved in the probe, spent innumerable private hours replaying our earlier experiences at FERC: wondering what patterns the investigators might be making out of past conversations and actions, wondering if any of them could be made to support the charges that Pusateri had mentioned—bribery, conspiracy, and fraud.

I made a special trip from Princeton to the inspector general's office in the Forrestal Building for my session with Special Agent Madden. He was agreeable and informal. He was not intimidating, but that might just have been a technique. Anyway, I answered all of his questions, citing names when a reply seemed to call for it and providing documents—photocopies of studies that I had completed under FERC contracts—when I had copies of relevant ones to give. Madden formally advised me of the Lebow allegation that affected me. McDonald was accused of having browbeaten FERC staff members into hiring me in violation of the rules of free-and-open competition required by the Competition in Contracting Act of 1984. Lebow's use of the term *sweetheart contracts* implied that bribes might have been passed.

I actually felt relieved at hearing this allegation, since bribery raises a clear-cut question of fact, not of interpretation or judgment. The thought that I might have kicked back portions of my consulting fees to McDonald was preposterous. I could deny it under oath, absolutely and categorically. Furthermore, I assumed that if anyone questioned my denial, I could just take a lie detector test to settle the issue once and for all.

But as the investigation deepened and everyone (I included) became more nervous, I began to understand why doubts exist about polygraphs as indicators of guilt or innocence. Certain anxieties are inherent in any inquisitorial process, be it a tax audit, the discovery phase of a lawsuit, or the lead-up to a possible criminal prosecution.

As the months wore on, the investigation grabbed constantly at my thoughts; "what-if" worries crowded everything else from my agenda.

In late September, the *Legal Times,* a Washington tabloid for lawyers and lobbyists, ran a four-page story on the mess at FERC (Effron, 1986). I told the chairman of my department at Princeton, Professor Fred Greenstein, that I had made the news as a possible investigatory target. I thought that notifying Greenstein of a possible embarrassment to the University would suffice for the time being and that Greenstein would simply hold the information privately unless complications developed. But no.

On hearing even a whisper of investigation, everyone's instinct is to run for cover. Given his official position, Greenstein felt obliged to alert the university's general counsel, its Washington representative (Princeton has a full-time lobbyist with a prestigious office address in the nation's capitol), and the dean of faculty— among others, in one of the world's most gossipy communities. Princeton's campus newspaper has its share of aspiring Woodward-Bernsteins, and I wasn't anxious for student journalists to pick up rumors and publish a "Prof Caught in Corruption Probe" headline. Nor was I cheered by the thought that the deans were probably already preparing contingency plans for action against me, should the Washington probe show that I had violated Princeton's expectations of ethical and decorous behavior by its professors. Deans are bureaucrats too, and they know as well as any Washington veteran does that there's no such thing as a good surprise. I imagined myself in a world of ex-friends, all racing as quickly as they could away from me, carefully covering their asses as they went.

Given the "what-ifs" that began to occur to me, I became less and less sure what my blood pressure and sweat glands would tell a lie detector. Fortunately, Agent Madden found the kickback allegation to be untrue on its face. Inspector General Layton apparently agreed with Madden. The charge was dropped, and I was spared the need to verify my denial before either a U.S. attorney or a polygraph operator.

The Integrity of the Procurement Process

The disposition of the bribery charge still left the allegations that my consulting contracts had been tainted by conspiracy and fraud.

Because so much of the public's business is conducted by outside contractors, a threat to the integrity of federal procurement procedures goes to the fabric of the governmental process itself. Nevertheless, we have seen that agency procurement officials often (and understandably) seek ways to avoid the competitive endurance course. As discussed in Chapter Two, task order contracting is one way to do so; layered subcontracting is another. Still a third way is through the awarding of small purchase orders using sole-source contracting.

Small Purchase Orders and Sole Sourcing

Because the process of competing a contract is so expensive and time consuming, contracts for relatively small jobs can usually be awarded directly. Were direct assignment of such jobs impermissible, the transaction costs of competing a small contract would often exceed the dollar value of the work that needs to be performed.

Interestingly, the vast majority of federal contracts are written for relatively modest amounts. No doubt the small-contract pattern is partly explainable by the desire of procurement officials and outside contractors alike to avoid competition when possible. Kettl (1988) has documented that more than 98 percent of all contracts are for $25,000 or less. Altogether, though, these small contracts add up to less than 10 percent of a typical year's federal contract expenditures. However, few tasks of any real significance can be completed for a total cost less than $10,000 or $20,000, typical thresholds during the early 1980s for small purchase orders in federal agencies. (In bureaucratese, $10,000 is "10K," or ten kilodollars.) Inevitably, contract officers feel the pressure to employ a subterfuge. Suppose that the agency has a 10K threshold and its staff members want consultant Z to do a job that will cost $40,000. The solution: give consultant Z a 10K purchase order to get the work started, with the understanding that three additional small contracts will be assigned in their turns. The agency gets the work it wants, consultant Z gets his $40,000, and no one gets tied up in a competition. Of course, consultants other than Z don't get a chance to bid for the work, either. Because a multiple purchase order agreement under this kind of understanding is an anticompetitive conspiracy, it is illegal.

Even if all requirements for purchase orders are observed in the spirit as well as the letter of the law, going directly to a specified contractor—sole sourcing—is permitted only if a relatively elaborate justification is submitted in writing. The crafting of acceptable justifications for sole-sourcing is one of the premier skills of the procurement officer. The sole-source justification typically ends with the boilerplate claim that "consultant Z is the only person who can complete the needed work at the required level of quality within the time required." The *only* person—in Washington, in the country, in the solar system? Taken literally, the conventional sole-source justification is usually fraudulent on its face.

Lawyers distinguish between deception and "puffery" in advertising, and members of the Washington federation of consultants and contractors are generally willing to put the claim that only one person can complete the work in the puffery category. In an investigative context, however, words written or spoken long ago under one set of understandings may be reinterpreted as part of a sinister pattern. I knew as well as McDonald presumably did that an auditor might object to the purchase order pattern that had been used to keep me on as a FERC consultant. A savvy researcher would have been able to identify contracts in which the specified deliverables were different from the work that was really desired. And surely, an investigator of Madden's obvious caliber might have found sole-source justifications that—especially in view of my initial inexperience in the computer field—had gone beyond mere puffery.

Did any of these practices invite the extreme judgment of conspiracy or fraud? That question was for Agent Madden to answer—if need be, with further review by Inspector General Layton, Justice Department prosecutors, and juries of our peers.

From Under the Microscope

McDonald and I had never discussed any intent to evade contracting requirements, but we knew that federal procurement practices are rife with "broad interpretations" and "ingenious devices." Our practices were well within the customary margins. Fortunately, the investigators again agreed. After an intense wringing out of all the evidence—indeed, after another eight months of interviewing people and studying FERC's files—the inspector general officially closed the inquiry not only on me but on McDonald and all the dozen or so others who had found themselves one way or another under the microscope (Layton, 1987).

But by then, the automation effort had dissolved, and the project team had long since been disbanded.

Living and Dying in a Bureaucracy

The living and dying to which the subtitle of this book refers is not that of the individual bureaucratic official. It refers instead to the life cycle of the automation effort at FERC, a typical special project in a fairly typical old-line agency of our federal government.

The disarray caused by the investigation had effects outside of the agency as well as within it. A friend of mine who is a lawyer in Washington advised me not to resubmit a bid for the diskette project even after Ken Williams's staffers asked that the project be restarted (personal communication with E. M. Zuckert, Oct. 24, 1986). It seemed too likely that potential competitors for the work would protest any procurement that did not imply a wholesale housecleaning at FERC. A protest, my friend warned, would be likely to renew publicity and perhaps reopen the investigation. The roiling of the waters would continue to toss lives about even if any new claims of impropriety were found to be without merit, as the old ones had been.

No one finally halted the automation project based on an adverse judgment of the record. Indeed, before it disbanded, the team recorded some creditable accomplishments. But there was no way to hold the team together in the face of a protracted probe by the inspector general.

The project, like much of the other work and even a few careers at FERC, became a casualty of an investigation caused by clashes of personalities, one that touched on the merits of the automation effort only tangentially. But even if the inquiry was the proximate cause of the death of the computerization initiative, the inspector general's probe probably could not have killed the effort all by itself. At the time that Lebow made his charges, the project had already been gravely weakened by forces that are inherent in the workings of any large, well-established organization. The factors that made the automation project liable to mortal wounding were the same ones, applied at the level of the task force, that theorists of the organizational life cycle like to apply at the level of an agency or firm as a whole. What may in the end have been most revealing about the project at FERC was its sheer ordinariness as it passed through the life cycle stages, from birth to death.

The Downside of the Automation Task Force

Task force thinking, as we have seen, begins with a decision by a manager that an organization needs a targeted zap of energy to start the process of change. This input of energy propels the project through the first phase of its trajectory. But the natural course of a special task force has its downside as well as its up. Three related lessons about the declining phase of a special project emerge from the FERC experience: (1) almost inevitably, the initial favoring psychology will erode over time—one way or another, a special project gradually ceases to be special; (2) changing priorities within the organization will eventually undermine the initial rationale for task force preferment on the agency's priority list; and (3) at some point, rising transaction costs will call into question the comparative advantage of the task-force mode. The inspector general's probe at FERC accelerated, but did not cause, movement along the downslope.

No Longer Special

Because change often must come selectively, by way of a special project, members of the project team may find themselves in a never-ending fight against the forces that resist change. Initial selection for membership on the project team is important for the psychology of specialness among the elect, but it implies the existence of a residual group of unselected individuals—those who remain outside to peer in, all the while wondering just how the task force will affect their working conditions and especially their own career prospects within the overall organization. Most projects potentially threaten someone. Even when a project responds to a clear

need (as the replacement of manual with automatic number crunch-
ing surely did at FERC), over time the task group responsible for
the project may itself become a new power center.

Because priorities change over time in any organization,
what may be a valid demand for organizational resources today may
rightly be viewed as a grab for undeserved privileges tomorrow.
Thus, more than mere jealousy or pettiness by left-out agency
members may contribute to the gradual erosion of the sense of specialness. Understandably (and probably correctly), FERC staff
members who were on the outside gradually reached a different
assessment than those on the inside did of the project's benefits
relative to its costs. What we on the team considered enhancements
(such as the diskette program), the outsiders came to regard as mere
bells and whistles.

The budget staffers who had to find extra funds for the project somewhere in FERC's appropriation thought that they were
being made to pay inordinately high costs to support automation.
So did the electricians who had to lay new cable on rush-rush schedules. So did the middle managers who lost some of their staff
members to assignment on the automation project team and others
to the "diversions" that automation necessitated (such as computer
classes).

Change in Agency Priorities

A task force is normally instituted because it promises to help solve
one or more of the biggest problems on an organization's agenda.
It follows that, once the initial problem has been reduced to man-
ageable proportions, other issues will almost automatically pop to
the head of the action-list. When such a reordering of priorities
occurs, the task force may lose its reason for being. Certainly it
forfeits much of the legitimacy of its claim for special status and
special support relative to competing demands on organizational
resources. To understand the tempos of organizational life is to
understand that the legitimate claims and priorities of different subunits change over time. Task force thinking is consistent with a
rhythm of rising and declining missions within an institution. One
benefit of this approach lies in the fact that when the need that

initially brought the project team into existence disappears, it is easier to disband an *ad hoc* group than it is to dismantle a permanent new subunit.

The inflection in the outlook of most FERC staff members was subtle but freighted with consequences. Its occurrence marked the point at which the task force ceased to be an effective means of reducing transaction costs within the agency.

Transaction Costs on the Downside

In the early days of the project, many FERC employees gave us spirited cooperation not just because Butler and McDonald wished it, but also because they foresaw genuine benefits from computerization for the regulatory process. However, once the main cost-of-service program (the one with all the options and trapdoors) had been written, most FERC employees concluded that the main benefits had been achieved. Everyone in the agency who had once deferred to the need for a basic automated data processing program began to see his or her own pet project X as a potential substitute for automation on the overall organizational priority list. The fair-minded staff member who had initially conceded that basic computerization should take priority over project X now saw an opportunity to argue that the diskette program (or any other "mere enhancement" to the basic computer network) should now yield its position to some alternative enterprise.

At first imperceptibly, and then in increasingly obvious ways, transactions started getting more, not less, costly. It gradually became harder to wheedle extra programming funds, special installations, and personnel arrangements. As long as Butler and McDonald were around to jab recalcitrant staff members, we could tell the budgeteers, the electricians, and the others what we wanted and expect quick action. But it became more and more tiresome to arrange for Butler or McDonald to intervene with the foot-draggers. And, of course, when Butler and McDonald both eventually left FERC, negotiating with permanent agency supervisors on behalf of an orphan project became still more difficult. As the costs of justifying and negotiating to keep the project funded, equipped, and staffed rose, the logic of even keeping it alive became less convincing.

Those with whom we had to transact business became more grudging, and sometimes downright resentful, when they found special requests from us in their in-out baskets. Telling them what we wanted no longer sufficed. Suddenly we had to bargain, requirement by requirement. As support for the project diminished, the expenditures of energy that were needed to overcome the barriers of higher and higher transaction costs increased.

When members of the team have to struggle across the various lines of internal and external organization in the same way that members of the old subunits do, the comparative advantage of the special status has vanished. Ordinariness and routinization have overtaken the erstwhile extraordinary organization within the organization. And the theory that explains so well why the task-force approach can succeed also helps us, on the downside, understand why it is in the normal course for a special project to undergo Bernstein's (1955) cycle of living and dying.

The Automation Project and the Life Cycle Model

Every project is born into a race with time, and the end may come in any of dozens of ways: investigation and scandal, budgetary starvation following a shift in agency priorities, abandonment of a going project by new agency leaders, gradual absorption of the project into the day-to-day routines. Since a project typically passes through phases of growth, maturity, and decline, in the end it is the entropy and inertia that win. Whatever may have been achieved between the project's birth and its death becomes just one more standard operating procedure amidst all the others. To life cycle theorists, the question is not whether a project will die but how long it can last and what it will have accomplished before succumbing.

What the Project Team Accomplished Before Succumbing

By the end of the third year of the project, FERC staff members had begun to do cost-of-service calculations for all new pipeline filings on that big mainframe computer over in the Forrestal Building's basement. The program that we finally wrote for this purpose was a huge one by almost any standard. It contained some 300,000 lines of computer code, about half the number of lines in the program that the National Aeronautics and Space Administration was using in the mid 1980s to control the orbiting space shuttle vehicle.

Interestingly, even this estimate of 300,000 lines had originated in a political calculation, and the comparison with NASA served a political purpose. A Princeton neighbor of mine, J. R. Thompson of the Plasma Physics Laboratory and previously a senior NASA official, suggested the orbiter comparison to me in 1985 as I was preparing for a briefing on FERC's computerization project to be given to examiners from the Office of Management and Budget. The OMB reviewers were impressed enough with FERC's automation progress to recommend an increased budget so that the agency could expand its computer efforts. In bureaucratic patois, 300,000 lines and the comparison to NASA became our standard "gee whiz story"—notwithstanding that it later turned out not to be a completely accurate representation.

Long after the OMB briefing, I came across published figures (Lin, 1985) suggesting that the program for the NASA orbiter vehicle actually contains on the order of a half-million lines of computer code, considerably more programming than in our rate-making software—but not by a factor of two. However, much of the coding in our program had been necessitated by the options and overrides that the professional rate makers had demanded. Had technical programming considerations rather than the need to negotiate for support controlled the automation effort, that impressive and politically useful "gee whiz" number would have been much smaller—and the program itself much more efficient.

Nevertheless, the usefulness of the rate-making program demonstrated not only the value but also the feasibility of automation in the federal regulatory process. Early in the fourth year of the effort, just as the inspector general's investigation was getting under way, the head of FERC's Office of Electric Power Regulation called on the automation team to develop a modified version of the cost-of-service algorithms to use in electric industry rate making. Unfortunately, the electric rate-making program, like the rate designers' system on the natural gas side of the agency, was to run on PCs rather than on a centrally controlled mainframe.

But at least within the cost-of-service area, computerization slowly replaced jury-rigged and idiosyncratic methodologies with standardized algorithms. Although a high-priority automation *project* proved unable to survive in the poisonous air of an investigation, the need at FERC for an automation *process* remained as compelling as McDonald had initially perceived it to be. The inspector general's probe marked an end to the work of the project team but only a pause in the broader process of computerization. The price of almost all gas sold in the United States today is set with the help of the automation team's program. Starting in the late 1980s, funds were found in FERC's budget for detailed maintenance and even modest upgradings of the original software. Thus the story ends not with the abandonment of automation but with its absorption into the low-priority everyday routines of the agency.

"Declaring Ourselves Winners"

Viewed retrospectively and with a recollection of the turmoil, fear, and ill will that attended its premature demise, the computerization project must be judged to have missed its full potential. In the end, our software package was, admittedly, a second-best performance. Its internal inelegancies would never have passed strict standards of programming sophistication. The CDSI programmers would have much preferred to have translated the pure mathematics of rate making into a program without trapdoors and exceptions. Instead, the dozens of compromise solutions that had to be made resulted in a much less economical and technically less advanced software package than could have been written if the rate-makers' expertise—and their egos, insecurities, and technophobia—had not been factors. But without the compromises, the professional rate makers would never even have used the final program. More likely, in fact, they would have gone out of their way to undermine its credibility.

When what was finally accomplished is measured against what agency procedures were like when the automation project began, the FERC rate-making program—compromised algorithms, trapdoors, linkups to PCs, and all—comes out looking not so bad.

But then, the art of management often involves a quest for "proximate solutions to insoluble problems," in the words of the political philosopher Reinhold Niebuhr (1944, p. 118; see also Hargrove and Glidewell, 1990).

One day, after the collective investigative neurosis had passed, I gathered with several former members of the automation team at The Dubliner for lunch and a postmortem discussion. There was no denying our disappointment. The debacle of the inspector general's investigation had made it certain that if the computerization of FERC were ever to be completed, some other group of analysts and programmers would get the chance to do it. But the disappointment was not unmixed with pride. In recognition of the natural obstacles to change that constrain any effort such as ours, we thought ourselves entitled to "declare ourselves winners," put the FERC automation project behind us, and turn to other matters in our lives.

part III

Whither Bureaucracy?

□   chapter 9

The Paradox of
Administrative Controls

Not only in the United States but also throughout the modernized
world, no substitute has yet been found for bureaucracy as an instrument to regulate an industrial economy. As long as we must rely
on administrative agencies to conduct the public's business, we
should try to make them work. The first requisite—and the main
subject of this chapter—is to recognize the obstacles to action that
are inherent in the bureaucratic form. The second requirement—
more fully discussed in the concluding chapter—is to acknowledge
the kinds of talents that nevertheless enable a few bureaucratic actors to overcome the stumbling blocks.

Directed and Natural Change

Broadly speaking, the changes to which organizations are subject fall
under the two headings, "directed" and "natural." *Directed changes*
are the work of organizational entrepreneurs who decide to move

183

their institutions this way or that (Doig and Hargrove, 1987). *Natural changes,* by contrast, need not be planned, and in fact tend to appear even when conscious efforts are made to prevent their emergence. Examples of natural change have been at the center of the narrative in Part Two: institutional aging (with its associated characteristics, resistance to change, and bureaucratic discretion) and the emergence of the informal organizations that are known as issue networks. A related phenomenon, which can also be considered an instance of natural change in our public bureaucracies, has been the growth of administrative controls.

To direct purposeful, constructive change against the opposing forces of natural change is a recurrent challenge in public management. The events at FERC present a case study in this by no means uncommon genre of bureaucratic activity. The forces of natural change can inhibit an entrepreneur, first, by pulling the organization in a perverse direction or simply retarding efforts to change it, and, second, by diverting managerial attention from projects of constructive change to the agonizing process of just staying even. ("I came to Washington to revolutionize regulation, not fight with subversive branch chiefs, importunate union leaders, demanding congressional staffers, and inspectors general who seem to have no sense of proportion!") The manager who loses against the adverse forces of natural change may never gain the momentum needed to win a campaign for directed change.

Even when directed change appears to have succeeded, employees may find ways to reinstitute certain preferred patterns of their own. However, they might have to do so at a price, as when FERC's rate designers repurchased some of their old freedom from supervision by adopting PCs, thereby implicitly acceding to McDonald's design for an automated agency.

Natural Change and the Contradictory Dynamic

The process of institutional aging, the emergence of issue networks that grow to encompass the formal public bureaucracy, and the elaboration of administrative controls form a single syndrome. At the core of this syndrome is a three-step dynamic, a dynamic driven (as any truly natural process of change must be) by a kind of inner logic of its own (see Simon and March, 1958.)

Step one of this dynamic involves the formation of an issue network, typically as a means of reducing transaction costs. The emergence of an issue network naturally leads to step two, the promulgation of new rules to regulate contacts across the public-private interface or to limit the discretion of public officials, who, it is feared, may act under the influence of private sector representatives. But the additional rules also add to transaction costs. The further buildup of transaction costs constitutes step three, and calls to mind the central teaching of the New Theorists. Because all participants in the network have an incentive to cut transaction costs, the process cycles back to step one.

I believe that today's public manager works within a system better described in terms of this paradoxical, even contradictory, dynamic than in terms of the Old Theory of public administration. The purpose of this chapter is, therefore, to unpack the concept of the contradictory dynamic, summarizing in the process the theory of the relationship between this phenomenon and the New Theorists' transaction-cost framework.

The Transaction-Cost Framework

The transaction-cost framework underpins the New Theory, but it is consistent with an old tradition in political science. That most prescient of all American political thinkers, James Madison, suggested in *Federalist 10* that economic prosperity and growth implied a diversity of crosscutting interests. A basic challenge of politics, Madison concluded, was to find ways to moderate and adjust competing interests while not destroying the underlying conditions of diversity, individual freedom, prosperity, and continuing economic growth that make conflicts of interest inevitable.

Whether in contemporary industrial America or in the kind of preindustrial economy that Madison had in view, the critical political problem is still to compose diverse, conflicting interests while keeping the peace and advancing the underlying good of all. How might reasonable men and women possibly hope to solve this problem except through processes of give-and-take? The issue net-

work naturally evolves as the institutional structure of these processes, and the New Theorists' transaction-cost framework explains
why.

Networks to Reduce Transaction Costs

As interdependencies have increased in the private economy, so have
the number of connections that must be considered when anyone
(whether a private actor or a public official) tries to change anything anywhere. Furthermore, as more actors do business with one
another and with the government, the transaction costs of interact-
ing increase as well. The day-to-day jostlings across the public-
private interface necessarily include the framing and discussion of
multiple alternatives, the interpretation of implementing rules (on
which reasonable people may disagree), the acquisition of technical
information, and, of course, the incessant give-and-take of bargaining. Often these transactions require that issues "ripen" through
the passage of time. These transactions may involve heavy data
processing requirements, and they frequently inflict considerable
emotional wear and tear on the participants.

Organizations come into existence when people try to arrange relationships in ways that tend to reduce these transaction
costs. The interested players within an industrial sector link up
with one another, often forming relationships that no one actor
anticipates. Indeed the outstanding characteristic of public decision
making is the way that it implicates private as well as public managers in a single decision-making complex. Today the relevant
decision-making structure is not an independent formal bureaucracy (the progressives' New American State) but a system of civil
servants supported by outside contractors—an effective bureaucracy
operating for the most part through issue networks.

An issue network is an informal organization that has been
superimposed on the artificially divided public-private structure. A
network reduces transaction costs by facilitating the flow of needed
information across the public-private boundary. It also helps regulatory officials and industry representatives reconcile opposing positions, for a network permits its members to set agreed-upon limits

on one another, thus enabling them to cooperate in holding conflict within bounds.

Among the examples of efforts to reduce transaction costs that the FERC case study has put before us is the increasing tendency to supplant formal litigation with settlement conferences and other informal decision-making procedures, including the various expedited rule-making actions that account for more than 80 percent of all such regulatory actions (Heffron and McFeeley, 1983). Procurement officers are always trying to find shortcuts through agency-contractor relationships—provided of course that they think they can do so with safety from the ever-looming auditor (Kelman, 1990). Other practices to reduce transaction costs include task order contracting and the development of institutions for information sharing and consensus building across the public-private boundary, including such prosaic events as the periodic FERC auditor site visit to a regulated pipeline company's headquarters. As was discussed in Chapter Six, the setting up of a special task force can also be viewed as a technique for reducing transaction costs.

The Proliferation of Transactions

I believe that critics who cry "agency capture" at every glimpse of an issue network mistake the nature of the modern administrative organization. To begin with, capture theorists usually ignore the complexity of the issue-network phenomenon and hence the real motivation for its appearance. Crosscutting interests underlie most network members' continuing relationships. Participants who hold some interests in common may be adversaries with respect to others. From the transaction-cost perspective, a network usually comes into existence as much because of its members' significant divergences of interest as because of their common aims. Regular pub'ic-private contacts emerge because participants try to reduce the transaction costs of dealing with goal-diversity, not because they are trying to form a conspiracy.

Here is an important insight of the New Theory: Organizations arise not only as instruments consciously and rationally designed to achieve clear-cut goals, as posited in the Old Theory, but also as informal, evolving structures that enable participants to consider diverse interpretations, conflicting interests, and potential distributions of the costs of partially achieving their respective objectives. The difference between the Old and the New Theories lies partly in the latter's attainment of this more subtle understanding of organizational purposes and dynamics.

I think, also, that capture theorists misunderstand the functions that public bureaucracies have to perform. The emergence of what today are called old-line agencies was part of a larger process of industrial development. That process required its participants to engage in many relatively high-cost transactions, not because bureaucrats or even lawyers wanted it that way but simply because the nature of industrial regulation required it to be so. The interactions that must take place among public and private actors in a complex economy involve far more than formal litigation. Debating, information gathering, and negotiation are inherently costly transactions. Public bureaucrats and private-sector decision makers alike have strong incentives to try to bring these transaction costs under control. Indeed, our civil servants—so frequently accused of fecklessness and indifference to the inefficiencies of governance—would probably be derelict if they did not, within the bounds of public trust, work with their private-sector counterparts to expedite the administrative process where possible.

Institutional Aging and Bureaucratic Discretion

At this point in the analysis of issue networks, the phenomenon of institutional aging—along with one of its consequences, the enlargement of bureaucratic discretion—enters the picture. For even as the effort to cut transaction costs through public-private networking goes forward, the public agencies that are at the center of our networks are growing older.

The Development of Discretion

Institutions, like individuals, age over time, and the FERC case study shows how the aging process can encourage the development of mutation-based discretion. As the Progressive Era bureaucracy gradually slipped toward old-line status, there emerged this and other problems that the reformers never foresaw. The progressives certainly did not expect that organizations born in excitement and optimism would become the tired spectacles that time has made many of them. In this sense, the Old Theory applied only as long as today's old-line agencies were still new!

Stodginess, aversion to risk taking, and routinization are traits that one particularly associates with the last stage in the aging of a bureaucratic institution. This image of an aging institution evokes the situation at FERC when Butler and McDonald took the reins. Most Washington hands would probably have declared that FERC displayed all the signs of organizational senescence. The "green eyeshade" operations within Ken Williams's staff presented a textbook situation for institutional renewal. Employees felt comfortable with the convoluted rate-making routines that had evolved over the years. Ironically, however, in some instances, the rigmarole that appeared to be mere repetitive routine when viewed by outsiders had come to mask the freedom of FERC employees to depart from standard procedures.

The issue-network pattern permits, even promotes, the development of "understandings" across the public-private boundary. Such understandings would obviously be of much less concern than they actually are if our public officials enjoyed no discretion in the way they react to influences from the other side of the boundary. Discretion gives its possessors room to maneuver. And because the employees who possess discretion are not necessarily those with formal supervisory responsibility in the agency, the mutational process may empower subordinates to sabotage, not support, programs of constructive change that their superiors are legally entitled to initiate.

Time was a necessary condition for the emergence of the kind of mutation-based discretion that many midlevel and lower-level bureaucrats had gradually acquired at FERC but not a sufficient one. According to the New Theorists, the first additional ingredient needed for the evolution of bureaucratic discretion is worker self-interest.

Self-Interest and Bureaucratic Discretion

The Old Theorists' preoccuption with corruption indicates how serious they considered the power of self-interest to be. Nor did the progressives underestimate the driving force of self-interest in private markets. As we have seen, however, the Old Theorists thought that higher standards could be applied in the public sector. They thought that "civil servants prepared by special schooling and drilled, after appointment, into a perfected organization" (Wilson, 1887, p. 216) could overcome the power of self-interest. In other words, the Old Theorists envisioned a world bifurcated into separate decision-making realms—one guided by public interestedness and an ethic of service, another driven by the urge to private gain.

The New Theorists, by contrast, suggest that it was naive to suppose that public sector employees would be any less susceptible than private workers are to the urgings of self-interest. What is more, the difficulty of reconciling diverse individual interests will be most acute in large organizations, such as government agencies, whose work is organized by classification. The larger the organization, the more elaborate its internal differentiation is likely to be. With subdivisions along specialized lines (line versus staff, "professionals" such as Ken Williams versus "administrators" such as Bill McDonald), confusion or competition over goals easily occurs. Organizations whose work is organized by classification also allegedly experience disproportionately large problems of adverse selection, resulting in the recruitment of workers who are inclined to shirk. In the extreme case, a bureau may become "a Club Med for government officials who undersupply policy decisions" (McCubbins, Noll, and Weingast, 1987, p. 247). *Undersupply policy decisions* is, of course, social science-eze for "goof off on the job."

In the midranks of the bureaucracy, as we have seen, mutation-based discretion can give employees the conditions in which shirking or subverting become possible. FERC's rate-making experience illustrates how subtle the process of genetic drift can be. Shortcuts and exceptions gradually accumulate. No revolution takes place; no abrupt break in agency work patterns can be discerned. Nevertheless, the day comes when an old-line civil servant inherits a set of alternative precedents, no one of which unambiguously applies in all cases.

A rule that admits of an increasing number of exceptions eventually ceases to be much of a rule. Obviously it ceases to be a limit on discretion. The bureaucrat then has no option but to balance competing agendas, interests, and values against one another. Even the midlevel official must begin to make essentially political choices—small choices, perhaps, that rarely attract the notice of journalists, but political choices nonetheless since they involve value judgments rather than mere expert assessments of facts followed by the application of clear-cut rules.

From time to time, tough-minded leaders such as Mike Butler appear, determined to learn about doings in their staffs. They can find ways temporarily to pierce the mystification and even to rerationalize and restandardize procedures. The pertinent example was the FERC automation project, which (at least for a while) forced a measure of uniformity on (at least a portion of) the ratemaking process. But in a massive bureaucracy, vignettes of demystification and rerationalization tend to be just that: vignettes, episodes in an encompassing process of slippage toward bureaucratic discretion.

Administrative Controls and the Contradictory Dynamic

Because the integrity of the administrative process can be threatened by certain practices that commonly occur in networks, such as cozy contacts across the public-private boundary, the issue-network structure creates a natural context for forbidden deal making. A senior public manager who is mindful of the position of trust that he or she holds will have to devote whatever energies are necessary to prevent improper conduct. The FERC automation project, we have seen, had its origin in Chairman Butler's judgment, based on concerns just such as these, that an "investigation" of his own ratemaking staff seemed in order.

Apart from specific actions that a specific leader may take to uncover or prevent improprieties, a general awareness of the possibilities for corruption in today's informal relationships has prompted efforts to control conduct at the public-private interface. The chain of causation to which the New Theory points—transaction costs leading to networking, leading in turn to the danger of corruption, and finally leading to the imposition of administrative controls—suggests why our public bureaucracies have become encrusted with rules. These rules are explicitly designed to regulate

contacts across the public-private interface (for example, procurement regulations) or are aimed primarily at limiting the
discretionary power of public officials (for example, the notice-and-
comment provisions of the Administrative Procedures Act).

The burgeoning of procedural controls seems an inexorable,
almost organic process. Not only at FERC but throughout Washington, the process has become cumbersome and ritualized as a
result of the multiple safeguards that have been added over the
years. An organizational entrepreneur finds hurdles and hindrances
at every step. And because the federal regulatory regime reaches to
the limits of the American economy, the encumbering of the administrative process affects literally millions of private citizens far
beyond the walls of any hearing room or civil servant's office.

Much of the red tape has a statutory origin, giving rise in
recent years to charges of inept micromanagement by Congress.
Other procedural safeguards have been amplified or even created
whole by decisions of the federal courts. The web of controls has
also tightened (especially around public managers) as a result of the
increased prominence of the federal investigatory regime. And the
advent of automation has expanded the ability of upper managers
to subject their subordinates to computer-based surveillance, raising
questions not only about workers' rights to privacy but also about
the point at which supervisory snooping destroys the morale of
employees and, ultimately, undermines their performance. All four
of these forms of administrative control figured to some degree in
the FERC story.

Detailed Legislation and Micromanagement

A public agency exists only because Congress has passed a law
setting it up and specifying its powers. Progressive Era legislators
typically used open-ended statutory charters to delegate discretionary powers to "experts," whose knowledge of the one best way was
supposed to be trusted to produce proper decisions. But over the
years, statutory prescriptions of bureaucratic procedures have become increasingly detailed.

Legislators relegislate when their own political antennae tell
them that administrative interpretations of the old laws are causing

problems rather than solving them. As Morris Fiorina (1985) has shown, lawmakers who want to limit the discretion of appointed officials can write statutes of extraordinary detail. One might quarrel with the wisdom of recent statutes such as the Clean Air Act of 1970 and its major amendments (1977, 1991); the Occupational Safety and Health Act of 1970; the Employees Retirement Income Security Act of 1974; or, for that matter, the Natural Gas Policy Act of 1978, which set up the phasing scheme that so vexed the Reagan appointees at FERC. But one cannot deny that these exceedingly complex laws—textbook examples of Congressional micromanagement—demonstrate the ability of elected officials to legislate in minute detail when they decide to reclaim vague discretionary powers from bureaucrats.

And then of course there is the Administrative Procedures Act itself—a.k.a. "the full employment act for lawyers" because of the way that it enmeshes agencies in legalism. Under the APA, elaborate prohibitions control who can talk to whom, in what forums, and about what topics—all in an attempt to structure by legal process the workings of issue networks. These prohibitions, known as *ex parte* rules from the Latin for "from a part," are meant to ensure completeness, fairness, and openness in administrative proceedings by preventing interested parties from advocating their special viewpoints in ways that would prevent legitimate opposing interests from challenging them (Administrative Conference of the United States, 1983; Riley, 1987).

The federal bureaucracy is surely more disciplined than it would be in the absence of today's elaborate procedural requirements. But agencies are also vastly less efficient than they might otherwise be. The costs of following all the rules sometimes seem to outweigh the benefits. As a result, the affected participants in issue networks constantly search for informal ways to get around requirements—one of the more obvious instances in micromanaged Washington of the contradictory dynamic.

Judicial Controls on Bureaucratic Procedures

Judges have displayed a tendency of their own to reduce bureaucratic discretion by prescribing, confining, and reviewing the procedures that federal bureaucrats use in their everyday decision making. What seemed to worry Chairman Butler most of all—more even than the discovery and revelation of improprieties by journalists—was the threat of an eventual judicial finding that FERC procedures failed the due process test.

In the 1970 case of *Goldberg* v. *Kelly,* the Supreme Court added significantly to the cost and fairness requirements of many types of administrative proceedings. And a series of federal appellate court cases involving the Department of Agriculture, the Environmental Protection Agency, and FERC's predecessor agency, the Federal Power Commission, added a judge-made amendment to the APA's provision for informal actions by creating a new category, called "hybrid rule making," with a number of additional procedural requirements (*Holm,* 1971, and related cases; Williams, 1975). Since the mid 1970s, the courts have backed off somewhat from detailed specification of procedures. They have shown more deference to regulatory officials and have acquiesced in the increasingly obvious preference of administrative decision makers for negotiation over adversarial procedures (Lassila, 1992). On balance, however, the legacy of judicial action continues to increase the burden of transaction costs in the federal administrative process.

Elaborate court-imposed requirements have also expanded the access of interested parties to the administrative process by embellishing the concept of legal standing and extending the notice-and-comment requirements of the APA (Stewart, 1975). Martin Shapiro (1988) has referred to the judicial expansion of the rights of interested parties as *superpluralism,* since the opening of access represented an effort to carry the pluralist view of democracy to its limit. The pluralists who rose to dominance in U.S. political science during the 1950s had taught that democracy worked not because it ensured the representation of millions of individuals' preferences but because it permitted organized interest groups to compete in an orderly way. If democratic government depended on group participation, then effective democratic government required all groups, not just those with the biggest budgets or most practiced lobbyists, to have full access to the corridors of power. Judicial superpluralism opened the administrative process to almost every conceivable directly affected, secondarily affected, indirectly affected, and even possibly affected group within sight, earshot, or mail service of a federal decision maker.

Additionally, the courts multiplied and ritualized the steps to be taken between the initiation of an agency action and its final disposition. To describe these steps, Shapiro adopted a term coined by the philosopher Braybrooke and political scientist Lindblom: *synopticism*—meaning, loosely, "seeing all at the same time." The synoptic test required agency decision makers to try to consider every possible means that might be employed to realize the legislative will; cursory or *pro forma* consideration of a few solutions would not do. Judicial synopticism marked a return to the gospel according to Gilbreth (Gilbreth and Gilbreth, 1953), for it required that administrators take all possible steps to find the one best way. Moreover, agency decision makers now had to prove that they had indeed made the search for the best way by building elaborate records documenting their extensive study of multiple alternatives.

The synoptic requirement has had its share of counterproductive results. Administrators, finding the judicial demands benighted and unrealistic, began to obfuscate decisions, sometimes conducting elaborate studies to give the impression of compliance and camouflaging the actual rationales for their decisions with facades of pseudoscience. These practices illustrate the abusability of asymmetric information and the way that experts can manipulate appearances—in this case, beneath the noses of kibitzing judges (Shapiro, 1988).

Control Through Threat of Investigation

As the number of government contracts has grown, so, of course, has the potential for abuse in the procurement process. Therefore, the auditing and investigatory functions of the federal government have also expanded along with congressionally imposed controls and judicial interventionism. It would be difficult to overstate the pervasiveness of sensitivity to the threat of auditing and investigation among seasoned civil servants. And as the story recounted in Part Two made clear, it was the investigative control rather than congressional oversight or judicial review that finally had decisive consequences for the process of directed change at FERC.

One cannot work for any length of time in the federal bureaucracy without coming into contact with the procurement specialists who are so critical to the interaction of the formal and the shadow bureaucracies. Nor (in my experience) can one engage a contracting officer very deeply in conversation without hearing an allusion to "doing it in a way that will withstand an audit" or an admonition about the investigative threat that hangs over every procurement action. The cautious attitude of most procurement specialists suggests that the auditing and investigatory threats probably do exactly what they are intended to—deter much of the corruption and even the carelessness that might otherwise occur. But does the level of caution interfere with the necessary work of government, particularly since so much of that work today has to be let by contract to outsiders? The question calls for a judgment and admits of no categorical answer. But the balance may already have tipped in the wrong direction.

An investigation is, in a sense, the ultimate multiplier of transaction costs. The mere rumor of an impending official inquiry guarantees that every transaction involving a targeted organization will be conducted with such scrupulous propriety as to put all operations into the slowest of slow motions. Following rules to the letter can ensure that nothing at all gets done, which is why union negotiators sometimes use "working to standards" instead of striking as a means of effectively halting production (see McCubbins, Noll, and Weingast, 1987).

Though it may deter malfeasance in some respects, the threat of investigation cannot keep the bureaucracy's version of barracks lawyers from exploiting ambiguities or loopholes in the rules. The threat of investigation fixes attention on paper trails and hence on compliance with formal rules. Nor can the fear of a future inquiry always keep bureaucrats from choosing the easy course today out of sheer laziness or carelessness. On the contrary, the threat of investigation encourages many bureaucrats to think first about appearances and only then about the substance of their actions.

Finally, the investigative regime contains no protections, other than the good sense of the investigators, against abuse by accusers who are motivated by their desires to settle scores. Every low-level functionary at FERC has learned how easy it is to record an anonymous charge on the inspector general's hot line, and every supervisor has now learned how important it is not to become the target of such a call. One can avoid incrimination by not acting illegally. But one can also often avoid it by not acting at all, so that in agencies already stereotyped as sluggish and risk-averse, the threat of investigation intensifies civil servants' disinclination to make waves.

Automation and Surveillance

In addition to external (congressional and judicial) safeguards and the mixture of external and internal controls that congressional investigations and inspector generals' probes represent, supervisors can exercise internal controls over lower-level employees. The automation of work and the installation of electronic monitoring systems will increase the surveillance under which staff members may have to work in the bureaucracies of the future.

The topic of organizational surveillance may seem somewhat distasteful, narrowly technical, and without implications for the general theory and practice of public management. But bureaucracy, itself an apparatus of authority and control, is also an instrument for acquiring, storing, selecting, and applying information. No important aspect of information management can be of indifference to a student of administration. The disparate surveillance possibilities of different automation techniques—for example, the different implications of mainframes and PCs for procedural standardization—underscore the relevance of this issue in a discussion of administrative controls.

The New Theory implies that careful supervision is needed to prevent abusive exercises of discretion by lower-level employees. The typical senior manager would like to have a lens capable of focusing on any group of employees within his or her jurisdiction. The kind of mainframe computer system that McDonald moved to install at FERC can give supervisers such a zoom lens capability, since in such a system the entire "memory" of the organization exists in a single location. Anyone who works in the organization must use the system, which can be programmed to screen for idiosyncrasies in the users' work. (The U.S. Internal Revenue Service, for example, uses such computer screenings to filter tax filings for returns that are out of line with norms.) And anyone with access to the organizational memory can recover information about goings-on in the unit. With reliance on the mainframe therefore comes some control over its users.

We saw in Chapter Seven that no comparable degree of control is possible with personal computers. Nevertheless there has recently occurred, within both business and government, a lemminglike migration to decentralized personal computer systems. As the migration to PCs at FERC illustrated, personal computers may reintroduce the very problem that mainframe automation can help solve because PCs permit subordinates to exclude their superiors from access to information. As personal computer users build up their own little floppy disk libraries, it gets more and more difficult for analysts to access one anothers' data bases. Even when PCs are linked by a local area network, users can devise ways to avoid logging their calculations into the central system more easily than when users time-share on a mainframe.

The less obtrusive the surveillance technique, the higher worker morale and loyalty are likely to be (see Ouchi, 1981a, and sources cited there). But less surveillance also implies less information for superiors about worker performance. The trick is to strike the correct balance. Like all other forms of bureaucratic control, mainframe-based surveillance of employees' activities carries indirect as well as direct costs. Direct costs include those of designing the screening algorithms, physically installing the surveillance network, and operating a system of checks to prevent workers from fooling the system. There may also be intangible surcharges in the form of worker resentment, guileful evasion, or employees' organizing to protest the Big Brother whom they fear is watching.

Selectively intensifying the use of centralized automated management information systems can expedite administration and also strengthen the framework of controls in an appropriate way. Underscore the need for *selectivity*—that is, for confining the use of so efficient (and abusable) a technique of control as central computer screening to areas of organizational activity that require strict accountability or a critically high level of quality control.

It is worth recalling in this connection that in some areas of public administration, particularly areas that lie within the penumbra of the due process clause, the civil servant fills a kind of fiduciary role, a role that justifies extraordinary efforts to exclude exercises of bureaucratic discretion. Rate making is one of the critical areas in which citizens have the right to expect standard treatment in accordance with published rules. Every customer of a regulated public utility is entitled to know exactly how his or her rates were computed and to be assured that the methodology is the same one used when computing the next-door neighbor's bill. For this reason, rate making is exactly the kind of public sector bureaucratic function for which the norm of rule-based decision making was formulated. Thus rate making is a natural candidate for automated data processing using a centralized computer system with a zoom lens capability.

A Critique of the Controls

The good news in all of this is that, in the short run, the controls and oversight capacities that are piled one on another in our system probably (or at least potentially) make for cleaner, more careful public administration than would otherwise be possible. The efforts by legislators, judges, investigators, and administrative supervisers to confine bureaucratic discretion and suppress corruption express principles of profound importance, for example, the "rule of law" principle and the principle of accountability. One must pause before quarreling with laws, rules, and surveillance procedures that are intended to prevent organized interests from ganging up on the public and careless civil servants from shirking their responsibilities. Americans have always favored a government of checks and balances, notwithstanding that such a system is inherently biased against both change and efficiency. The contradictory dynamic probably presents the extreme example of this bias.

I therefore do not suggest that disciplines and controls can be dispensed with. Still, it would be simplistic to pretend that the controls can never lead to effects worse than the original problem. The sometimes overlooked reality is that the effort to control bureaucratic discretion increases transaction costs in the long run and intensifies the search for new shortcuts that will eventually call for more rules.

Each incremental addition to the framework of controls may make eminent sense when it is considered by itself; it is almost always possible to find a reason somewhere along the line for a given bit of red tape (Kaufman, 1977). Yet the bureaucratic routine that may have originated to protect a legitimate interest or plug a procedural loophole cannot be judged in isolation. It is the totality of controls that defines the lived experience of bureaucracy. It is the overall ambience of niggling, numbing rules that suggests what we can continue to expect in the way of official behavior as long as the agency experience is as the story of the FERC automation project suggests it to be.

The web of controls has a demoralizing, depressive effect— exactly the effect that de Tocqueville ([1840] 1956, pp. 303–304) described when, more than a century and a half ago, he foresaw the emergence of "a network of small complicated rules, minute and uniform, through which the most original minds and the most energetic characters cannot penetrate. . . . [S]uch a power does not destroy, but it prevents existence; it does not tyrannize, but it compresses, enervates, extinguishes, and stupefies."

The web of controls constantly irritates those public officials who are committed to action and achievement. Every new restriction creates an additional incentive to cut corners, to find circumventing interpretations, to blink the bothersome requirements away. As for the others, the less ambitious and less energetic among our civil servants: Given the existence of controls that are so unconducive to the exercise of initiative, can we be surprised if some bureaucrats refuse to break their necks at hard work? Well-intentioned procedures that are intended to check abuses by exhaustively controlling, monitoring, and auditing workers can have a by-product effect—the breeding of discouragement or indifference. Thus ironically, the reputed lackadaisicality of old-line bureaucrats may be a consequence of the attempt to solve the classic bureaucratic problem of discretion.

In the Realm of the Second Best

The thesis of this chapter has been that the public manager typically labors (somewhat in the manner of Sisyphus) under a peculiar burden of frustration and against a steep gradient of resistance to change.

The public sphere is by no means unique in the kinds of barriers to change that vex would-be entrepreneurs. The proliferation of regulatory controls on corporate decision makers as well as on public managers means that *any* organizational leader must contend with the contradictory dynamic to some degree. And since movement from the public sector to the private cannot eliminate difficulties that originate in human nature itself, *any* manager has to deal with problems of employee quality and behavior (read: "problems of adverse selection and moral hazard"). Nevertheless, a consensus of sorts seems to exist among both practitioners and scholars to the effect that managers must expect to encounter greater difficulty in public sector than in private sector decision making (Allison, 1992; see also Perry and Kraemer, 1983).

Whether the inhibitors of action have become too powerful, the controls too overwhelming; whether bureaucratic practice has been condemned by its own internal logic to perpetual slow motion and the larger process of governance to political gridlock—these issues, again, raise questions of degree. Those who think (as I do) that the challenge today is to reactivate our public bureaucracies must ponder how to control the controls. A balance must be struck between resistance to change and adaptability, between efficiency and incorruptibility.

Should we, under any circumstances, aim to recover the Old Theorists' image of public bureaucracies that would be more efficient, more businesslike than are the best private sector organizations? The answer seems to be that no one in the complicated decision-making loops of public management can realistically expect better than halfway satisfactions or more than second-best solutions. In the context of the contradictory dynamic, even to conceive a project of change may be a feat. To plan, execute, and institutionalize a significant reform is a doubly praiseworthy achievement. And the manager who wants action but knows that others (particularly subordinates) may not share his or her enthusiasm for new policies may face the toughest challenge of all.

One hears much talk of "new ideas" and "bold initiatives" from candidates for electoral office. But definitive solutions are more often than not figments of political rhetoric. Rarely are they realistic possibilities in the bureaucratic battle zone or the defiles of the issue network. The leadership aspirations—and in the end, the achievements—of our senior political appointees (such as Mike Butler) and our senior public managers (such as Bill McDonald) should be judged in a context defined by this system of limits. Restrictions war with ambitions in the land of the bureaucrats, and the order of battle more often than not determines that the restrictions eventually will win.

chapter 10

To Meet the Challenges of Public Management

I have tried in the foregoing pages to present some glimpses of the lived experience of bureaucracy. Notwithstanding the rationalizations of the classification system and the organizational chart, that experience is untidy with ambiguities and personal conflicts. Life in a public agency is also conditioned by the dynamics of the issue network in which the formal organization is usually embedded. The essence of the issue-network structure is the porosity of the public-private interface. Without that porosity, the governance process would be more transaction-costly and even less efficient than it is. Yet from this porosity, some of the characteristic problems of American public bureaucracy arise. Specifically, the perceived danger that private actors may exert undue influence on public officials, combined with the potential for abuse of discretion within the formal bureaucracy, largely accounts for the growing system of administrative controls.

There is no escaping the problem of discretion in public management or its twin, the problem of control. The urge to control bureaucratic discretion goes back at least to the late nineteenth century interpretation of the "rule of law" principle. It is consistent with this Diceyian tradition that our public servants work within a net of rules, regulations, red tape, and required procedures—*bureaucracy* in the common, pejorative sense of the word. Moreover, insofar as the institutional aging process tends to widen the latitude enjoyed by civil servants, the danger of renegade discretion increases with each passing year in an agency's life. But the apparatus of controls that has been set up to confine discretion and prevent corruption also becomes more monstrous and obstructive over time.

An understanding of bureaucracy begins with the recognition that resistance to change is the one real constant in an old-line agency. The potential for innovation in an organization such as FERC is constrained at all critical points by the self-interested behavior of individuals, by controls that seem to grow constantly under the impulse of the contradictory dynamic, and often by counterbalancing forces in the surrounding issue networks. Much of an official's time has to be spent bargaining, compromising, reporting, requirement-checking, and backside-covering. The would-be policy entrepreneur can undertake a project of directed change only with the energies that remain after the business of staying even has been seen to. In this environment, unrealistic expectations evidence hubris or delusion rather than the needed quality of optimism.

The leader who would sustain a project of directed change in these unforgiving circumstances needs a full satchel of managerial techniques and the staying power that may give him or her enough time to employ them. The experience at FERC underscores the importance of certain how-to's of public management—task force initiation and trust-building, management by indirection, favor-trading across organizational lines, using contracting options in an opportunistic way. But it takes more than the right kit bag of techniques to meet the challenges of public management. It also takes public managers with the right instincts, character traits, and values.

At FERC, Butler and McDonald combined purpose and guts with sensitivity to the political forces at work in their relevant organizations—the issue network in Butler's case, the formal agency in McDonald's. Both missed some signals: Butler by insouciantly touting accelerated deregulation in the earliest days of his chairmanship; McDonald by exposing his position to attacks that led to an investigation. But by any realistic measure, the tenures of both were eventful, constructive, and successful. Overall, the record of the Butler-McDonald team suggests that the list of essential traits for would-be public managers includes political acumen informed by a sense of limits and a willingness to work within them; opportunistic management skills; acceptance of certain personal and institutional values that are essential to good government—honesty and moral courage, respect for the "rule of law" principle and for the obligations of democratic accountability; and—probably the architectonic virtue—prudence.

Political Acumen: Butler's Agenda of Deregulation

At FERC, Mike Butler took the position of "Mr. Outside" to McDonald's "Mr. Inside." As agency chairman, Butler had to play in the industry network, where he dealt with more powerful forces than those buffeting McDonald inside the agency. The coalitional balances also tend to be more difficult to discern in the issue network than they are in the formal agency, where an explicit hierarchical structure (at least theoretically) clarifies who can do what to whom.

In the noise that fills the air inside the Washington beltway, messages of impending danger may be indirect, equivocal, and easily confused with contrary communications from others in the network. Had the intent of the law under which Butler was operating (the Natural Gas Policy Act) been absolutely clear, had there been a technically unambiguous one best way to advance "the public interest and necessity" (the classic formulaic expression of regulatory purpose), had Butler's ideological commitment to President Reagan's agenda been the sole consideration in his decision making, there need have been no wavering or maneuvering on his program of directed change. Certainly there need have been no final surrender on the goal of accelerated deregulation.

But in an environment of technical uncertainty and legal

ambiguity, one uses political assessments to determine what is possible—and what is not. A presidential appointee, even an appointee
to a politically independent position such as Butler's, deals with
dozens of significant others outside of the home agency: legislators,
judges, auditors and investigators, counterpart officials in neighboring agencies and bureaus, other notables from the relevant issue
networks (including journalists from the trade press and watchdogs
from public interest firms). Butler's desire to move forward aggressively on deregulation called for a whole sequence of judgments
about the desirability, saleability, and long-term political supportability of policies that he thought it his duty to advance. Because
he had no objective metric with which to gauge either President
Reagan's deregulatory expectations or Congressman Dingell's determination to keep tight controls on gas pricing, the new chairman
had to probe incrementally, experimentally for the point at which
his partisan agenda would exceed the limits of the statutes or the
flash points of important political opponents.

The agency head who neglects to exploit whatever tolerances
exist within this complex of counterbalancing forces fails to exercise the kind of aggressive leadership that bureaucratic torpor makes
necessary if change is ever to occur. But the appointee who exceeds
the allowances is likely to find his or her program trimmed back in
Congress or repudiated in the courts. And for the good of the
agency, it is almost always more important for a leader to preserve
political support—to maintain what prior agency leaders have
managed to win from a grudging political and bureaucratic environment—than it is to make the flashy new score. Butler's determination to uncover any due process irregularities, irregularities that
might have foiled any chance of forward movement on deregulation, exemplified the political acumen needed by one in his
position.

"It is not incumbent on you to complete the work," Rabbi
Tarfon admonishes in the Talmud, "but neither are you at liberty
to desist from your portion of it." Butler's portion of the Reagan
revolution was to advance his agency whatever distance he could
toward deregulation. For his efforts, he had to settle for a second-
best, compromised version of the work. Butler pressed his agenda
about as far and fast as the political realities permitted. He headed

off the looming battle with the Democrats in Congress. That spelled victory for Dingell. But it also was a victory for FERC, since the defeat that Butler avoided was more valuable than the complete victory he could never have won.

McDonald and the Givens of Public Management

The constraints on Bill McDonald, though different in nature from the ones that limited Butler's freedom of action, could not have felt any less binding in McDonald's position.

The main given in public management is the quality of the workforce that is to be managed. When McDonald arrived at FERC, he found himself in the midst of a typical population of federal bureaucrats. He had no way to deal himself a new staff but was required instead to work with what he had. The FERC complement included workers who would have been counted as outstanding performers by any definition of the term. But intermixed with them were hundreds of staff members of middling talent and motivation. And unfortunately, the occasional incompetent or shirker could also be found in the FERC cadre.

A new leader in an existing organization may be able to rearrange some job assignments here and redouble commitments of budgetary or personnel resources there. But the organization's over-all personnel allotment is usually a given, not a variable subject to easy manipulation, and the appointee to a high bureaucratic post typically must operate within an overall organizational structure legislated from above.

The "Good People" Catchphrase

"Good people," one sometimes hears, "can make *any* organization work." This catchphrase, when true at all, is often so only in a rather trivial sense. It may amount to little more than a redefinition of personnel quality. In a poorly designed organization, inordinate energies have to go into the completion of ill-conceived transactions rather than into the production of the substantive results that efficient transactions are supposed to ensure. So in a bad organization, the "good people" frequently are simply those who have a knack for dealing with the transaction costs that a more efficient structure might have eliminated to begin with. One test of sound organization is the salience of workers' ability to do the primary substantive work of their unit compared with their skills as wheeler-dealers, red tape cutters, and fixers.

Even if the "good people" catchphrase were not simply incorrect (see Simon, 1947), it would be irrelevant to the situation that actually faces a public sector manager. When, as is typical, the appointee inherits a personnel ceiling that is fixed by legislation, there is simply no way to replace the existing staff, even a mediocre one, with "good people" unless inferior staff members can be removed to make room for new hires. But who are the inferior staff members? To answer that question takes time and close observation, time that a new leader usually prefers to spend getting started on his or her special agenda.

At FERC, civil service rules would have prevented McDonald, had he actually tried to change the overall complexion of the agency staff, from turning the workforce over. Permanent reductions in force are notoriously difficult to bring off in the federal service. What is more, RIFs are often counterproductive even when top officials do manage to trim an agency's staff (Rubin, 1985). Even if McDonald had been able to fire half of the FERC staff without worrying about civil service protections, where could he have found significantly better people to take the same old jobs in the same old classification scheme? Thus we return to the critical factor, organization of work by classification, which the New Theory suggests is a basic source of personnel problems in our public bureaucracies.

The Classification System

The New Theory implies that the General Schedule, originally instituted to prevent cronyism and nepotism, can also attract mediocrity into the civil service and protect incompetence in the ranks. If so, then at a time when job requirements are, on average, becoming more demanding—a result of the evolution of the industrial economy that most of our public bureaucracies exist to regulate—the organization of work by classification makes it relatively more, not less, difficult to attract "good people" into government employment.

Although the government's inability to recruit and retain the most talented individuals may account for some of the malaise that observers have noted in the federal service, other sources of demoralization are equally noteworthy. One should neither forget nor underestimate the depressive effect that bureaucracy bashing, especially during the Reagan presidency, had on the morale of civil servants and the attractiveness of civil service positions. Young Americans heard from the bully pulpit itself that government is the problem, not part of the solution. The thousands who believed that message of denigration belong to the ranks that are missing from today's public service. The lost recruits of the 1980s would have been the midlevel public officials of the late 1990s.

Historically, the formal bureaucracy's rigid classification system encouraged the growth of a shadow bureaucracy of highly skilled contractors, from which there gradually grew the shadow bureaucracy as it exists today—an all-purpose source of supplementary workers, from the most specialized technical consultants to contract janitors and security guards. What is more, current efforts to retard the growth of government, although perhaps desirable on fiscal, political, or philosophical grounds, can hardly help but intensify the trend toward reliance on private contractors to deliver public services. Virtually no one expects demand for such services to decrease over the long term.

The accelerating trend toward privatization and third-party government (Kettl, 1988; Salamon, 1988) suggests that private sector jobs with public sector functions will continue to be available to qualified individuals. These jobs typically promise higher pay levels and often higher-quality professional associations than applicants are likely to find in the civil service. The situation tends to beggar the public service by deterring young candidates from seeking employment at entry levels and by driving more senior civil servants through the revolving door. One expects to find today's Gifford Pinchots and Harvey Wileys not in the formal bureaucracy but in "Nader's Raiders" or Physicians for Social Responsibility— or in beltway bandit firms that can offer higher pay, better working conditions, and more career flexibility than the classified service will ever allow.

Notwithstanding all of which, the senior public manager

must continue to seek for ways to attract "good people" into government service and then must try to move them in diligent pursuit of organizational (as opposed to self-dealing personal) objectives. Here again the New Theorists reason that the system is defective, for it impairs rather than reinforces the kinds of material and professional incentives that even altruistic workers require.

Mitigating Incentive Impairment

By definition, any impairment of employees' incentives demotivates workers and detaches their goals from those of the larger organization. The typical demotivated worker is the shirker, who wants to expend as little effort as possible for as much pay as he or she can continue to collect. Williamson (1985) argues that incentive impairment is most likely to occur in nonmarket settings that fail to reward individuals when they apply extra care or undertake the risks of productive innovation—in other words, when career progression approximates the lockstep promotion system of a classification scheme.

Because incentive impairment is in part a consequence of the structure of work, it should be possible to mitigate shirking by altering institutional arrangements. Change the incentive structure and certain behavioral changes should follow as well. One hears frequent calls from knowledgeable commentators for improvements in civil service salary schedules and physical conditions of work. Thus, in 1989, the National Commission on the Public Service urged a thoroughgoing reform of the pay scales that today discourage bright, ambitious people from governmental employment (Volcker, 1989).

But better pay is only a start. Needed too is more flexibility to promote superior performers, demote or fire mediocre ones, and transfer workers among jobs within agencies. Though it would not be feasible or even desirable to abolish the General Schedule, there is no reason why the equilibrium of the effective bureaucracy cannot be shifted toward a more loosely structured personnel system, for example, by increasing the proportion of "fire-able" Schedule C appointees within the federal professional ranks or by extending the bonus system established by the Civil Service Reform Act of 1978.

Arguably, a civil service system organized more nearly on the basis of contract than of classification might mitigate adverse selection and moral hazard in the public sector workforce. It might, in other words, enable the formal bureaucracy to begin attracting and motivating more of the kinds of workers who now often prefer employment in the shadow bureaucracy. Fortunately, action of the right kind—toward deregulation or at least toward decentralization of the appointment process—is already under way. In the late 1980s, some 45 percent of federal career civil service appointments were made by direct action of the appointing agency rather than by the central Office of Personnel Management. Another 40 percent represented so-called direct hire jobs in occupations deemed to be so specialized or so critical that normal procedures could not be used. All but 15 percent of federal civil service positions, then, had been excepted in some way from the most rigid requirements of the traditional centrally administered classification process (Ingraham and Rosenbloom, 1990).

Further movement in this direction seems desirable. In fact, Office of Personnel Management officials have launched a series of experimental programs to test more flexible applications of traditional classification principles (U.S. Congressional Budget Office, 1991). David Osborne and Ted Gaebler (1992) have made a persuasive case for the adoption of a much more flexible personnel system than the current classification scheme permits and have documented examples of successful experiments along these lines at the municipal, state, and federal levels of government.

Opportunistic Management

If increased flexibility in the civil service personnel system is the first prescription for improvement in the workings of our public bureaucracy, the rapid promotion and professional encouragement of opportunistic senior managers is the second, complementary, prescription. Only a decision maker with what McDonald used to call "moxie"—a mix of imagination, courage, and organizational savvy—can take full advantage of any flexibility that exists in the institutional structure.

When bureaucracy works, it is usually because an opportunistic leader sees a way though the obstacles and presses an agenda to its limit: Seek the chance, take the risk, push the project. But the concept of the limit is as important as is that of the venture itself. Opportunistic management is visionary leadership tempered by realism. It is what remains after the would-be radical transformer of structures or processes reckons with the constraints of public sector management.

At the organizational level, opportunistic management implies *task force thinking* when wholesale restructuring is impossible. In day-to-day operations, it involves *transactional manipulation* of whoever and whatever resources happen to be on hand, when, as is usual, no way exists to go out and get exactly the people or materials that the manager would want.

Task Force Thinking

In the end, the test of personnel quality is performance, and performance invariably has an important organizational component. In fact, improvements in the governmental workforce through personnel upgradings may yield only marginal improvements in the output of public services unless corresponding organizational and procedural changes also occur. For this reason, the "good people" issue leads quite naturally to a consideration of organizational techniques.

Decidedly average people can sometimes be organized in ways that will produce better than average performance. Then average workers become "good people" from the perspective of the institution, even though their raw abilities, natural incentives, or professional skills might belie such a characterization. It may not be standout workers in any absolute sense, but leaders able to convert followers into the good people of the catchphrase, who manage "to make any organization work."

In the public sector, even temporary reorganizations take place in a context constrained by prior legislation, limited by administrative controls, and conditioned by workers' habituated practices.

Thus, the restructuring possibilities that are typically available involve incremental adjustment rather than radical transformation. The manager must watch—as McDonald always watched—for his or her chances, and then must make whatever interstitial improvements the opportunities permit.

Because the line-staff structure at FERC separated the professional rate makers from the executive director's line of authority, McDonald had no direct way to reach the majority of the staff members on whom he would eventually have to rely if his pet enterprise, the automation of the agency, were to succeed. Within the existing FERC structure and budget, however, McDonald did have the freedom to set up an efficient focusing organization: a special task force targeted on gas pipeline rate making.

The special project has become the public manager's vehicle of choice for efforts of directed change in large part because it offers a way to draw the greatest output from an available workforce when neither extensive personnel replacements nor new hiring are realistic options. With Chairman Butler's backing, McDonald was able to ensure that some of the best rate makers from Ken Williams's office were assigned to the automation task force. The "good people" principle, though of limited or trivial validity when applied to the agency as a whole, became a sound managerial criterion when combined with an opportunistic approach to the organization of work at FERC.

Transactional Manipulation

The special project represents a kind of halfway solution between the creation of a permanent new bureau (which will eventually develop its own pathologies of senescence) and an attempt at change using the existing permanent structure (which will be likely to present formidable problems of resistance to change and internal transaction costs). But even the most carefully calibrated system of special task forces will leave some wobble spaces within an agency's official structure. The FERC case illustrates how loosely coupled the units of a "rationally organized" bureaucracy tend to be. After organizational rationalization and organizational opportunism have both gone as far as they can go, resources that can be manipulated will remain.

To exploit the residual opportunities in an organization is to exercise what the political scientist James McGregor Burns (1978) called "transactional leadership." The transactional leader (contrasted with Burns's more radical, revolutionary "transforming leader") accepts the existing organizational structure more or less as it is given and then manipulates followers' preferences to achieve desired goals.

Transactional manipulation involves the exercise of power in a highly rational way, but ironically, it fully succeeds only when incomplete rationality within the organization releases resources to be manipulated by the agent of change. In Weber's ideal type, bureaucracy involves a rational assignment of roles and tasks. It supposes a perfect fit between the employee's skills and the needs of the office. To the extent that the Weberian version of the bureaucratic program succeeds, any personal aspirations that would conflict with organizational goals are eliminated. But it is precisely such personal aspirations that the transactional manager must identify and orchestrate into the basis for a coalition in support of his or her own agenda.

To be a bureaucrat is to play an official role, but the role never completely absorbs the role player. Therefore, officialdom never reaches that efficient, idealized—and dehumanized—limit toward which the bureaucratic idea as explicated by Weber inclines it. The looseness that always persists in the couplings between organizational subunits, the crannies in which workers' personal idiosyncrasies may be indulged (or personal empires built), and the very existence of resources unallocated by rational plan are all imperfections when viewed from the perspective of classical bureaucratic theory. But they are also handles that the opportunistic manager may grab onto and use as levers of change. The transactional leader takes advantage of organizational imperfections to mobilize and manipulate resources that would be eliminated entirely if the Weberian model were fully realized. Friction and even waste represent exactly the kind of looseness in the bureaucratic gears that permits the transactional leader to perform (Burns, 1978).

Transactional leadership may even call for a willingness to

initiate and exploit conflict within an organization. Conflict, properly orchestrated, fosters a "we versus they" sense that would have been anathema to the Old Theorists. But the transactional leader knows that by cultivating a group of loyalists he or she might be able to create the team of committed supporters needed to do battle against the outgroup. Here again, a psychological dimension that was absent from the machine model becomes a dominant factor in organizational analysis.

The striking conclusion is that a bureaucratic organization can thrive only if it never reaches the perfection of its form—in other words, only if room remains within its interstices for the exercise of leadership. It is not in the ideal type of a bureaucracy, but rather in departures from it, that the opportunistic manager may find unexpected reserves of human and material resources and hence possibilities for imaginative coalition building.

McDonald as a Transactional Leader

It is paradoxical, this concept of a bureaucracy that can work best only if, when judged by strictly bureaucratic norms, it works imperfectly. Yet this paradoxical concept gives us a useful perspective from which to assess the qualities that Bill McDonald brought to his job at FERC. As a hands-on administrator dealing every day with dozens of FERC officials and hundreds of ongoing actions, McDonald had to amass support by cultivating loyalists, both within FERC and without, and by accumulating small increments of goodwill, personal power, and privileged knowledge of the agency.

Transactional leadership feeds on unfulfilled personal ambitions and surplus organizational resources—these being the chits and bargaining chips that the leader can trade for support. For this reason, the best manager is sometimes the one who first finds ways to increase efficiency in an organization, but then, instead of using the savings to reduce costs, salts the surplus away in recesses of the organization known only to himself. Cyert and March (1963) coined the term *slack* for the reserve of decision-making power that an effective manager collects from these sources (see also Moe, 1984). The manager who has created the slack resource and knows where it has been hidden (for example, where and under what aliases extra funds have been secreted in the agency's budget) can mobilize it when he or she—not the congressional appropriations committee—wants to.

McDonald was a master at accumulating and manipulating slack. The knowledge, skills, and loyalty of his inner entourage of staff subordinates represented slack in the FERC organization. So in a sense did McDonald's network of outside contractors, informants, and favor traders throughout the larger effective bureaucracy. McDonald considered these contacts and reserve resources as assets to be drawn upon when opportunities arose. His way of waving a wand and producing tangible results (such as the CDSI computer programmers, hired by task order to be part of the automation effort) qualified McDonald as a most effective transactional leader, and one with a keen appreciation of the paradox of bureaucracy.

A Remarkable Civil Servant

McDonald's aggressiveness and "field sense" were precisely the traits that Americans prize in business leaders, military tacticians, even professional athletes. He played a game of inches, as any civil servant must, but he played it aggressively, opportunistically, and as close to the limits as he could. McDonald's "are we in trouble?" study, his addition of the automation deliverable when Mike Butler directed him to arrange for an investigation of the rate-making process, and his wheeling-dealing to secure the services of high-paid outside computer programmers all exemplified McDonald's way of pushing opportunistically through apertures of change when they presented themselves.

Stephen Bailey (1992) once singled out optimism as the first moral requisite of the effective administrator. Then in a second thought, noting that the term *optimism* failed quite to catch the essence of his idea, Bailey went on to define this most essential of character traits as "an affirmation of the worth of taking risks" (p. 497). Bill McDonald was the most optimistic civil servant (in Bailey's redefined sense) that I ever encountered. But risk takers may not be able to calculate all the odds and so eventually become hostages to fortune. At the end of the day, the bureaucracy showed itself unable to appreciate one of its own finest practitioners.

Notwithstanding his lifetime of public service and years of recorded achievement at FERC, McDonald too was a casualty of the inspector general's inquiry. The inspector general found a single charge amongst all the allegations against McDonald that could be sustained by the evidence. What puts all the investigatory time and effort into perspective is not the fact that one lone charge against McDonald finally stuck but rather that it proved to be a charge of almost unutterable triviality—specifically, that McDonald had failed to get written (instead of merely informal) approval from the General Services Administration before exercising his authority to allocate more than 10 percent of the parking spaces at 825 North Capitol Street to senior FERC officials (Layton, 1987).

In the words of the late comedienne Judy Holliday, "It'd be laughable if it weren't so funny."

Tempering Opportunism with Judgment and Values

The FERC case demonstrates that a leader with imagination and initiative can use a mixture of organizational and personal techniques to induce a process of constructive change. At least temporarily, the manager who comes at the job opportunistically may work through, over, or around the briar patch of administrative restrictions. Yet opportunism—or anyway, *mere* opportunism—also has its underside. Public management remains a public trust, and governance to the highest standards is impossible in a society of *mere* opportunists—mere grabbers at the main chance. In the issue-network context, the threat comes both from public servants who abuse their discretion and from private self-dealers who take advantage of easy opportunities to advance their own interests at the public's expense.

To control unprincipled opportunism is a problem of special poignancy today, given a popular culture and a persuasive academic theory (the New Theory) that accentuate the human trait of self-interest. A general heightening of the egoistic impulse seemed to have occurred in the United States in the 1980s. But when citizens in large numbers begin really to believe that "greed is good," society is in trouble. The touting of self-interest by political and intellectual leaders as if it is an entirely benign driver of human conduct tends to sharpen the natural urges of some citizens to exploit the porosity of the public-private interface.

Good governance needs some minimum support in a broader culture of civic virtue. Our civil servants are recruited from the general populace. They reflect the mores of society in their own values and commitments, and (because of the issue-network structure) they constantly react to private actors' concerns. The propensities of economic man, if accentuated to the point of encouraging mere opportunism, may encourage public officials to abuse the discretion that they possess, either in their own interests or in the interests of the importunate private actors with whom they have regular contact through the process of continuing consultation.

The control techniques emphasized in the New Theory do little more than the New Theorists' assumptions about human nature do to ameliorate the problems of unprincipled opportunism. No one doubts that worker self-interest may be harnessed to move a public agency, like a private firm, toward efficiency. But more than efficiency is involved in public service—a fact well appreciated by the Old Theorists. Incentive impairment occurs only in part as a consequence of an institution's career structure. Only in part can it be mitigated by more cunningly devised material incentives or by artful transactional manipulation. As the New Theorists themselves argue, in any large technically based bureaucracy, organizational distance and increasing information costs limit a superviser's ability to monitor subordinates. To try to remedy this deficiency with a self-regarding rewards-and-punishments calculus would be to reaffirm precisely the wrong values among our public servants. For this reason, I would end with a nod (and a good deal more than a nod) of approval for the progressives' ideal—an internalized standard, an *ethic* of public service.

The Moral Burden of Governance

No precise formula can be written for an optimum mix of the Old Theorists' faith in internalized values (Frederick Mosher's "government by the good") and the New Theorists' emphasis on self-interest, surveillance, and control. Both approaches have their places in the scheme of public management.

Better pay for civil servants is a must, and so are improved flexibility and selective worker oversight arrangements. But after the last affordable set of material incentives has been adopted, an organization needs a sense of common dedication among its employees. If we must appreciate the inevitability of self-interestedness in our public servants, perhaps the most compelling teaching of the New Theorists, we must also recognize that individuals ultimately demand fulfillments beyond those that are immediate, material, and self-regarding. The theologian Pascal (1966) once observed that the human heart knows reasons that reason itself does not know. In virtually every person's makeup there exists the capacity—indeed, the yearning—to transcend narrow calculations of self-interest and to respond to factors other than rationally measured personal gain.

Culture and Self-Interest

That groups of individuals, when properly led, can indeed be inspired to identify with larger values is precisely the argument that the proponents of an organizational culture and corporate culture approach have advanced over the years (see Barnard, 1938; Selznick, 1957; Peters and Waterman, 1982; Wilson, 1989). What today's thinkers call organizational culture was implicit in the Old Theorists' ideal of public servants as participants in a collective, public-interested movement first, and as self-interested individuals second. The New Theorists, with their atomistic, individualistic view of organizations, tend to undervalue a communitarian, social concept such as culture. For unlike rational calculations of self-interest, culture cannot be referred back to an egoistic individual, even for purposes of building a theoretical model. Culture is a product of human experience in a society, a group, a larger collectivity of some sort. Culture therefore exists only in the context of a social organization. Conversely—and this key point is insufficiently appreciated in the New Theory—under certain circumstances, the society, the group, or the organization can provide acculturative experiences to offset the incentive impairment that may occur when individuals cease transacting in markets and become members of an organization.

The problem today lies in the fact that the relevant organization is, for most purposes, the issue network rather than the progressives' formal bureaucracy. The Old Theorists' difficulty lay not in their implicit acceptance of an organizational culture approach but in their failure to anticipate the organizational context in which an ethic of service would eventually have to be developed. Recent scholarship on organizational culture suggests how hard it is to cultivate an ethic in an organization (Doig and Hargrove, 1987; U.S. General Accounting Office, 1992; DiIulio, 1993). The "value-infusing" task (Selznick, 1957) must be vastly more difficult when the outlines of the organization are themselves in the process of dissolution—which is exactly what has happened to the New American State as, over the years, the progressives' public versus private system of agencies and business firms has given way to systems of public and private consultation.

Some years ago Judge Learned Hand (1958) warned that Americans cannot ultimately depend on courts to preserve free government. Hand argued that no special class of lawyers or judges can preserve vital political values unless the people as a whole hold them dear as well. Similarly, Americans must put aside the notion that public managers by themselves can solve problems that are organic to the broader organizations, the issue networks, that underlie so much of the modern governance process.

The values that must underpin good governance have been discussed by some of the most thoughtful students of public administration in the post–World War II period. Scholars such as Paul Appleby (1945, 1949, 1952), Dwight Waldo (1948, 1955), and more recently John Rohr (1978) and David Hart (1989), while rejecting Woodrow Wilson's concept of a policy-administration gap, have reemphasized the progressives' ethical vision. Above all, Appleby and the others have stressed the need for deep commitments by our public officials to civic virtues, democratic values, and constitutional procedures. According to these thinkers, the traditions of republicanism, democracy, and constitutionalism ground the common values of the cadre of civil servants that we need today as they did the corps of expert administrators envisioned by Woodrow Wilson.

General Obligations of Citizenship

The admonitions of Appleby & Co., however, help rather little when we try to describe the kind of culture that seems appropriate for decision making in issue networks, *unless* we identify the ideals to which they appeal as *general obligations of citizenship* rather than as peculiar requirements of the call to public service. Such an identification implies an extension of the public service ethic to all who actually participate in the public policy process, whether from the public or the private side of the boundary.

What would an extension of the ideals of citizenship in this way mean in practice? It would mean that if, to reemphasize the New Theorists' point, we must appreciate the element of private interestedness in our public officials, we must also demand public-interestedness from private decision makers. Our canons of public administration should not ask civil servants to bear the whole moral burden of governance in the issue-network context—to live with the ambiguities and pressures of rules, to decide rightly when exercising discretionary power, to deflect the importunities of private sector advocates, to control the impulses of egoism and greed. Neither should an impoverished conception of citizenship imply absolution for private decision makers who shirk their fair shares—and, by doing so, exacerbate the pressures under which their public sector counterparts must work.

With all the talk these days of deregulating and even reinventing government, one must expect that some public sector conduct will begin looking more like the conduct of private, profit-motivated actors. But the call to citizenship implies a further requirement: that the private participants in issue networks become more like the public servants envisioned of old—guided by a public ethic instead of merely driven by individualistic self-interest. This tempering of the traditional selfishness of market-oriented activity should be seen as fair exchange for the easy access to public policy making that issue-network membership provides to the private actor in our system.

Conclusion

That one cannot always look for first-best solutions in our public bureaucracies owes partly to the change-defeating characteristics of the system's formal controls, partly to change-resistant habits of mind that career bureaucrats themselves tend to develop, and partly to the fact that bureaucracy itself often selects against the promotion of managers with the qualities—Machiavellian qualities, if you will, rather than Weberian (or Wilsonian) ones—needed to make the system function more effectively. That one can *ever* look for a record of accomplishment from civil servants is a tribute to the drive, stamina, and sheer coping abilities brought by certain managers to public service despite the obstacles that they must expect to encounter all the days of their professional lives.

If in the public bureaucracy as it has actually evolved it is unrealistic to expect agencies of government to set new standards for efficient, businesslike operations (as the Old Theorists expected they would), it is not unreasonable to ask for enough "control of the controls" so that our public managers have running room to administer effectively. Adequate responses to that request must, of course, come mainly from Congress and the courts.

There is even less reason why public officials should not be expected to set certain standards of civic virtue for society at large. To members of the public, the image of the civil servant is that of the drone, the obfuscator, or the pettifogger. These deprecatory stereotypes should no more be the first assocations in the minds of Americans today than they were in the progressives' minds a century ago. Nor is it untoward to hope for a return to the original vision of public servants as general exemplars of citizenship—of ethical decision making and social responsibility. Gaebler (1992) has pointed out that public sector decision makers faced up to issues such as affirmative action, handicapped workers' rights, and sexual harrassment well before private managers did. These issues turn primarily on moral values rather than on criteria of efficient production.

After the last set of surveillance techniques has been put in place, it remains necessary to trust workers to use good judgment— the kind of judgment we hope to have from our political appointees when they frame broad agency policies, the kind bureau chiefs must exercise when they decide whether to give the regular staff a new job or to contract out another chunk of the public's business, the judgment implicit in midlevel civil servants' decisions when they tilt their rate designs to favor one group in society over another, even the judgment of auditors and inspectors when they are reviewing the reasons why a particular contract was let or a particular tilt was chosen.

No rule book or monitoring scheme can compensate for motivational or judgmental deficiencies in a decision maker who has managed not to develop the sense of standards that the use of discretion requires. To ensure that bureaucrats exercise discretion with responsibility, while at the same time making it possible to hold administrative controls to a tolerable level, the "faceless bureaucrats" on whom Americans rely must be men and women of judgment, probity, and dedication.

The most hopeful sense of what ought to be, however, should not cause anyone to blink away the difficulties that actually are. In their study of history as a source of lessons for policy makers, Richard Neustadt and Ernest May (1986, p. 268) stressed that "the prize in the package is prudence." If the history of U.S. governance, viewed in the large, teaches us anything, Neustadt and May observe, it is that the future is always likely to be "like the present in confounding previous hopes" (p. 254). The FERC story suggests much the same.

The FERC story also suggests that the how's of public management matter if we are interested in effective governance. The why's—the values and motives of the actors in our issue networks—matter even more if we want governance in the public interest rather than in the service of organized private constituencies. And if we want governance that is both effective and honest, the who's of public service matter most of all.

References

Ackerman, B., and Hassler, W. *Clean Coal/Dirty Air*. New Haven, Conn.: Yale University Press, 1981.

Administrative Conference of the United States. *A Guide to Federal Agency Rulemaking*. Washington, D.C.: U.S. Government Printing Office, 1983.

Administrative Procedures Act (APA), Act of June 11, 1946; 60 Stat. 237.

Airline Deregulation Act—P. L. 95-504, Oct. 24, 1978; 92 Stat. 1705.

Albrow, M. *Bureaucracy*. New York: Praeger, 1970.

Alchian, A., and Demsetz, H. "Production, Information Costs, and Economic Organization." *American Economic Review*, 1972, *62*, 777.

Allison, G. T. *The Essence of Decision*. Boston: Little, Brown, 1971.

Allison, G. T. "Public and Private Management: Are Fundamentally Alike in All Unimportant Respects?" In R. Stillman (ed.),

Public Administration: Concepts and Cases. (5th ed.) Boston: Houghton Mifflin, 1992.

Anderson, A. D. *The Origin and Resolution of an Urban Crisis: Baltimore, 1890–1930.* Baltimore, Md.: Johns Hopkins University Press, 1977.

Appalachian Power v. *EPA,* 477 F. 2d (4th Cir., 1973).

Appleby, P. *Big Democracy.* New York: Knopf, 1945.

Appleby, P. *Policy and Administration.* University, Al.: University of Alabama Press, 1949.

Appleby, P. *Morality and Administration.* Baton Rouge: Louisiana State University Press, 1952.

Argyris, C. *Integrating the Individual and the Organization.* New York: Wiley, 1964.

Arnold, T. *The Symbols of Government.* New Haven, Conn.: Yale University Press, 1935.

Arrow, K. "Uncertainty and the Welfare Economics of Medical Care." *American Economic Review,* 1963, *53,* 941.

Arrow, K. "The Organization of Economic Activity: Issues Pertinent to the Choice of Market or Non-Market Allocations." In J. Margolis (ed.), *The Analysis of Public Output.* New York: Columbia University Press, 1970.

Arrow, K. *The Logic of Organization.* New York: Norton, 1974.

Axelrod, R. *The Evolution of Cooperation.* New York: Basic Books, 1984.

Bailey, S. K. "Ethics and the Public Service." (1965), in R. Stillman (ed.), *Public Administration: Concepts and Cases.* Boston: Houghton Mifflin, 1992.

Barnard, C. *The Functions of the Executive.* Cambridge, Mass.: Harvard University Press, 1938.

Barzel, Y. *Economic Analysis of Property Rights.* New York: Cambridge University Press, 1989.

Behn, R. D. "Management by Groping Along." *Journal of Policy Analysis and Management,* 1988, 7, 643.

Bernstein, M. *Regulating Business by Independent Commission.* Princeton, N.J.: Princeton University Press, 1955.

Blum, H. *Time's Arrow and Evolution.* Princeton, N.J.: Princeton University Press, 1955.

Bowen, D. E., and Jones, G. "Transaction Cost Analysis of Service

Organization–Customer Exchange." *Academy of Management Review*, 1966, *11*, 428.

Bozeman, B. *All Organizations Are Public: Bridging Public and Private Organizational Theories*. San Fransisco: Jossey-Bass, 1987.

Brandl, J. "How Organization Counts: Incentives and Inspiration." *Journal of Policy Analysis and Management*, 1989, *8*, 489–493.

Braybrooke, D., and Lindblom, C. E. *A Strategy of Decision*. New York: Free Press, 1963.

Breyer, S., and MacAvoy, P. *Energy Regulation by the Federal Power Commission*. Washington, D.C.: Brookings Institution, 1974.

Buchanan, J. *Constitutional Economics*. Cambridge, Mass.: Blackwell, 1987.

Buchanan, J., and Tullock, G. *The Calculus of Consent*. Ann Arbor: University of Michigan Press, 1962.

Burns, J. M. *Leadership*. New York: HarperCollins, 1978.

Byner, G. C., *Bureaucratic Discretion*. Elmsford, N.Y.: Pergamon Press, 1987.

Calvert, R., McCubbins, M., and Weingast, B. "A Theory of Political Control and Agency Discretion." *American Journal of Political Science*, 1989, *33*, 588.

Cary, W. L. *Politics and the Regulatory Agencies*. New York: McGraw-Hill, 1967.

Chevron v. NRDC (Natural Resources Defense Council), 467 U.S. 837 (1974).

Chubb, J. E., and Moe, T. *Markets, Politics, and American Schools*. Washington, D.C.: Brookings Institution, 1990.

Civil Service Reform Act, P. L. 95-521 (Oct. 26, 1978); 92 Stat. 1824.

Classification Act, Act of Mar. 4, 1923; 42 Stat. 1488.

Classification Act of 1949, Act of Oct. 28, 1949; 63 Stat. 954.

Clean Air Act Amendments (CAA), P. L. 91-604 (Dec. 31, 1970), 84 Stat. 1676; P. L. 97-375 (Dec. 21, 1982), 96 Stat. 1820; P. L. 101-549 (Nov. 15, 1991), 104 Stat. 2399.

Coase, R. "The Nature of the Firm." *Economica*, n.s. 1937, *4*, 386.

Coase, R. "The Problem of Social Cost." *Journal of Law and Economics*, 1960, *3*, 1.

Cohen, M. D., March, J., and Olson, J. "A Garbage Can Model of

Organizational Choice." *Administrative Science Quarterly*, 1972, *17*, 1-25.

Competition in Contracting Act—P. L. 98-369, July 18, 1984; 98 Stat. 1175.

Congressional Record. 95th Cong., 2nd sess., 1978. Vol. 124, pt. 28.

Cook, B. *Bureaucratic Politics and Regulatory Reform.* Westport, Conn.: Greenwood Press, 1989.

Crenson, M. A., and Rourke, F. E. "American Bureaucracy Since World War II." In L. Galambos (ed.), *The New American State: Bureaucracies and Policies Since WW II.* Baltimore, Md.: Johns Hopkins University Press, 1987.

Croly, H. *The Promise of American Life.* New York: Macmillan, 1909.

Cyert, R., and March, J. *A Behavioral Theory of the Firm.* Englewood Cliffs, N.J.: Prentice Hall, 1963.

de Tocqueville, A. *Democracy in America.* New York: New American Library, 1956. (Originally published 1840.)

Demkovich, L. "The Cautious Approach of Cannon's Commerce Committee." *National Journal*, May 27, 1978, p. 846.

Denhardt, K. G. "The Management of Ideals: A Political Perspective on Ethics." *Public Administration Review*, 1989, *49*, 187.

Department of Energy Organization Act—P. L. 95-91 (Aug. 4, 1977), 91 Stat. 565.

DiIulio, J. J., Jr. "Recovering the Public Management Variable: Lessons from Schools, Prisons, and Armies." *Public Administration Review*, 1989, *49*, 127.

DiIulio, J. J., Jr. "Principals, Agents, and Principled Agents." Paper presented at the Harvard University Center of American Policy Studies, Cambridge, Mass.: December 1990a.

DiIulio, J. J., Jr. "The Public Administration of James Q. Wilson." Paper presented at the American Political Science Association National Meeting, Public Administration Section, San Francisco, August 1990b.

DiIulio, J. J., Jr. *Principled Agents: Leadership, Administration, and Culture in a Federal Bureaucracy.* New York: Oxford University Press, 1993.

Dobzhansky, T. *Mankind Evolving.* New Haven, Conn.: Yale University Press, 1962.

Doig, W. J. "If I See a Murderous Fellow Sharpening a Knife Cleverly . . . : The Wilson Dichotomy and the Public Authority Tradition." *Public Administration Review*, 1983, *43*, 292–304.

Doig, W J., and Hargrove, E. C. *Leadership and Innovation*. Baltimore, Md.: Johns Hopkins University Press, 1987.

Donahue, J. M. *The Privatization Decision*. New York: Basic Books, 1989.

Edelman, M. *The Symbolic Uses of Politics*. Urbana, Ill.: University of Illinois Press, 1967.

Effron, E. "Allegations of Improprieties Rock FERC." *Legal Times*, Sept. 29, 1986, p. 1.

Employees Retirement Income Security Act (ERISA), P. L. 93-406 (Sept. 2, 1974), 88 Stat. 829.

Ethics in Government Act—P. L. 95-521 (Oct. 26, 1978); 92 Stat. 1824.

Federal Power Act—Act of June 10, 1920; 41 Stat. 1063.

Fenno, R. *The Power of the Purse*. Boston: Little, Brown, 1966.

Fiorina, M. "Group Concentration and the Delegation of Legislative Authority." In R. Noll (ed.), *Regulatory Policy and the Social Sciences*. Berkeley: University of California Press, 1985.

Frankfurter, F. *Cases and Other Materials on Administrative Law*. Chicago: Foundation Press, 1935.

Freedom of Information Act (FOIA)—P. L. 89-487 (July 4, 1966); 80 Stat. 250.

Fritschler, L. and Ross, B. *The Executive's Guide to Government*. Cambridge, Mass.: Winthrop, 1980.

Frug, G. E. "The Ideology of Bureaucracy in American Law." *Harvard Law Review*, 1984, *97*, 1277.

Gaebler, T. "Entrepreneurial Government." *On Achieving Excellence*, June 1992, 10.

Galbraith, J. K. *The New Industrial State*. New York: New American Library, 1967.

Galbraith, J. K. *The Great Crash*. Boston: Houghton Mifflin, 1979.

Garvey, G. *Strategy and the Defense Dilemma*. Lexington, Mass.: Lexington Press, 1983.

Garvey, G. *The Natural Gas Pipeline Ratemaking Automation Project*. Report prepared for the Office of the Executive Director, U.S. Federal Energy Regulatory Commission, April 1984.

Garvey, G. E., and Garvey, G. J. *Economic Law and Economic Growth*. Westport, Conn.: Greenwood-Praeger, 1990.

Gellhorn, W. *Federal Administrative Proceedings*. Baltimore, Md.: Johns Hopkins University Press, 1941.

Gilbreth, F., and Gilbreth, L. In W. Spriegel, and C. Myers (eds.), *The Writings of the Gilbreths*. Homewood, Ill.: Irwin, 1953.

Goldberg v. *Kelly*, 397 U.S. 254 (1969).

Goldman, E. F. *Rendezvous with Destiny*. New York: Random House, 1952.

Gormley, W. *Taming the Bureaucracy*. Princeton, N.J.: Princeton University Press, 1989.

Graham, O. *Toward a Planned Society: From Roosevelt to Nixon*. New York: Oxford University Press, 1976.

Gruber, J. *Controlling Bureaucracies*. Berkeley: University of California Press, 1987.

Gulick, L., and Urwick, L. (eds.), *Papers on the Science of Administration*. Clifton, N.J.: Kelley, 1937.

Haber, S. *Efficiency and Uplift*. Chicago: University of Chicago Press, 1964.

Habermas, J. *The Theory of Communicative Action*. Vol. 2: *Lifeworld and Systems*. Boston: Beacon Press, 1987.

Halperin, M. *Bureaucratic Politics and Foreign Policy*. Washington, D.C.: Brookings Institution, 1974.

Hand, L. *The Bill of Rights*. Cambridge, Mass.: Harvard University Press, 1958.

Handler, J. F. *Law and the Search for Community*. Philadelphia: University of Pennsylvania Press, 1990.

Hannaway, J. *Managers Managing*. New York: Oxford University Press, 1989.

Hargrove, E., and Glidewell, J. *Impossible Jobs in Public Management*. Lawrence: University of Kansas Press, 1990.

Harmon, M., and Mayer, R. R. *Organization Theory for Public Administration*. Boston: Little, Brown, 1986.

Hart, D. K. "A Partnership in Virtue Among All Citizens: The Public Service and Civic Humanism." *Public Administration Review*, 1989, *49*, 101.

Hartman, R. W. *Pay and Pensions for Federal Workers*. Washington, D.C.: Brookings Institution, 1983.

Hatch Act—Act of Aug. 2, 1939; 53 Stat. 1147.

Hawley, E. "Herbert Hoover, the Commerce Secretariat, and the Vision of an Associative State." *Journal of American History,* 1974, *67,* 116.

Hayes, C. J. *A Generation of Materialism. 1871–1900.* Westport, Conn.: Greenwood, 1983. (Originally published 1941.)

Hays, S. *The Response to Industrialism, 1885–1914.* Chicago: University of Chicago Press, 1957.

Hays, S. *Conservation and the Gospel of Efficiency.* New York: Atheneum, 1975. (Originally published 1955.)

Heclo, H. *A Government of Strangers.* Washington, D.C.: Brookings Institution, 1977.

Heclo, H. "Issue Networks and the Executive Establishment." In Anthony King (ed.), *The New American Political System.* Washington, D.C.: American Enterprise Institute, 1978.

Heffron, F., and McFeeley, N. *The Administrative Regulatory Process.* White Plains, N.Y.: Longman, 1983.

Henke, S. (ed.). *Prospects for Privatization.* New York: Academy of Political Science Press, 1987.

Herring, E. P. *Public Administration and the Public Interest.* New York: McGraw-Hill, 1936.

Heyman, P. B. *The Politics of Public Management.* New Haven, Conn.: Yale University Press, 1987.

IG Act—P. L. 95-452 (Oct. 12, 1978); 92 Stat. 1101.

Ingraham, P. W. "Building Bridges or Burning Them? The President, the Appointees, and the Bureaucracy." *Public Administration Review,* Sept./Oct. 1987, *47,* pp. 425–435.

Ingraham, P. W., and Rosenbloom, D. H. "The New Public Personnel and the New Public Service." *Public Administration Review,* 1989, *49,* 116.

Ingraham, P. W., and Rosenbloom, D. H. *The State of Merit in the Federal Government.* An Occasional Paper Prepared for the National Commission on the Public Service, Washington, D.C.: June 1990.

International Harvester v. *Ruckelshaus,* 478 F. 2d 615 (D.C. Cir., 1973).

Jaffee, L. "The Effective Limits of the Administrative Process: A Revaluation." *Harvard Law Review,* 1954, *67,* 1105.

Jones, A. R. *The Constitutional Conservatism of Thomas McIntyre Cooley*. New York: Garland, 1987.

Kaufman, H. *The Forest Ranger*. Baltimore, Md.: Johns Hopkins University Press, 1960.

Kaufman, H. *Are Government Organizations Immortal?* Washington, D.C.: Brookings Institution, 1976.

Kaufman, H. *Redtape*. Washington, D.C.: Brookings Institution, 1977.

Kaufman, H. *The Administrative Behavior of Federal Bureau Chiefs*. Washington, D.C.: Brookings Institution, 1982.

Kaufmann, W. *The McNamara Strategy*. New York: HarperCollins, 1964.

Kelman, S. *Making Public Policy*. New York: Basic Books, 1987.

Kelman, S. *Procurement and Public Management*. Washington, D.C.: American Enterprise Institute, 1990.

Keohane, R. *After Hegemony*. Princeton, N.J.: Princeton University Press, 1984.

Kettl, D. F. *Government by Proxy*. Washington, D.C.: CQ Press, 1988.

Kimberly, J. R., Miles, R. H., and Associates. *The Organizational Life Cycle: Issues in the Creation, Transformation, and Decline of Organizations*. San Fransisco: Jossey-Bass, 1981.

Kimura, M., and Ohta, T. *Theoretical Aspects of Population Genetics*. Princeton, N.J.: Princeton University Press, 1971.

Kolko, G. *Railroads and Regulation*. Princeton, N.J.: Princeton University Press, 1965.

Landis, J. M. *The Administrative Process*. New Haven, Conn.: Yale University Press, 1938.

Lassila, K. D. "See You Later, Litigator." *Amicus Journal*. Summer 1992, pp. 5-6.

Lax, D., and Sebenius, J. K. *The Manager as Negotiator*. New York: Free Press, 1986.

Layton, J., Memorandum to Martha O. Hesse, Chairman, Federal Energy Regulatory Commission, "Alleged Improprieties Regarding Procurement, Award of Contracts, and Conduct of Employees, FERC (I83HQ004)," July 27, 1987.

Lerner, A. "The Economics and Politics of Consumer Sovereignty." *American Economic Review*, 1972, *62*, 258.

Levine, E. *The Irish and Irish Politicians.* South Bend, Ind.: University of Notre Dame Press, 1966.

Lin, H. "The Development of Software for Ballistic-Missile Defense." *Scientific American,* 1985, *253,* 46.

Lindblom, C. E. "The Science of 'Muddling Through.'" *Public Administration Review,* Spring 1959, *19,* 1.

Lineberry, R., with Edwards, G. *Government in America.* Glenview, Ill.: Scott, Foresman, 1989.

Lynn, L. *Managing Public Policy.* Boston: Little, Brown, 1987.

McConnell, G. *Private Power and American Democracy.* New York: Knopf, 1966.

McCubbins, M., Noll, R., and Weingast, B. "Administrative Procedures as Instruments of Political Control." *Journal of Law, Economics and Organization,* 1987, *3,* 243.

McCubbins, M., and Schwartz, T. "Congressional Oversight Overlooked: Police Patrols vs. Fire Alarms." *American Journal of Political Science,* 1984, *28,* 165.

McCurdy, H. E. "Organizational Decline: NASA and the Life Cycle of Bureaus." *Public Administration Review,* 1991, *51,* 308.

McDonald, W. G. "Welcome to Washington, Reagan Man!" *Fortune,* Dec. 15, 1980, p. 100.

McGregor, D. "The Human Side of Enterprise." In W. Bennis and E. Schein (eds.), *Leadership and Motivation: Essays of Douglas McGregor.* Cambridge, Mass.: MIT Press, 1966.

Mashaw, J. L., and Harfst, J. *The Struggle for Automobile Safety.* Cambridge, Mass.: Harvard University Press, 1990.

Maslow, A. *Toward a Psychology of Being.* New York: Van Nostrand Reinhold, 1962.

Mason, A. T. *Brandeis: A Free Man's Life.* New York: Viking Penguin, 1946.

Mayer, K. R. *The Political Economy of Defense Contracting.* New Haven, Conn.: Yale University Press, 1991.

Mayo, E. *The Human Problems of an Industrial Civilization.* New York: Macmillan, 1933.

Melnick, S. *Regulation and the Courts.* Washington, D.C.: Brookings Institution, 1983.

Mintzberg, H. *Structure in Fives: Designing Effective Organizations.* Englewood Cliffs, N.J.: Prentice Hall, 1983.

Mobil Oil v. *FPC,* 483 F. 2d 1238 (D.C. Cir., 1973).

Moe, T. "The New Economics of Organization." *American Journal of Political Science,* 1984, *28,* 733.

Moe, T. "Control and Feedback in Economic Regulation: The Case of the NLRB." *American Political Science Review,* 1985, *79,* 1094.

Moe, T. "The Politics of Strategic Choice: Toward a Theory of Public Bureaucracy." In O. Williamson (ed.), *Organization Theory: From Chester Barnard to the Present and Beyond.* New York: Oxford University Press, 1990.

Moore, S. "Contracting Out: A Painless Alternative to the Budget Cutter's Knife." In S. Henke (ed.), *Prospects for Privatization.* New York: Academy of Political Science Press, 1987.

Mosher, F. C. *Democracy and the Public Service.* New York: Oxford University Press, 1968.

Munn v. *Illinois,* 94 U.S. 113 (1877).

Nathan, R. P. "The Reagan Presidency in Domestic Affairs." In F. I. Greenstein (ed.), *The Reagan Presidency: An Early Assessment.* Baltimore, Md.: Johns Hopkins University Press, 1983.

Natural Gas Act—Act of June 21, 1938; 52 Stat. 821.

Natural Gas Policy Act—P. L. 95-621 (Nov. 9, 1978), 92 Stat. 3350.

Neustadt, R., and May, E. *Thinking in Time.* New York: Free Press, 1986.

Niebuhr, R. *The Children of Light and the Children of Darkness.* New York: Scribner's, 1944.

Nye, J., and Keohane, R. *Power and Interdependence.* Boston: Little, Brown, 1977.

Osborne, D., and Gaebler, T. *Reinventing Government.* Reading, Mass.: Addison-Wesley, 1992.

Ouchi, W. "A Framework for Understanding Organizational Failure." In J. R. Kimberly, R. H. Miles, and Associates, *The Organizational Life Cycle: Issues in the Creation, Transformation, and Decline of Organizations.* San Fransisco: Jossey-Bass, 1981a.

Ouchi, W. *Theory Z.* New York: Avon, 1981b.

Pascal, B. *Pensees* (Thoughts). (A. J. Krailsheim, trans.) New York: Viking Penguin, 1966.

Pauly, K. "The Economics of Moral Hazard: Comment." *American Economic Review,* 1968, *58,* 531.

Pendleton Act—Act of June 16, 1883; 22 Stat. 403.

Perry, J. L. (ed.). *Handbook of Public Administration.* San Francisco: Jossey-Bass, 1989.

Perry, J. L., and Kraemer, K. *Public Management.* Mountain View, Calif.: Mayfield, 1983.

Peters, T., and Waterman, R. H. *In Search of Excellence.* New York: HarperCollins, 1982.

Phillips Petroleum v. *Wisconsin,* 347 U.S. 672 (1953).

Portland Cement v. *Ruckelshaus,* 486 F. 2d. 375 (D.C. Cir. 1973).

Pound, R. *An Introduction to the Philosophy of Law.* New Haven, Conn.: Yale University Press, 1922.

Pratt, J. W., and Zeckhauser, R. (eds.). *Principals and Agents: The Structure of Business.* Boston: Harvard Business School Press, 1985.

Quirk, P. J. *Industry Influence in Federal Regulatory Agencies.* Princeton, N.J.: Princeton University Press, 1981.

Rakove, M. *Don't Make No Waves, Don't Back No Losers.* Bloomington: University of Indiana Press, 1975.

Rehfuss, J. A. *Contracting Out in Government: A Guide to Working with Outside Contractors to Supply Public Services.* San Francisco: Jossey-Bass, 1989.

Reich, R. "Regulation by Confrontation or Negotiation?" *Harvard Business Review,* 1981, *59,* 82.

Reich, R. "Policy Making in a Democracy." In R. Reich (ed.), *The Power of Public Ideas.* New York: Ballinger, 1981.

Riley, D. *Controlling the Federal Bureaucracy.* Philadelphia: Temple University Press, 1987.

Ripley, R., and Franklin, G. *Congress, Bureaucracy, and Public Policy.* Glenview, Ill.: Scott, Foresman, 1989.

Roethlisberger, F., and Dickson, W. J. *Management and the Worker.* Cambridge, Mass.: Harvard University Press, 1939.

Rogers, J. E. *A Primer on Functionalization, Cost Allocation, Classification, and Rate Design Current Rate Design Issues.* Washington, D.C.: Office of General Counsel, U.S. Federal Energy Regulatory Commission, 1982.

Rohr, J. *Ethics for Bureaucrats.* New York: Dekker, 1978.

Rourke, F. G. *Bureaucracy, Politics, and Public Policy.* (2nd ed.) Boston: Little, Brown, 1976.

Rubin, I. *Shrinking the Federal Government: The Effect of Cutbacks on Five Federal Agencies.* White Plains, N.Y.: Longman, 1985.

Salamon, L. "Rethinking Public Management: Third-Party Government and the Changing Forms of Government Action." In R. Stillman (ed.), *Public Administration: Concepts and Cases.* (4th ed.) Boston: Houghton Mifflin 1988.

Schick, A. "A Death in the Bureaucracy: The Demise of Federal PPB." *Public Administration Review,* Jan./Feb. 1973, *33,* pp. 146–156.

Schick, A. "The Road to PPB: The Stages of Budget Reform." In F. J. Lyden and E. G. Miller (eds.), *Public Budgeting.* Englewood Cliffs, N.J.: Prentice Hall, 1982.

Schlesinger, A., Jr. *A Thousand Days.* Boston: Houghton Mifflin, 1965.

Schwartz, B. *Administrative Law.* (2nd ed.) Boston: Little, Brown, 1982.

Scott, W. G., and Hart, D. K. *Organizational America.* Boston: Houghton Mifflin, 1979.

Scott, W. G., and Hart, D. K. *Organizational Values in America.* New Brunswick, N.J.: Transaction, 1989.

Seidenfeld, M. "A Civic Republican Justification for the Bureaucratic State." *Harvard Law Review,* 1992, *105,* 1511–1577.

Selznick, P. "Foundations of the Theory of Organizations." *American Sociological Review,* 1948, *13,* 25.

Selznick, P. *Leadership in Administration.* New York: HarperCollins, 1957.

Shapiro, M. *Who Guards the Guardians?* Athens: University of Georgia Press, 1988.

Sharkansky, I. "Policymaking and Service Delivery on the Margins of Government: The Case of Contractors." *Public Administration Review,* 1980, *40,* 116.

Simon, H. *Administrative Behavior.* New York: Macmillan, 1947.

Simon, H. "The Organization of Complex Systems." In H. Pattee (ed.), *Hierarchy Theory.* New York: Braziller, 1973.

Simon, H., and March, J. *Organizations.* New York: Wiley, 1958.

Skowronek, S. *Building a New American State.* Cambridge, England: Cambridge University Press, 1982.

Small Business Act—Act of July 30, 1953, 67 Stat. 232.

Stanley v. *Illinois*, 405 U.S. 645 (1972).

Steinbruner, J. *The Cybernetic Theory of Decisions*. Princeton, N.J.: Princeton University Press, 1974.

Stewart, R. B. "The Reformation of American Administrative Law." *Harvard Law Review*, 1975, *88*, 1667–1813.

Stillman, R. (ed.), *Public Administration: Concepts and Cases*. Boston: Houghton Mifflin, 1992.

Taylor, F. W. *The Principles of Scientific Management*. New York: HarperCollins, 1947. (Originally published 1911.)

Thompson, J. *Organizations in Action*. New York: McGraw-Hill, 1967.

Tolchin, M. "Senators Accused Inspectors of 'Pattern of Wrongdoing.'" *New York Times*, Sept. 9, 1990, p. 26.

Tullock, G. *Trials on Trial*. New York: Columbia University Press, 1980.

Tullock, G. "Negotiated Settlement." In J. M. van der Schulenburg and G. Skogh (eds.), *Law and the Economics of Legal Regulation*. Dordrecht, Netherlands: Kluwer, 1986.

U.S. Congress. *Senate Resolution 331*. 97th Cong., 2d sess., 1982.

U.S. Congressional Budget Office, *Changing the Classification of Federal White-Collar Jobs*. CBO Papers. Washington, D.C.: U.S. Congressional Budget Office, 1991.

U.S. Federal Energy Regulatory Commission. *Staff Cost of Service Manual*. Washington, D.C.: Office of Pipeline and Producer Regulation, U.S. Federal Energy Regulatory Commission, 1983.

U.S. General Accounting Office. *Organizational Culture: Techniques Companies Use to Perpetuate or Change Beliefs and Values*. Washington, D.C.: U.S. Government Printing Office, 1992.

U.S. Federal Energy Regulatory Commission. "Notice of Inquiry: Impact of NGPA on Current and Projected Natural Gas Markets." *Federal Register*, 1982, *47* (19), 157.

U.S. Office of Management and Budget. *Management of the United States Government, Fiscal Year 1989*. Washington, D.C.: U.S. Government Printing Office, 1989.

Van Riper, P. *History of the United States Civil Service*. New York: HarperCollins, 1958.

Veljanovski, C. G. *The New Law-and-Economics: A Research Review*. Oxford, England: Centre for Socio-Legal Studies, 1982.

Verkuil, P. A. "The Emerging Concept of Administrative Process." *Columbia Law Review*, 1978, *78*, 258.

Volcker, P. A. *Leadership for America: Rebuilding the Public Service*. Washington, D.C.: National Commission on the Public Service, 1989.

Waldo, D. *The Administrative State: A Study of the Political Theory of American Public Administration*. New York: Ronald Press, 1948.

Waldo, D. *The Study of Public Administration*. New York: Random House, 1955.

Walter Holm v. *Hardin*, 449 F. 2d 1009 (D.C. Cir., 1971).

Weber, M. "Bureaucracy." In H. H. Gerth and C. W. Mills (eds.), *From Max Weber*. New York: Oxford University Press, 1946a. (Originally published about 1910.)

Weber, M. "Politics as a Vocation." In H. Gerth and C. W. Mills (eds.), *From Max Weber*. New York: Oxford University Press, 1946b. (Originally published 1918.)

Weick, K. *The Social Psychology of Organizing*. Reading, Mass.: Addison-Wesley, 1979.

Weingast, B., and Moran, M. "Bureaucratic Discretion or Congressional Control: Regulatory Policymaking by the Federal Trade Commission." *Journal of Political Economy*, 1983, *91*, 765.

Weiss, P. "Conduct Unbecoming?" *New York Times Magazine*, Oct. 29, 1989, p. 41.

Wildavsky, A. *The Politics of the Budgetary Process*. Boston: Little, Brown, 1964.

Williams, J. "Cornerstones of American Administrative Law." In D. Barry and H. Whitcomb (eds.), *The Legal Foundations of Public Administration*. (2nd ed.) St. Paul, Minn.: West, 1987.

Williams, S. F. "'Hybrid Rulemaking' Under the Administrative Procedure Act: A Legal and Empirical Analysis." *University of Chicago Law Review*, 1975, *42*, 401.

Williamson, O. *Markets and Hierarchies: Analysis and Antitrust Implications*. New York: Free Press, 1975.

Williamson, O. *The Economic Institutions of Capitalism*. New York: Free Press, 1985.

Williamson, O. *Organization Theory: From Chester Barnard to the Present and Beyond.* New York: Oxford University Press, 1990.

Wilson, J. Q. *Bureaucracy: What Government Agencies Do and Why They Do It.* New York: Basic Books, 1989.

Wilson, W. "The Study of Administration." *Political Science Quarterly,* 1887, *2*, 197.

Wright, S. "Evolution in Mendelian Populations." *Genetics,* 1931, *16*, 97.

Index